A

[signature: Philip E. Lilienthal]

■   ■   ■

BOOK

The Philip E. Lilienthal imprint
honors special books
in commemoration of a man whose work
at University of California Press from 1954 to 1979
was marked by dedication to young authors
and to high standards in the field of Asian Studies.
Friends, family, authors, and foundations have together
endowed the Lilienthal Fund, which enables UC Press
to publish under this imprint selected books
in a way that reflects the taste and judgment
of a great and beloved editor.

The publisher gratefully acknowledges the generous support of the Philip E. Lilienthal Asian Studies Endowment Fund of the University of California Press Foundation, which was established by a major gift from Sally Lilienthal.

Eating Bitterness

Eating Bitterness

*Stories from the Front Lines of
China's Great Urban Migration*

Michelle Dammon Loyalka

UNIVERSITY OF CALIFORNIA PRESS

Berkeley Los Angeles London

University of California Press, one of the most
distinguished university presses in the United States,
enriches lives around the world by advancing scholarship
in the humanities, social sciences, and natural sciences.
Its activities are supported by the UC Press Foundation
and by philanthropic contributions from individuals and
institutions. For more information, visit www.ucpress.edu.

University of California Press
Berkeley and Los Angeles, California

University of California Press, Ltd.
London, England

First paperback printing 2013

© 2012 by The Regents of the University of California

Library of Congress Cataloging-in-Publication Data
Loyalka, Michelle Dammon, 1972-
    Eating bitterness : stories from the front lines of
China's great urban migration / Michelle Dammon
Loyalka.
        p.   cm.
    Includes bibliographical references and index.
    ISBN 978-0-520-28036-6 (pbk. : alk. paper)
    1. Rural-urban migration—China—History.
    2. Migration, Internal—China—History.   3. China—
Social conditions—1976-2000.   4. China—Social
conditions—2000-   I. Title.
    HB2114.A3L73 2012
    307.2'40951—dc23

                                        2011036187

Manufactured in the United States of America
20   19   18   17   16   15   14   13
10   9   8   7   6   5   4   3   2   1

In keeping with a commitment to support environmen-
tally responsible and sustainable printing practices, UC
Press has printed this book on Rolland Enviro100, a
100% post-consumer fiber paper that is FSC certified,
deinked, processed chlorine-free, and manufactured with
renewable biogas energy. It is acid-free and EcoLogo
certified.

CONTENTS

Introduction

I

1. The Veggie Vendors

9

2. The Impenetrable Knife Sharpener

36

3. The Teenage Beauty Queens

64

4. The Ever-Floating Floater

97

5. The Landless Landlords

119

6. The Nowhere Nanny

153

7. The Opportunity Spotter
182

8. The Big Boss
206

Epilogue
240

Research Notes   247
Acknowledgments   257
Index   261

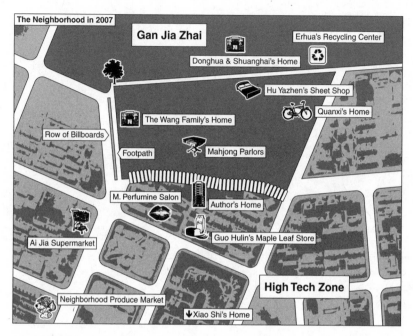

Map of the Gan Jia Zhai and High-Tech Zone neighborhood in 2007 before demolition began.

INTRODUCTION

Little more than sixty years ago, China was an impoverished and underdeveloped nation. Though among the world's most advanced civilizations throughout much of history, in the middle of the nineteenth century it was debilitated by opium addiction and invaded by imperial powers. In the first half of the twentieth century, the nation's progress was stymied by the collapse of its four thousand-year-old dynastic system, hampered by eight years of conflict with the Japanese, and stalled by an outbreak of civil war. When the Communist Party came to power in 1949, the country made initial gains, but those advances were soon disrupted by a wild ride through collectivization, the Great Leap Forward, and the Cultural Revolution.

Three decades ago, the government launched a series of reforms to help modernize the country and invigorate its economy. Since then, China has lifted a record 230 million people out of poverty. Its nominal GDP has increased seventy-five times over, and today it boasts the world's second largest economy. It is also the second largest producer of energy on earth and the third largest manufacturer.

Perhaps nowhere is China's spectacular transformation more evident than when it comes to urbanization. While most Western nations took nearly two hundred years to transition from agrarian to urban societies, China is on track to accomplish this in little more than fifty. Over the past thirty years the country's urban population has more than doubled, and over the next thirty it is expected to nearly double yet again, reaching a whopping one billion people and making China's cities more populous than the entire North and South American continents combined. By 2025 it will boast 221 urban centers, each with more than a million people; all of Europe, by comparison, has a mere thirty-five. The country's major metropolitan areas will likely include fifteen supercities that, with populations over 25 million people, are each the size of the entire state of Texas. To accommodate its lightning-fast development, the nation will have to pave five billion square meters of roads and erect five million new buildings, including up to fifty thousand skyscrapers, or ten New York Cities.

Clearly, China is rising at a pace and an intensity never before seen in human history, and that alone is destined to have a dramatic impact on the nation and the world at large. But *Eating Bitterness* is not about the magnitude of these accomplishments or the fervor surrounding the country's coming of age; it is about the underlying pain, self-sacrifice, and fortitude upon which the nation's advances are built. It takes as its focus the smallest, the humblest, and yet arguably among the most vital, participants in the process: peasants hunting for a better life than rural China can provide.

At any given time, over 200 million such people leave their families and farms behind and flock to China's urban centers, where they provide a profusion of cheap labor that helps fuel the country's massive city-building process as well as its staggering economic growth. Long recognized for making the nation's factories an international juggernaut, these migrants are also inextricably involved in every aspect of China's own domestic life. They raise buildings, lay highways, sweep streets, and shine shoes. They clean houses, cut hair, babysit children, and wash cars. They sell produce on busy street corners, peddle clothes in open-air stalls, and hawk all manner of conveniences from the back of bicycles. They snap up the lowest-paying jobs and carve out the pettiest of entrepreneurial niches. They are light on their feet, quick to seize opportunity, and able to continually remold themselves to meet the changing demands of the Chinese economy. As a result, there isn't a single Chinese city—nor hardly a neighborhood—that functions without them.

Despite their pivotal contributions, China's rural migrants tend to be overworked, underpaid, and largely without the benefit of labor law protections. In the cities, they typically lack access to affordable health care, education, and other social services and are relegated to the most meager housing. A great number of cultural and economic barriers keep them living on the outskirts of society, rarely able to enjoy the fruits of their labors. To make matters worse, for them, "rural" is not simply an adjective but, rather, a legal designation assigned at birth that makes it nearly impossible for all but the most educated or successful to fully integrate into urban life. Even the term given to them—the *liudong,* or "floating population"—is emblematic of their status as outsiders temporarily residing in the nation's cities.

In recent years, China's leadership has increasing hailed the contributions of the country's rural migrants. Policies to protect their rights and foster their assimilation into urban life are being created, but in practice improvements have been slow to come. That will need to change. Until now, such peasants have been left largely to fend for themselves, relying on their own resourcefulness to survive, but over the next twenty years a full 300 million migrants are expected to descend on China's cities. A group of people equivalent in size to the entire American nation cannot be overlooked without serious repercussions. For all the rosy forecasts and sheer exuberance surrounding China's rise, if the country doesn't adequately address the inequalities these people face, its current goal of creating a harmonious society and moving smoothly to the next stage of development may be impossible; maintaining social stability itself may even prove challenging. That makes people like those featured in *Eating Bitterness* one of China's most pressing domestic issues.

Most news reports out of China come from Beijing, Shanghai, Guangzhou, and a few other select cities that, while alluring and easily accessible to the Western media, are far from representative. After decades of heavy investment and foreign influence, the eastern part of China now brims with boomtowns and business centers that serve as the flashy new face of the nation. By comparison, landlocked western China is still steeped in history and tradition and largely unknown to the outside world. It is synonymous with rural China, poor China, underdeveloped China. And yet it is also the largest part of the country, the cradle of Chinese civilization, and the center of Mao's Communist revolution.

Whether in terms of earning power, productivity, or urbanization, western China invariably comes in last. This disparity is not an accident; it is, in fact, entirely purposeful. When the Communist Party initiated opening and reform policies in the late 1970s, it did so with the idea of allowing some to get rich first and letting the wealth trickle down from there. The country's southeastern seaboard was chosen to lead the nation to prosperity, while western China was left to languish behind.

In 2000 the Chinese government launched the *Xibu Da Kaifa*, or "Great Opening of the West," policy to step up the development of and close the gap between western China and the country's central and coastal provinces. The ancient capital of Xi'an— home to the Terra Cotta Warriors and one of the world's largest and most modern cities some 3,000 years ago—became the focal point of this new policy. A torrent of investment money poured into the city, as did plans to double the metropolis' population by expanding its emerging High-Tech Zone into a "New Xi'an." As the money flowed in, so too did a flood of peasants, each hoping to snatch up a portion of the region's newfound prosperity.

Having moved to Xi'an in 1999, a year before this grand undertaking began, I witnessed firsthand the rapid, relentless development that ensued. From my apartment in the High-Tech Zone, I watched as dozens of impressive new buildings suddenly sprang up on the horizon. And yet there, in the middle of all this newness, sat Gan Jia Zhai—a decrepit old village that, though not much more than five city blocks in size, now burst with an estimated thirty thousand migrants who had come to work in the neighboring new district. Its dusty footpaths and sagging concrete block houses stood in marked contrast to the High-Tech Zone's orderly streets and soaring skyscrapers, as did its mounting crime rate and rough-and-tumble night life.

Like most of my neighbors, I simply avoided the area. But when long-circulated rumors of Gan Jia Zhai's demolition were finally confirmed in 2006, many of the people with whom I regularly

Construction in the High-Tech Zone.

interacted—from the vegetable peddlers and waitresses to the shopkeepers and security guards—were suddenly looking to move. That's when I realized that the entire High-Tech Zone was built and maintained by people who could never afford to live there, people putting in incredibly long hours for a city they could never hope to enjoy. I started asking questions and soon became engrossed in life stories so full of ingenuity and determination—as well as misfortune and adversity—that I felt compelled to share them.

Eating Bitterness: Stories from the Front Lines of China's Great Urban Migration takes readers into the lives of eight rural migrants who have come to Xi'an in pursuit of the newly imported American Dream. By day most of them find opportunity in the bustling High-Tech Zone, but by night their lives play out mainly in the dilapidated old village of Gan Jia Zhai. The book is structured to show, in rough progression, how successfully these individuals

Gan Jia Zhai's main street.

assimilate into city life and how conflicted the relationships between their familiar rural roots and newly minted urban aspirations become. Each chapter introduces a new story and a new set of social issues that, taken together, present a panorama of what it means to embark on the migrant journey.

Eating Bitterness starts with a family of vegetable vendors who would like to return to the countryside but believe only a lifetime of urban labor will open the doors of opportunity for their young daughter. It follows an itinerant knife sharpener who is painfully aware that he represents a rapidly dying breed in the New China; a group of teenage beauty-industry poster girls who are eager to forget all things old in pursuit of their new material dreams but have no idea how or where to begin; a free-spirited recycler who drifts from job to job just waiting to find an opportunity worthy of his heart's attention; a former farmer who is racked by addiction and plagued with idleness after receiving a huge payout in exchange for his land; a cash-strapped mother who leaves her own children back in the village only to take care of rich people's kids in the city; and a successful storekeeper who lives with her family of four in the back of her linen shop because she has not yet found a way to attain a normal urban life. *Eating Bitterness* ends with a second-grade runaway turned wealthy philanthropist wannabe who is consumed by a restless longing for meaning indicative of a growing dissatisfaction with the ultra-materialistic direction in which China is headed.

Though tales of China's economic miracle abound, as do portraits of its peasant poor, little attention has been paid to this vital and growing class of new urban workers who are caught in between. Their stories present the human side to China's seemingly unstoppable development machine, and their resilience, determination, and grit all attest to the human spirit's time-tested ability to persevere. Over and above providing a vast and inexpensive labor pool, by pressing ahead in the face of seemingly insurmountable obstacles and enduring all manner of hardships, this stalwart band of people may well be the unsung hero behind China's rising success on the world stage. There is no exact term for it in English, but in Chinese this indomitable spirit is called *chiku*, or "eating bitterness."

CHAPTER ONE

The Veggie Vendors

The sun sets on the High-Tech Zone as a hazy-orange disk sinking beneath a blanket of smog. It is soon replaced by a muted moon shining down on the day's last surge of activity. Gradually the traffic clears, the glitzy shops close, and the interminable construction work grinds to a halt. The last stragglers head home shortly after midnight and finally even the ever-present battalion of taxis camps along the empty roadways for the night.

By 3:00 a.m., the High-Tech Zone is a dead zone.

Suddenly, out of the silence bursts Li Donghua, reining in his three-wheeled motorcycle as it bounces and lurches along the city's deserted avenues. His wife, Chuan Shuanghai, sits behind him in a rickety metal cart, head tucked between her knees to avoid the brutal autumn wind. As they whiz through the district, they catch up with a nearly identical vehicle—right down to the tightly bundled woman riding in the back. Another three-wheeler cuts in from a side street, and then another, and another. Donghua guns ahead, jockeying for position at the front of the caravan.

Within minutes they pull into a sprawling, iron-gated compound and their daily trek comes to an end. Bright stadium lights extinguish the early-morning darkness and the clamor of frenzied business transactions engulfs them from every side. Donghua squeezes the motorcycle into a parking space and peers off toward a sea of flatbed trucks filled with eggplant, zucchini, cucumbers, and countless other vegetables, all stacked high and selling fast.

This is rush hour at the High-Tech Zone's wholesale market, an outdoor foodstuff super center of sorts where Donghua and Shuanghai start each day. They have a little over three hours to stock up on veggies, load them into the cart, race back to their local retail market, and unpack everything before their own customers start trickling in. Donghua looks at the throng of other small-time vegetable peddlers already scouring for deals and starts to feel antsy. It's 3:30 a.m., time to get to work.

When Donghua and Shuanghai finally arrive at their own neighborhood market, their three-wheeler stacked high with the morning's freshly purchased produce, it's nearly 7:40 a.m. and they are running late. They navigate through the mob at the front entrance and push their motorcycle toward the interior, where small-time entrepreneurs stand over coal-block heated woks, cooking up local specialties hot and fast throughout the day and late into the night. With the cheapest breakfast selections in the neighborhood—piping-hot soy milk, tea-boiled eggs, and a batch of salty fried donuts, all for well under a dollar—business is already booming. Donghua's stomach growls faintly, but there's no time to stop and eat today.

Instead the couple moves past the dining area to the rickety, market-supplied wooden tables where more than twenty vegetable merchants display their wares. If there's one thing that makes Shuanghai and Donghua extraordinary, it's how painfully ordinary they are among their peers. Like all the other vendors here, they grew up in the countryside; they have low education and even lower life expectations. They dress simply, clad most often in hand-knit sweaters and old-style cloth shoes. And though the circumstances that compelled each of these peddlers to head city-ward vary, their purpose here in the market—and, for that matter, the purpose of the more than 200 million rural migrants residing in China's burgeoning cities at any given time—is very often the same: a quest for financial stability and opportunity that simply doesn't exist back in their villages.

And so for 200 yuan a month—the equivalent of about $30—Donghua and Shuanghai rent out one of the market's shaky little tables and hope for the best. Seeing that the other tables are already overflowing with a potpourri of red, green, yellow, and orange vegetables, Donghua quickly parks the motorcycle beside a small cement fish pond and then makes a beeline for the last and arguably worst spot in the market—the table right across from the dinky, hardly used back entrance, the table they call home.

They scramble for the next twenty minutes to lay out their produce, Donghua muttering all the while about the morning's already lost opportunities. They're not usually late—in fact, they almost always arrive first so that they can snatch up as many early-bird customers as possible. But tomorrow is October 1, the beginning of China's week-long National Day celebration, and they had spent a little extra time at the wholesale market stocking up for what they hope will be a big holiday rush.

Among the last items to make it onto the table are dried red pepper strings—hot sellers as popular as they are hard to get. As soon as Donghua sets them out, a customer materializes and, without even asking the price, snaps up two *jin*, a standard half-kilo measure used across China. An older lady with hair cut in a trendy Japanese-style shag and streaked with color scoots down the aisle, with grandson in tow, eager to get a look at their peppers. Donghua stretches a string between his arms. "I can cut this to any length you want," he encourages her.

"How much?" Grandma asks.

"1.5 per *jin*."

"1.5?" she says. "That can't be. That's way too expensive."

From across the table, Shuanghai looks up from the Chinese cabbage she's preening. "They were 1.3 wholesale," she says flatly.

Grandma isn't ready to pay that much and so she shuffles away, pointy-toed shoes clacking against the pitted concrete floor. Shuanghai returns to her cabbage, while Donghua moves on to the yams. But a minute later, Granny's back, arguing for a price of 1.3 yuan and hinting that anything more would be a rip-off.

Shuanghai's cheeks flush red. It doesn't bother her so much that these wealthy city people want everything so cheap. What really gets to her is their impression that all small-time vegetable peddlers are dishonest. Sure, some sellers—especially those with a prime location up front—mark prices way up when they think they can get away with it. Those are the same people who slide the market's management extra money to secure the best tables. But other than that, for the most part, they're all just people like Shuanghai and Donghua, trying to squeak out a decent living. That's hard enough without all these rich folk wanting their peppers and potatoes practically for free and yet still feeling like they're getting cheated over every cent. "We bought these peppers for 1.3, so how can we sell them to you for that price?"

Shuanghai snaps at Grandma. "We should be selling them for 1.8, but we're only asking 1.5."

"Yesterday I saw them for…"

"Yesterday? Yesterday!" Shuanghai brews. "Today's wholesale prices are not the same as yesterday's!"

Donghua pipes in, voice calm, playing the good cop to Shuanghai's bad cop as he explains to Granny what a good deal she's getting. He shows her how tightly the peppers are tied on the string and how thoroughly they've been dried. Just then, another lady swoops in to get a closer look, and Grandma, noting the dwindling pile and waxing enthusiasm, quietly relents. She'll take 4 *jin* at 1.5 yuan.

Shuanghai tucks a loose strand of hair into her ponytail and turns back to her produce with a hint of a smile.

Midafternoon is the slow time at the market, but even so the din can reach deafening proportions. From the whining of motorized steamers warming impossibly high stacks of *mantou*, or steamed buns, to the squawking of chickens as they're weighed, killed, and shoved into brightly colored plastic bags, layer upon layer of noise builds into a single buzz of activity that, for the uninitiated, can be nearly unbearable. But none of it even registers for Shuanghai—not the individual sounds, and surely not the hum itself. No, her attention is on adding right now, and that, for the moment, is her world.

"1.2, 2.4, 3.6…right?" she asks as she pulls a sack of zucchini off the scale and hands it across the table. An old man with an MP3 player tucked neatly in the front breast pocket of his fading blue Mao suit simply grunts, tosses a few crumpled bills her way, and walks further down the aisle. As he goes, he catches sight of Shuanghai's round, black eggplants—the ones that are a little harder to find than the typical oblong ones, the ones Shuanghai knows sell well, despite their slightly higher price, the very ones she and Donghua scoured the wholesale market for early this morning until, triumphantly, she snagged a 10-kilo sack of them. When they got here this morning she noted, with a glint of satisfaction, that only a few of the other vendors had them.

And so the old man stops, pulls the headphones off of his ears, and picks up one of her black beauties. "How much for these?"

"1.8 for a *jin*."

"That's too much," he whines. But there's no way she'll go down on the price, not with eggplants that look this good, and so he nods at her to hand him a plastic bag.

Soon Donghua arrives, back from his afternoon nap, and he and Shuanghai fall into their unspoken rhythm: she manages the front of the table, answering pricing questions up between the scale and the blue silk money box, while he works the back half, stacking and restacking the heavier veggies. Donghua thwacks a *donggua*, or winter melon—a watermelon-like vegetable with green outer skin and white flesh—and presses his fist down its length, subconsciously calculating how much longer it will last.

A little lull descends on the market, and he starts chatting with a neighbor who's peeling a pear with a butcher knife, working the giant blade from his body outward so that the peels fly onto the floor's ever-growing pile of discarded scraps. When he finishes, he hands the fruit to Donghua and starts working on one for himself.

Shuanghai points under the table to the pears they bought the other day, the ones that are already going bad. "You can't keep pears, they rot too quickly," she tells Donghua. It's the first time they've spoken about anything other than vegetables all day.

An old man wearing oversize glasses appears and asks about the price of their tomatoes. "1.6 yuan," Donghua and Shuanghai chime in unison, as if it were a rehearsed script. Even after so many years it sometimes still surprises them that they can do that. Though prices fluctuate each and every day, depending on what they pay at the wholesale market in the morning, they can still spit out the current price of any of their thirty-plus vegetable varieties without a second thought, despite the fact that they never discuss what the day's new amount should be. That, according to Donghua, is because "it's impressed on our hearts."

Yes, Shuanghai agrees, their hearts are full of many of the same impressions, full of vegetable prices and seasons and sellers and locations. But it hasn't always been that way, especially not at the beginning of their marriage. Shuanghai's two older sisters had already married men from villages several hours from theirs, and her mother didn't want to lose her third and final daughter in the same way. She was determined that Shuanghai should stay by her side, and the best way to make sure that happened was for her to marry someone local. And so it was that Shuanghai's mom picked Mr. Li Donghua, a young man whose parents worked the plot of land adjacent to theirs. He was the last of seven kids from a family not nearly as well off as theirs—which wasn't saying much, except that they'd surely be glad to marry their son off to her. And so her mom decided he was the one.

The only problem was that Shuanghai didn't agree. She couldn't stand the thought of it, to be more precise. It wasn't that she didn't like Donghua—she "never thought about that too much"—but, rather, that she didn't want to stay in their village, didn't want to live such a tired peasant existence tending the land. Simply put, she wanted a better life, and that, to her, meant life in the city.

But now, as she stands behind their table at the open-air market, feet and back and neck and knees aching from years of long, incredibly long, hours—3:00 a.m. to 8:00 p.m., 360-some days a year—every inch of her body concedes that life here is certainly more tiring than anything she could have experienced in the countryside. She examines her fingertips, calloused, peeling, and stained black with dirt that won't wash away no matter how hard she scrubs. Then she laughs and thrusts her palms into Donghua's. "I'm only in my thirties and already they're like a sixty-year-old lady's hands."

Migrants like Shuanghai and Donghua may drudge through each day with their own financial concerns in mind, but their collective endeavors form a key component of China's double-digit economic growth. It's not just that they provide a nearly endless supply of cheap labor, but that they do so with unimaginable tenacity and grit—a strength of character and work ethic reminiscent of America's early immigrants and the country's struggles through the Great Depression.

In Chinese, that ethic is called *chiku* or, literally, *eating bitterness,* a term that has no direct correlate in English but that means, roughly, to endure hardships, overcome difficulties, and press ahead all in one. While long considered a virtue in Chinese culture, the country's upheavals over the past sixty years—including the Communist and cultural revolutions, market reforms, and the recent spread of materialism—have honed this ability to a new degree of perfection. This is especially true among peasants, who have had to be far more savvy and entrepreneurial than their urban counterparts to survive this tumultuous period.

And so it is that no matter how greatly city life may differ from their expectations, China's peasants don't often turn tail and head back home at the first sign of difficulty. Instead, they *chiku*, accepting and enduring and adapting as each situation demands and ultimately filtering into distasteful factory or service jobs, searching out petty business opportunities, and even inventing new channels of their own. In so doing they provide the country with an unusually resolute and yet highly flexible workforce that is helping vaunt China onto the world stage. But when all is said and done, by molding themselves to the vagaries of a society in extreme flux, Shuanghai and her peers often find that they no longer belong to the nation's traditional past and yet neither do they have a place in its modernized future; they are a people caught in between.

Nobody needs to tell Donghua that it's almost dinnertime. He knows by the eerie glow of the market's fluorescent lights, by the clouds of chili-laced smoke drifting over from the dining area, and by the merchants hustling back and forth to their motorcycles to grab extra provisions. But most of all he knows by the way customers are suddenly pressed three-deep around their table, eager to get hold of some fresh produce for the night's meal. This is prime time at the market, and he and Shuanghai are working double-time.

From the very beginning, when Donghua first saw the High-Tech Zone six years ago, with its wide roads and new schools, he was hooked. "I knew that this place was better than others. I knew there'd be development potential here," he says.

Despite the district's obvious wealth, the open-air market itself was slipshod and simple, thrown up for the temporary convenience of nearby residents. But that didn't daunt Donghua and

Shuanghai—after all, how else were they going to get a chance to work in such a ritzy area? Besides, they weren't planning to strike it rich. This just seemed to be a better opportunity than the petty peddling they'd been doing out of the back of a manual three-wheeled bike—a step up the mercantile food chain, so to speak. So they scraped together 2,000 yuan to buy a motorized three-wheeler—a necessity for hauling large quantities of veggies from the wholesale market—and that was that. "We never really thought about it too much," Shuanghai says. "We just did it."

At times like this, with customers swarming the mushrooms, the potatoes, the spinach, and the bamboo shoots, Donghua has to admit that things have worked out okay. They could, of course, always be better—he and Shuanghai could be renting out one of the tiny shops at the perimeter of the market where people sell things like grains, meats, noodles, and spices. Those vendors pay more for their spot, but then they make more, and they get running water, a cooking space, and even enough room to cram a little bed inside. As it is now, Donghua and Shuanghai get nothing more for their 200-yuan rent than a barren table.

And so it is that when their twelve-year-old daughter, Ming, comes back from school a half hour later, there's no hot meal waiting for her, nor even a hard surface on which to do her homework. Instead she sits on a six-inch-high mini-stool next to a pile of turnips and tries to study. Donghua hovers over her shoulder for a minute, shaking his head as she opens her English book. "I don't understand any of it," he says, finally, and turns his attention to a shrinking heap of carrots.

A well-dressed businessman with a Bluetooth headset plugged in his ear approaches the cucumbers as he talks on his cell phone. He points to them silently, and Donghua indicates a price of 1.8 yuan. The man sighs and starts filling a plastic bag, only inter-

Li Donghua stands by his table at the produce market.

rupting his phone conversation to mutter "*Zhe me gui*," or "That's so expensive."

Zhe me gui is a constant refrain here at the market, but what, Donghua often asks himself, do these urbanites with their nice clothes and expensive electronics really know about *zhe me gui?* In recent decades pennies have become increasingly irrelevant, and now the smallest unit of change is the *mao*, a ten-cent piece. In the last few years, many businesspeople have stopped dealing with that too; it's simply too small for big-time concerns. But here, for Donghua and Shuanghai, the *mao* is their lifeblood.

Donghua's Bluetooth-wielding customers may choose not to acknowledge it, but the lifestyles they enjoy are made possible in large part by these *mao*-dependent migrants. Never mind the convenience of having cheap produce available on virtually every block; thanks to them, regular facials and foot massages are within reach for even lower-middle-class urbanites, as are housekeepers, nannies, and tailors. Thanks to them, there's someone to re-sole shoes, repair zippers, or copy keys hovering in every neighborhood, and eating out is almost as cheap as eating in. In essence, it is thanks to migrant labor and ingenuity that people like Mr. Bluetooth are able to focus the bulk of their time and energy on the much more glamorous business of becoming upwardly mobile.

But all that is lost on Donghua, who feels more like a piece of the city's hardware than a real, live contributor to progress. Poorly educated, unsophisticated, and uncultured, he is unconvinced that he and his wife have much to offer the China of the future. "We are the people at the lowest level," Donghua says, hefting a load of potatoes onto a woman's bike for her. "The people here have knowledge as their foundation. All we have is the power of our bodies, so all we can do is hard labor."

He's thought about trying to do something else, something with shorter hours, something less tiring, but each time he comes to the same conclusion: "Anything else we wouldn't understand. We don't make much now, but we don't lose money, either. It's not guaranteed that every business will be like that."

One thing Donghua and Shuanghai hadn't counted on when they moved here was just *how* fast the area would develop. Since the 2000 inception of *Xibu Da Kaifa*, the central government's policy to develop China's western region, Xi'an—and particularly its High-Tech Zone—has undergone rapid transformation. The couple's vegetable market, once nestled in what was considered one of the district's lower-end neighborhoods, is now sandwiched between towering apartment complexes and sparkling-new office buildings. Although established only six years ago, the market has already become an anachronism in this zone, sure to face extinction in the near future. "The location is super good," Shuanghai says. "They can't possibly leave it empty like this—the market definitely isn't long term; it could be torn down any minute."

That's already happening to their current residence, located in Gan Jia Zhai, one of the few old villages left in the midst of the rapidly expanding High-Tech Zone. Though Gan Jia Zhai starts just a block and a half up the street from their market, it might as well be another universe. Composed mainly of ramshackle three- and four-story buildings rented out room by room, it houses an estimated thirty thousand rural migrants who, like Donghua and Shuanghai, work in the High-Tech Zone but could never afford to live there. Most of the vegetable market's middle-class customers have never been to Gan Jia Zhai, since traffic seems to flow in one direction only—out of the village and into the High-Tech Zone.

For years, rumors of its imminent demise have run rampant, but this time the threat seems real. Still, that's months away, and Donghua and Shuanghai plan to stay put as long as possible. It may not be glamorous, but their so-called home—a windowless, one-car garage on the bottom level of a crumbling apartment house—is cheap and familiar.

As usual, tonight Shuanghai and Ming walk home around 8:00 p.m., leaving Donghua at the market to pack up for the night. When they arrive, Shuanghai unlocks and lifts the garage's sliding metal door, and Ming rushes in to pull the string on the room's lone lightbulb. Two beds, pushed end to end, line one wall, with a flimsy curtain between them to give Donghua and Shuanghai a small degree of privacy. Along the opposite wall is an old cardboard box, turned on its side to serve as a countertop on which to place their electric rice cooker. There's also a small table for cutting vegetables and stacking cooking supplies, as well as the centerpiece of the room, a three-drawer dresser with a sizable new television set on top.

But there's no time for TV now. Ming immediately launches back into her homework, sitting on a tiny stool and using the top of her bed as a writing surface. Shuanghai uncovers lunch's shredded potato leftovers and then goes out into a common hallway where the building's first-floor tenants keep their kerosene-powered cookstoves. She begins heating water to make *miantang*, or thickened flour water "soup."

Once dinner is under control, Shuanghai peels a pear, letting the skin fall onto the room's cement floor, and hands it to her daughter. Then she sits on Ming's bed and peers down at her homework.

"Mama, how do you write this character?" Ming asks.

Shuanghai thinks for a moment, but she isn't sure. "Let's look in the dictionary," she says, finally, and pulls an ancient volume off a shelf above the bed. While she leafs through the book, Ming sweeps up the pear skins.

Shuanghai and Donghua worry about their daughter's studies as much and as often as they can. When she was young, they left her with her grandma in the village while they worked in Xi'an, some six hours away. When she got older, they wanted her to live with them and go to a higher-quality city school, but they had no way to look after her properly, given their crazy work hours. So they settled instead on sending her to live with Shuanghai's sister, who, though still in the countryside, was only an hour away from Xi'an. Finally, when Ming turned nine, they decided she was old enough to get herself up and off to school in the morning, and she came to live with them. But somehow it seems those first few years in village schools left her so far behind in her studies that even now, three years later, she can't catch up. They pay for special after-school and weekend classes, but so far that hasn't seemed to help much. Maybe, they fret, she's simply just too dumb.

The sound of a pot boiling over interrupts Shuanghai's thoughts, and she looks up from the dictionary, momentarily confused, and then rushes into the hallway to tend her flour water soup. Ming laughs at her mother, a woman who might be able to remember the fluctuating prices of more than three dozen produce items without any effort but who is renowned for her forgetful spells at home. Just last week she cut up a pile of green onions and then absentmindedly dumped them into the trash before she could use them.

In the midst of all this, Donghua arrives, befuddled that he can't get the three-wheeler up over the curb and into the building's entryway, where he parks it at night. The bricks he usually uses as a ramp are suddenly missing, so all three of them file out into the dark street, first scouring for the missing bricks and then, when they can't be located, working together to push the vehicle inside. When they've finished their task, Ming grabs a flashlight and a few *mao* from her dad and disappears down the dark alley toward the public restroom on the next block.

"Living in the city is such a hassle," Shuanghai sighs. "Everything takes money, even going to the bathroom."

"Yeah, in the city if you have money you have everything," Donghua agrees. But here in their garage, with its high ceiling stained with mold and draped with years of black cobwebs, it's clear they don't have everything and probably won't any time soon. Sure, Donghua is quick to concede, if you use the village standard, where a laborer might only make 15–20 yuan per day, selling vegetables isn't bad business at all. But if you use the city standard, the 2,000 yuan they usually bring home in a month is not much more than two factory workers would make. And if you use the High-Tech Zone standard, well then they don't even make enough to pay rent for a proper apartment. As it is, they're paying 120 yuan just to live in a garage.

Ming returns and they slide the metal door closed behind her, revealing a host of phone numbers scrawled in chalk across its surface—Shuanghai's way to make sure important information doesn't get lost. Donghua tips a yellow plastic crate on its end and balances a large cutting board on top to serve as a makeshift table. Shuanghai puts the potato dish on it, scoops out three big bowls of *miantang*, and dinner is ready. They tend to eat simply—most meals consisting of just one dish and one staple—not, Donghua says, in order to save money but simply because it's too inconvenient to prepare big meals in such a tiny room.

"Our place here is very small, very messy," he says. "Not like our home in the village. There we've got everything."

From the day Shuanghai's mom first brought up the idea of marriage, Donghua started thinking about how he could afford to build them a house. Never mind that Shuanghai hadn't yet consented to be his wife; he knew she wouldn't refuse forever. So he started doing construction work for a local contractor, and by the time Shuanghai finally did agree, he had scraped together just enough to build and furnish a little two-room house. But now there it sits, locked up and unused for the past ten years, while they've stayed in rundown places like this.

Sometimes Donghua talks about going back to the village, and Ming is always quick to jump in, extolling every stone and pebble of her idyllic childhood. But Shuanghai will hear none of it. "We definitely want to go back, but there's no opportunity for development there," she says.

"Yeah, but selling vegetables doesn't give us any opportunity to grow, either," Donghua replies.

"You have to go back to the village on a solid financial foundation," she explains. "If you have money, you can go back and open a store or a factory. If you have money, you can do a lot back there. But if we go back without money, what are we going to do, live off a farmer's salary again?"

It's a logic that Donghua knows is right. Though he loves to talk about going home, he can't imagine actually being able to do so until he's old, until his body wears out and there's nothing more he can do here. Besides, right now their goal is to let Ming study and grow up with chances they never had, and that means staying in the city where they can make more money and she can attend better schools.

"If she goes to a university, we'll need 20,000 to 30,000 yuan per year. If she doesn't get in, then we'll want her to go to trade school or do some other type of study," Donghua says. "As long as our daughter's life is better than ours, it's all worth it."

Shuanghai agrees: "You see we're so tired, it's all for her. Our child is our biggest responsibility. We don't want her to be as tired as us. We don't want to let her follow in our footsteps."

After they've finished dinner, Shuanghai flips on the TV and they clear away the dishes. Most nights they don't finish eating until almost 10:00 p.m. If they're not too tired, they'll watch television for half an hour before they fall asleep, mindful that their 3:00 a.m. wake-up call is just around the corner. Ming likes to spend that time drawing, but for Donghua indulging in any sort of recreation is unthinkable.

"My dad just loves sleeping," Ming says. "That's his hobby."

"I'm always so tired," he agrees, yawning. "There's no time to think about liking anything else."

It's too soon to tell yet whether Shuanghai and Donghua's dreams for Ming's future are realizable. It's not a mere question of funds, or ability, or even desire; for children of rural migrants, the equation is more complex.

Until recently, kids from the countryside had to pay substantially more than their urban counterparts to attend city schools. Though the law now mandates that they are charged the same price as everyone else, good schools are typically so expensive as to be non-options and many schools simply refuse enrollment to migrant children. Even at the cheaper urban schools, competition is extreme, and there's a huge gulf between kids like Ming and her city-born-and-bred classmates. To address these problems, unofficial schools for migrant children are popping up in many of China's metropolitan areas. Unfortunately, the quality of the education there isn't much better than countryside schools, where typically almost half of the students don't test past junior high, much less make it to college.

Many parents simply avoid these hassles by leaving their children with relatives back in the village, telling themselves that the monetary gains are worth the separation. Though they took that route for Ming's first few years of primary school, it was hard on Donghua and Shuanghai—if they allow themselves one indulgence at all, it's an uncharacteristic touch of sentimentality toward their daughter. But their dilemmas are lost on Ming, who looks at the rundown market, their rundown living quarters, and her parents' increasingly rundown faces and can't understand all the hype about city life. And though her parents continue to plow ahead, hopeful for her future, Ming longs to go back to the village where she remembers spending a tranquil, playful childhood.

Early mornings at the wholesale market can be dangerous. Never mind the overcrowding and the freezing cold. By 4:00 a.m., its cement floor is covered with discarded veggie scraps that have been trampled into a thick, slick paste. Shuanghai skids a bit as she hustles between trucks, looking for the perfect batch of cauliflower. They've been here forty minutes now, and she has yet to make a purchase. That's because yesterday Donghua bought cauliflower that was already turning black, and they lost 50 yuan on it alone. She's determined to do better today, but the challenge to buying vegetables here—in addition to being tired and pressed for time—is that, unlike the way business is done at their own market, there is no negotiating on prices and no rummaging to find the best-quality merchandise. Instead, most produce is already bound up in big clear plastic bags, leaving buyers to judge from the ones that are visible and hope for the best. But of course the best doesn't always happen, and so most days Shuanghai and Donghua end up losing money on something.

Unable to make up her mind about the cauliflower, she decides to buy some chives first. She heaves them up onto her shoulder—the transport method of choice for heavy parcels—and scurries across the pulpy ground to deposit them in the motorcycle cart. Donghua also happens to be there, dropping off 16 *jin* of shallots that he just bought for 30 yuan. He's excited, as this is the first day they've been available. "I haven't seen these yet this season," he says. "But 30 yuan...is that too expensive?" Shuanghai is busy unloading the chives, and in her silence he decides that, indeed, he's paid too much. "I'm already regretting this," he sighs.

Before they part ways again, he tells her to buy some cucumbers, but she's not willing. These days they're too expensive and haven't been selling well. Besides, it's already 4:35 a.m., and so

far all that she's bought are these chives. Instead, she tells Donghua, she's off to buy cauliflower, since she's seen some that's very
white, if not a bit big. He snorts. "When you look at them here
they seem so white, but when you get them back to the market,
they're not white at all."

Funny how life is like that—never quite what it seems, and
certainly never what one is expecting. When Shuanghai refused
to marry Donghua it was because she wanted out of the
countryside—but when she finally gave in, she had reconciled
herself to staying put, she really had. It was destiny itself that
thrust city life upon them. Near the end of their first year of
marriage, just a month before Ming was born, Donghua was still
doing part-time construction work when a building collapsed on
him. He came within inches of dying, and recovery meant numerous surgeries and nearly two years in and out of the hospital.

They borrowed more than 40,000 yuan to cover the medical
expenses—an amount so astronomical that they would have no
chance of ever paying it back, at least not on a farmer's income.
And still he needed more medicine, more trips to the hospital.
They'd already tapped all their friends and family dry, and so
Shuanghai headed to Xi'an—not to satisfy the wanderlust that
had consumed her just a few years earlier but to see if she could
start sending money back home to pay off their skyrocketing
debts. She scrounged up one last round of charity, borrowing
about 2,000 yuan to get started in the city, and left Donghua and
Ming—now almost two years old—in her mother-in-law's care.

Once she got to the capital city she looked up a fellow villager who was making a fairly decent living selling vegetables,
and she decided to give it a try. She invested 800 yuan in a three-
wheeled pedal bike, and the very next day she was in business.
Early each morning she'd ride forty-five minutes to the nearest

wholesale market and then spend her day tooling around the city selling produce out of the back of the bike. She was able to make enough to fund the final stages of Donghua's recovery, and about a year later, he joined her in Xi'an.

Living in the city is nothing like she'd dreamed it would be, but still, she says, she can't complain—not about their life, or their setup, or her husband. Whether they're happily married or not, whether giving in to her mother was the right thing to do or not—these are things she's never really thought about much. They're married now and need to focus all their attention on providing for Ming's future; for Shuanghai, thinking about anything else is just a waste of time.

By 6:10 a.m. the sky is starting to lighten and the market traffic is thinning. They meet back up at the motorcycle, which is now heaped with the morning's purchases. There is no room left in the cart for Shuanghai to sit, so instead she stands on the cart's narrow back bumper and clings to the metal side railing. Though it's precarious, she doesn't sit or stand in the back simply because that's what wives are expected to do. In fact, Donghua would like it very much if she would take the reins, but she can't because she doesn't know how to drive, and despite his urging, she has no desire to learn. "If I know how to drive, he won't get up in the morning," she says. "He's really lazy." Funny for a guy who's gotten up at 3:00 a.m. every day for nearly a decade.

If she could drive, not only would Donghua have the option of sleeping in sometimes, but he could also go back to the village for a visit on occasion. As of now, he's only gone home once in all these years, and that was to commemorate the third anniversary of his father's passing—a tradition in western China's countryside that can't be missed. Besides that, he has to stay put; otherwise they would have to close shop completely in his absence.

"No doubt he'd like me to learn how to drive. It'd be a great advantage to him," Shuanghai says. But she is not ready to go down that road just yet. As they pull out of the parking lot, she lets out a belly laugh. "I know my idea's not right, but still…"

Another thing Donghua hadn't anticipated when he chose this retail market six years ago was the advent of the superstore. Before moving here they'd heard that mammoth chain stores were popping up in big cities in the south, but they'd never actually seen one in Xi'an, where small-time street sales were still the norm. Who would have thought that just two years later *Ai Jia*, a leviathan literally called Love Home, would be built just half a block away.

At first *Ai Jia* didn't affect business much, since people were used to buying ultra-fresh veggies like theirs, not the wilted ones that *Ai Jia* had to offer. But recently even that has started to change. People are busier and are no longer willing to shop for groceries every day, and *Ai Jia* has begun selling some of its produce at a loss just to bring customers in the door.

To make matters worse, the High-Tech Zone has started clamping down on pedal-bike vendors, no longer allowing them to display their wares on busy street corners or in front of local housing complexes. And in some neighborhoods, small-time open-air markets like theirs don't even exist anymore. As integral as rural migrants may be to China's city life, it turns out that, as individuals, they are equally dispensable.

Ai Jia may be the wave of the future, but Donghua has no time to think about that tonight. Instead he looks down at their table, still flush with inventory, and knows what's in his immediate future—losing money. Their clever little plan to stock up before the National Day break backfired: the last few days have been nothing but clear and sunny skies, which means a lot of people headed out of town and vegetable sales plummeted, leaving them with a whole lot of goods that are not moving anywhere. As it is, he's out 100 yuan today, and he doesn't even want to think about what tomorrow may bring.

"*Zen me ban*," Donghua mutters to himself as he surveys the spread before him, asking "What can be done?" Shuanghai and Ming just left for the night, and it's time for him to begin packing up. He starts where he always starts—sorting the vegetables according to those that are still in excellent condition, those that will have to be sold at a discount tomorrow, and those that won't make it another day.

He picks up an old zucchini with several brown spots. Shaking his head, he grabs his butcher knife and cuts off the sides to reveal inner flesh that's perfectly white. "In the countryside we'd definitely still eat this. If it's something you grew yourself, you'd think it's such a pity to waste over just a few spots. But if you have to pay for it, I guess you want it to be perfect," Donghua laments, chucking it onto the floor.

A lady in a navy-blue blazer comes around the table, looking at his cauliflower. She wants to buy a fresh new head for 8 *mao*, but Donghua offers her an older, barely passable one for 5 *mao* instead.

"That cauliflower is bad," she says. "It's turning black already."

"You won't even buy it for 5 *mao*?" he asks.

"Give me the good stuff for 8 *mao* and I'll buy it," she insists. "Otherwise I won't buy from you."

"Then it looks like you won't be buying anything from me," he replies, in no mood for bargaining tonight. "Bye-bye."

Donghua turns his attention back to his vegetable sorting. Soon there's a pile of keepers towering in the corner of the table, but it's the floor, littered with rotting discards, that still has him grumbling *zen me ban* over and over. Before long, the navy-blazer lady is back, this time under the guise of buying tomatoes—though she's clearly still eyeing the cauliflower.

"8 *mao?*" she asks hopefully. Donghua merely shakes his head. "Don't regret this," she warns, starting to turn away again.

Donghua wonders sometimes if people like her understand, if they've ever even thought for a moment how hard people like he and Shuanghai work for each and every *mao*, and if they have any idea what those *mao* mean to them. It took almost ten years for them to save up enough to pay back all the people who helped him cover his medical bills. But then, just when they started to build up a tiny bit of savings, his brother's wife got sick and needed their nest egg. Now, finally, they've started saving again, but so far they've only amassed a few thousand yuan, nowhere near what they'll need to get their daughter a proper education. No, he muses as the lady walks slowly down the aisle, waiting for him to call her back and offer the premium cauliflower at a losing price, he surely won't regret it. Not tonight anyway.

Donghua is still pressing, squeezing, and ruing his plight when the market's custodian of sorts—an old man with a home-made broom in one hand and a shovel in the other—pulls up a stool and sits at the end of the table smoking. Once the peddlers have put their veggies to bed, his task each night is to sweep the produce from the floor and cart it away in a wheelbarrow. Most of the others have already finished and gone home; now he's simply waiting for Donghua to do the same.

Across the aisle the boys who work the *mantou* shop are singing as they wash their clothes in a big red basin, carefully hanging their pants along the rim of the tiny shack's sliding metal door. They're in no hurry, since they live right here in the market. After all, someone needs to guard all those steamers at night; unlike veggies, they're worth something.

Donghua eventually gets all the leftovers stowed under a tarp. He uses an old bunch of parsley to dust the table off and pronounces himself ready to go. As he revs his three-wheeler, the custodian gets up from his stool and starts sweeping and shoveling his way down the aisle. For him, there's still a long night ahead.

A month later, in mid-November, the neighborhood market closes down unexpectedly under the pretense of cleaning and repair. There was no advanced warning—the merchants were doing business as usual one day and then simply told not to come the next. Donghua and Shuanghai began the sudden respite from work in good spirits, using the first two days off to move out of the garage in Gan Jia Zhai and into a room on the top floor of a five-story house in one of the only nearby villages that has not already been torn down. Though still just a single room with no bathroom, no heating, and no running water, it is noticeably bigger and brighter than the previous one, with a tiled rather than cemented floor and a large window looking out onto the High-Tech Zone. They definitely like the new place, but they're still not convinced it's worth the extra 60 yuan a month—the price of a haircut in one of the High-Tech Zone's moderately priced salons.

By their third day off, they don't know what to do with themselves, having no hobbies or interests to fill up their time. And so they spend the next two days watching TV and getting terribly depressed. Being exhausted but busy, Donghua concludes, is much better than being relaxed but bored.

Only during rare occasions like this, when there's suddenly nothing to fill his mind, does he allow himself the luxury of worrying about the future. They say the market will open up again after a week or so, but who knows? What if it closes for good? What, he wonders, would they do then? "We don't have much education. We don't have any profession or any specialty, so we can just do small-time buying and selling," he says. "Even if our daughter can't get into university, she can study something else, some other kind of craft. Then she can go out and work for someone else and use her talents. But we don't have any."

"We can do something else, or find another place to sell vegetables. Everything's possible," Shuanghai reassures him. "We don't have to worry. When it happens, we'll look at the situation, see how the society's developing, and find our place in it. That's the way you do things when you have no other way."

In a strange sense it's that lack of other options, that being battered about by the country's march toward modernization and capitalism, that keeps them going. If they are to survive here in the no-man's-land between old and new, they must stay nimble, light on their feet, and ready at any moment to seize new opportunities. With so little to lose, everything is possible.

And even in times of self-doubt, Donghua admits that having come from the countryside and living—and surviving—in Xi'an for so many years gives them a degree of self-confidence that farmers who've never left the village don't have. They may be among the lowest level of society here in the city, but if there's one thing they know how to do, it's persevere.

And so today, their fifth day off from work, they decide to have pork dumplings for lunch—a rarity for them because they're expensive and time-consuming to make. But it's something to keep them occupied, they decide, as they pull out the makeshift crate-and-cutting-board table. Shuanghai rolls out the dough skins, and Donghua stuffs in the filling and pinches them closed. When Ming gets home for lunch, Shuanghai fires up the kerosene stove in the hallway and starts boiling water. Within minutes there's a bowl of steaming hot dumplings in front of each of them, and they settle in to watch a Chinese women's volleyball match on TV, though none of them are totally sure they understand the rules.

As Donghua reclines on his bed, remote in hand, full, and a bit sleepy, it strikes him how different this life is from what he knew growing up. "When we were young in the countryside, we were starving, and you couldn't make even one cent. Then the big impossible dream was to have a bicycle," he says with a laugh. "Society's developed so fast. Back then there wasn't electricity in the village, we just had candles. Now most of the farmers there have motorcycles. And look at us, we have a big TV. We couldn't have even imagined it before, and we don't dare think of wanting anything else."

CHAPTER TWO

The Impenetrable Knife Sharpener

Wang Quanxi has never read a book. He's never used a calculator or owned a telephone, never opened a bank account or sat in a car. He's never seen a computer. And the Internet... well, he's never even heard of that.

But if there's one thing he knows, and knows well, it is knives. Butcher knives, carving knives, paring knives, and boning knives. New knives, crooked knives, warped knives, and rusty knives. During the past two decades he's spent trolling the streets of Xi'an, he's seen knives of every cast and condition, and he's sharpened them all.

This morning he found his first knife just minutes after emerging from his room in Gan Jia Zhai, but now he's been wandering the streets for more than an hour and still hasn't unearthed another. As he pushes his ancient bicycle past some of the High-Tech Zone's newest housing developments, he flips on a battery-powered bullhorn and the refrain of "Knife sharpening! Cutting board sanding!" blares out loudly enough to reach even the twentieth-story penthouses. He trudges ahead slowly, not because his cast-iron bike and associated gear weigh even more than he does, or because his sixty-something-year-old feet are sweating and slipping in his blue plastic flip-flops. No, he creeps along slowly simply to give potential customers enough time to get to their windows and let him know they're bringing their knives down for him to sharpen.

But, alas, there are no takers today, and so when he reaches the entrance to a gated community—the point beyond which people like him are categorically not allowed—he parks his bicycle at the curb and sits down next to a couple of rice peddlers who are already resting there. Then he opens up a flip-top container of Extra gum, cantaloupe flavor, and takes a whiff. He's never tried the stuff and is not sure why anyone would want to pay good money for "mouth fragrant candy," as gum is literally called in Chinese, but the container has kept his tobacco well preserved for years now. Quanxi shakes a little line of it out onto a newspaper scrap and then rolls it up and licks the end to ensure that his homemade cigarette sticks together.

As he sits there enjoying his smoke, he leaves the bullhorn on—more out of laziness than in an effort to keep scouting for dull-knife customers. Eventually, though, a security guard comes over and tells him he's disturbing the public peace with all that clatter. No doubt he's also disturbing the public sense of modernization with a funnel-shaped straw peasant hat perched atop his head, an unkempt goatee sprouting from his chin, and a battered Flying Pigeon bike parked at his feet, but that's not an issue this particular guard attempts to address.

Without a word, Quanxi reaches up and turns off the bullhorn nestled in his bicycle basket. He savors another minute of silent camaraderie sitting among others who work hard for their money and don't give a damn about their place in society. Then he gets up and starts pushing his bicycle again, flaming bits of newspaper drifting from his cigarette as he goes. He flips the bullhorn back on and his hunt for knife number two begins anew.

He decides to give up on the ritzy part of the High-Tech Zone for now and heads instead toward Shajingcun, an old-time village that, like Gan Jia Zhai, is now nestled within the Zone's protective embrace. He's barely set foot in the village when a woman pokes her head out of a tiny noodle joint and asks if he sharpens knives. He gives a confirmatory grunt and the lady disappears into her restaurant, returning a few moments later with a butcher knife in hand.

It's 9:27 a.m., and Quanxi has finally found his second knife of the day. As soon as it hits his palms, he is in his element. He's no longer a man searching for work; he's a knife sharpener, as he's called on the streets, and he has a job to do.

He starts by pulling a ragtag assortment of sharpening paraphernalia off the hooks he's strategically fixed onto his bicycle. The centerpiece of his operation is a wobbly wooden bench with an old couch cushion strapped to the middle. He seats himself on this makeshift saddle of sorts with the intensity of a bullfighter mounting his steed. Then, after finding just the right grip on the knife, he leans forward and begins sliding it rhythmically back and forth over a grinding stone roped to the end of the bench. After several minutes he turns around in the saddle and repeats the entire process, this time using the more finely grained stone attached to the other end.

His concentration is broken when a car pulls up behind him and honks to let him know he's blocking the way. He gets up, subconsciously fingering the blade while moving his equipment off to the side. Deciding that the knife is not yet honed to his professional standards, Quanxi settles back into the saddle for another quick round of sharpening.

By 9:35 he proclaims the knife thoroughly sharp and the noodle bar owner hands him 2 yuan. It's not bad money for eight minutes of work, and if he could pocket that much every eight minutes for the entire twelve to fourteen hours that he usually spends on the streets each day, he could have gone back home to live with his wife in the countryside long ago. Unfortunately though, most days the bulk of his time is spent searching for customers, and some days he's lucky even to find one knife every hour. This morning's pace has proven even worse, so Quanxi shoves the money into his pocket, hooks his gear back onto the bike, and hurries off in pursuit of knife number three.

A few minutes later Quanxi turns down a dilapidated alleyway where a load of bricks is being hoisted in a wheelbarrow to the top of a building. As he approaches, the bricks come crashing five stories down at him, but he simply steps out of the way and presses ahead. Further on, as he passes a restaurant with a cooking station set up along the roadside, a pot of hot soup explodes up into the air, but again he simply shuffles out of the way and keeps going. After that, a mangy yellow dog with a menacing growl storms after him, but he simply stamps a plastic-sandaled foot at it and moves on.

In his two-plus decades sharpening knives on China's city streets, there's not much Quanxi hasn't seen or sidestepped, but all these potential hazards seem so minor compared to the days he's lived through that he hardly even notices them. He sees no danger in this job at all ... as long as he keeps his fingers out of the way.

As he winds through the village, another woman flags him down and, like the customer before her, asks if he sharpens knives.

Wang Quanxi sharpens a knife in Gan Jia Zhai.

"Yep," he replies, not sure why the bike full of gear and the bullhorn's blaring announcement are not clear enough indications of his profession.

"How much?"

"2 kuai," he says, using a slang term for the Chinese yuan.

"2 kuai? Follow me." The woman leads him down the street and around the corner before disappearing into her home. Quanxi rolls a cigarette while he waits and is just about to light it when the woman returns with two knives in tow. He sets to work immediately, unlit cigarette dangling from his lips while he unpacks his gear and launches into his sharpening routine.

"We Chinese have to *chiku*," the woman says as she stands on the sidewalk watching him. "All that"—she points as Quanxi's scrawny body blends into a single blur of motion with the blade—"just to make a little bit of money."

It's no secret that when China's peasants arrive in metropolitan areas, they are typically relegated to the low-level, labor-intensive jobs snubbed by local urbanites. But for old-timers like Quanxi, who lack even the most basic literacy skills, the options are even more limited.

It didn't have to be like this. Back when Quanxi was growing up in the 1950s, he had the chance to be at the forefront of his generation. Most village kids didn't go to school at the time, but though his parents were among the poorest of the poor, they wanted their children to have the opportunities an education could bring. And so young Quanxi headed dutifully off to school, but it didn't take him more than a couple hours stuck behind a desk to deem it meaningless; after a week in first grade, he simply stopped going.

With the country fresh off the Communist revolution and farm production lagging, his parents were too occupied elsewhere to make a fuss; sending a peasant kid to school seemed more of a novelty than a necessity anyway. But over the next two decades the new government made great strides in providing a basic education to urban and rural kids alike, and the literacy rate, which stood at a mere 20 percent in 1949, began to rapidly climb. While an obvious boon for the country and its people, that left Quanxi and his poorly educated compatriots outdated well before their time.

Back on the farm it doesn't seem to matter so much, but with nine-year compulsory education now nearly universal throughout the country and the literary rate among the youth population at a full 99 percent, many factory and service jobs require at least a junior high school education—which means Quanxi is not qualified even for what is typically deemed unskilled labor.

The logical choice for people like him, then, is to engage in some form of petty entrepreneurship with no barriers to entry. Even so, Quanxi is admittedly among the smallest of the small-time entrepreneurs still found on China's city streets. There are simply not that many avenues left for people looking for an opportunity with virtually no start-up costs, no overhead, no paperwork, and no oversight. But it's that simplicity that makes knife sharpening ideal for him. "If you do a real business, then you're going to have overhead. I don't have any costs and as soon as I sharpen one knife, I immediately get my money," he explains. That, in his mind, is the only way for someone like him to survive in today's urban China.

Without the ability to read or write and a memory that he says has long since abandoned him, Quanxi has to rely heavily on his sixth sense to get things done. And so it is that he wakes up one blistering hot morning and knows it's time to head over to the fancy two-story restaurant that is the closest thing to a regular customer he's ever had. He doesn't know this because he called the boss or made an appointment or checked a calendar; he just suddenly has the feeling that their blades must be pretty worn down by now. Since the restaurant usually has six knives to sharpen and six cutting boards to sand, it's a feeling he's not inclined to ignore. He hurries through his already short morning routine, pulling on his clothes and wolfing down a crusty piece of steamed bread before rushing off to the restaurant as fast as his loaded-down bike will allow.

This is a high-class place, and though it's not open for business so early, Quanxi doesn't dare come in through the front door; instead, he climbs up the back stairway into the kitchen, where he waits for someone to acknowledge him. Two girls squatting over a tub of potatoes finally look up from their peelers. Yes, they confirm, they are indeed in need of his services, but since the boss isn't around right now, they advise him to come back in the afternoon.

As he heads downstairs, his mind darts for a moment to his younger brother and sister, who both went to school and stayed in school. Along with most of the other village kids of their generation who actually made it through junior high, his siblings eventually became teachers in neighboring villages. Now they're retired, with pensions, and have nothing to do all day, while Quanxi is still out pounding the pavement looking for dull cutlery. "I started regretting my decision a long time ago, but it was already too late for me," he says. "It's a real pity, but there's nothing I can do about it now."

After leaving the fancy restaurant, Quanxi starts scouring the neighborhood for other customers. As he passes a diner with a row of red paper lanterns swaying out front, a cook rushes out to ask how much he charges. Quanxi tells him 2 yuan per knife and 5 per cutting board. The cook starts haggling with him, but Quanxi is not in the mood to lower his price.

"We'll give you 5 kuai for each knife-cutting board set, and we've got a bunch of sets," the young man tells him. "If you do a good job, we'll always call you." He sizes Quanxi up and then asks, "You've got a phone, right?"

"Nope."

"No phone?" the cook snorts. "How can we connect with you next time then?"

Quanxi simply shrugs. "I come through here a lot."

They quibble a bit longer, but Quanxi eventually agrees to the lower price. He pulls an electric sander off his bicycle and unwinds a twisted extension cord while two other cooks stack cutting boards on the sidewalk next to him.

These are not cutting boards in the traditional sense of the word, and they bear little resemblance to the sheets of flimsy plastic or pressed wood used in Western countries. Like most heavy-duty restaurant-grade chopping blocks in China, they are simply circular slabs taken out of a tree trunk, measuring about 4 inches thick and 20 to 25 inches across and sporting a layer of bark around their outer edge.

Quanxi squats down beside the first board, which is still full of minced garlic, and starts sanding right over the sticky surface. Younger members of the kitchen staff crowd around, watching as he moves the shrill power tool in circles across the board. This proves to be a great advertisement, and before long a server from a café across the street hustles over to tell Quanxi that they have work for him when he's finished here. A few minutes later a pedestrian stops to inquire about his services, promising to bring her family's knives out shortly.

The diner's boss, a pudgy man sporting a white tank top and bad teeth, drinks his morning tea and follows Quanxi's seemingly booming business from the window. "In one day this guy can make at least 100 kuai. Not bad at all. He doesn't look like it, but he's got money all right," he tells his nearby employees. They disagree, but the boss insists. Only after he starts walking through Quanxi's daily financial opportunities does he begin to backtrack. "Okay, so some days maybe he can only make 50 or even 20 yuan, but when he finds places like this, he's making a lot more."

Wang Quanxi doesn't know his own age, or the year he married, or even the decade in which his four children were born. He can't remember names or numbers, and sometimes he's not even sure what year it is. But if there's one date he knows, one date that is so deeply engraved on his soul that he can never forget, it is 1958, the year the Great Leap Forward ushered in collectivized farming across rural China. Depending on the day he's trying to recollect, he was as young as eight or as old as thirteen when the policy started. Whatever his age, 1958 brought his school-free days of running wild to a sudden halt and commenced a crash course in eating bitterness that has proven indispensible during his twenty-year stint on the city streets.

Under communal agriculture, everyone was assigned a specific job: farming, cutting trees, making bricks, or even cooking for the entire collective. Work received no remuneration beyond simply getting to eat, and everyone, no matter whether they applied themselves or not, got a serving from what became known archly as *Da Guo Fan*, or the "Big Rice Pot." "There was no question of whether we were used to the new system or not," Quanxi recalls. "We were all poor, and our main thought was just to fill our stomachs." Unfortunately, that turned out to be difficult: three years of starvation ensued, and the country lost an estimated twenty to thirty million people. No one in his village died, but they endured their share of hardships. "After 1958 we were hungry and couldn't find enough to eat. We were eating bark and grass and roots and weeds. That's not something you can forget."

After those terrible first few years, the country modified the collective system somewhat. Labor still had no substantial cash value, but now at least it earned points that could be redeemed for additional food provisions. As Quanxi grew up, he gained a reputation for being a strong, hard worker and before long he was assigned to the commune's brick factory. It wouldn't have been so bad if he'd gotten one of the easier tasks, like digging dirt or pouring mud into molds, but he was put in charge of firing the bricks—the absolute worst job of all. Not only was it incredibly hot and dirty, but if he accidentally tripped, death was almost certain.

Though he can't remember the details anymore, Quanxi is pretty sure he stayed at the brick factory for at least six or seven years, if not a decade or more. Regardless, it was long enough to ensure that no job has ever seemed too dangerous or dirty or distasteful to him again—especially not when there's some real cash involved. Now the younger generation—those who've never endured the likes of 1958 and beyond—thinks something as simple as sharpening knives is a bitterness that's too big to be eaten, but for Quanxi and those who lived through that bygone era in Chinese history it's one that's too small to even notice. "Life here is so much easier," he says. "In Xi'an there's no such thing as eating bitterness."

Eating bitterness is subjective.

Sanding is not as quick and easy as knife sharpening tends to be, and it takes more than an hour for Quanxi to finish the restaurant's cutting boards. When they are eventually sanded to his satisfaction, Quanxi turns his attention to the knives. They're in pitiful condition, with warped edges, big grooves, and whole chunks of metal missing, and he'll need to pull out all the stops to get them back in top condition.

When he finishes the first knife the head cook gives it a thorough inspection. Not only does it pass the test, but he's so impressed with the knife sharpener's craftsmanship that he sends an assistant to round up any blades they might have overlooked. Though never one to pass up a chance to make more money, Quanxi starts to feel anxious; he knows that if he doesn't get to the café across the street before the lunch crowd begins pouring in, they won't be able to relinquish their cutting equipment to him. Sure enough, it isn't long before they send someone over, urging him to hurry.

"I'm still busy here," Quanxi grunts, without looking up.

"Then forget it," says the young man, as he starts walking away. "Don't bother coming."

"How many sets do you have?"

"Four."

Quanxi doesn't respond; he just slides the knife across the grinding stone with enhanced vigor. He finishes up within a half hour and is packing up his gear when the buck-teethed boss comes out of the diner, waving a knife in the air and yelling that it isn't straight enough.

They bicker for a minute, but in the end Quanxi knows he doesn't really have a choice; they'll only hand over his money when they're fully satisfied with his work. In this regard, he's a bit like an indentured servant, only in hour-long spurts. So he slides the couch cushion back into position and climbs into the saddle once again. He works another fifteen minutes before the boss begrudgingly hands over 22 yuan.

Quanxi originally agreed to 20 yuan for four knife-cutting board sets. He didn't actually keep track of how many extra knives they brought out to him in the end, but he knows it was more than 2 kuai' worth. Though he wants to protest, he can see that it will do no good with this boss, and he doesn't have time to waste anymore; the café's four sets are worth more than the couple yuan this guy is shorting him, so he snatches up the money and hurries across the street.

Quanxi can deal with long, hard work for unfair pay—especially since the first part of his life was all about long, hard work for no pay whatsoever. But it's still hard for him to just walk away from cheapskate bosses like this. During the era of collectivization, when labor had little to no cash value, perseverance was one of the most valuable commodities a person could possess. In recent years, though, as he's struggled to survive in the city's ever-morphing landscape, he's learned that time is money, and that sometimes the most lucrative course of action isn't to persevere but, rather, to just keep moving.

It's not a lesson that has come easy to him, considering how stubbornly he's had to struggle for everything else in his life. Take his wedding, for example. Though his parents chose a wife for him in his late teens, actually getting married was impossible; weddings required money, and his family had none. So he kept plodding away at the brick factory, waiting until he could afford a traditional wedding banquet. It took five or six years, but in the end his perseverance paid off and he earned himself a wife.

Perseverance was also the only way he and his bride were able to build a home for themselves at a time when money was still scarce. He could do the construction himself—the problem was simply how to get the bricks he needed. If he bought them directly from the brick factory, he could only afford enough to build a one-room house. But since brick-making required an excessive amount of coal, the factory agreed to give him twice as many bricks if he paid in coal rather than cash. Without hesitation, he trundled through the woods with a wheelbarrow for two days to the nearest coal mine, filled it with several hundred kilos of coal, and immediately started on the long—and now much heavier—journey home. He made three trips and spent a total of 60 yuan, less than $10, before he had enough coal to trade for 3,000 poor-quality bricks; two weeks later, he completed their new three-room house.

As he finishes telling the story, Quanxi pauses to twirl a blade of grass between his teeth. On second thought, he admits ever so sheepishly, maybe the bricks-for-coal swap wasn't the way he built a home for himself but, rather, for his oldest son after his wedding. Granted, the two events happened nearly two decades apart, but nowadays everything after 1958 runs together in his mind. The hand of fate might have made him more than able to deal with long, hard work no matter what the pay, but it didn't equip him to retain all the details. "I can't remember that far back," he says, deciding once again that the brick trade was how he and his wife built their own home. "It's not something that happened three or four years ago. Now the only thing I think about every day is how to make money. I've forgotten all that other stuff."

By the time Quanxi arrives at the café it's nearing noon and, as expected, the kitchen staff can't surrender their boards and knives to him anymore. So he squats instead against the building's faux picket-fence exterior and rolls the first cigarette he's had time for all day. He blows out a huge cloud of smoke, flips on the bullhorn, and then heads off down the street. As he passes a strip of tiny, five-table eateries, a man sitting outside waves him down. He asks the standard pricing questions and then, without negotiation, heads into his restaurant to retrieve a cutting board. Before he even reaches the entrance, however, his wife rushes out and screeches, "Not now! The restaurant's full!" She sees Quanxi unloading his sharpening supplies and shoos him away as if he's a fly on her food. "No, no, no! Come back after 2!"

Obediently, Quanxi packs back up and moves on. A few minutes later he turns onto a main thoroughfare and immediately silences his bullhorn. Leaving it on in the High-Tech Zone's busier neighborhoods is a sure way to get his stuff confiscated by the police. When Quanxi first hit the city streets two decades ago, people like him were the norm, and no one thought a thing about such peddlers canvassing the streets. But now, though ultra-petty entrepreneurs are still an important part of city life, they've also been deemed a part of the underground economy that needs to stay a bit more underground. Now it's a love-hate relationship in these areas; urbanites need the services and appreciate the convenience, but they still don't want to have to stare it in the face. Local officials likewise recognize the contributions these entrepreneurs make to the city's development, but they still don't want them to mar its gleaming-new image.

The key for small-time businesspeople, then, is to stick to the back streets as much as possible. So when Quanxi turns into a village two blocks later, he's not at all surprised to find another knife sharpener working a blade over a grinding stone in the alleyway. He's equally unsurprised that this sharpener has a setup nearly identical to his own. After all, almost all the knife sharpeners in this part of Xi'an are from the same village in neighboring Henan province and have helped each other work the system for a very long time now.

Many generations ago their village was full of blacksmith artisans, and even now it's a place known for producing sickles and scythes, so knife sharpening seems like a logical and familiar choice for those looking to make extra money in the city. But none of them are out here now because of history or tradition or pride in craftsmanship, Quanxi says. As he sees it, there's only one reason they're all still sharpening knives in the new millennia: "None of us have any ability, so we have to do this kind of work."

Quanxi doesn't say this in a self-deprecating way but, rather, with a hint of relief: knowing that his fellow knife sharpeners are as outdated and unskilled as he is constitutes his only form of job security. They, like Quanxi, don't have phones or clocks or calendars to help them keep track of business, so they too must rely on luck and intuition to survive. If someone came in and made this a real, organized business, with customer lists and times and dates, there's no doubt they'd all be wiped out in a matter of months. He's already seen it happen to the people who used to bike around the city delivering jugs of purified water. Eventually some wise guys with motorcycles and minivans got together and just like that most of the bicyclers were forced to find something even more menial to do. But if that happened to them, Quanxi is not sure how much smaller-time he and his fellow knife sharpeners could go.

displaced by advancing technology.

After parting company with his village mate, Quanxi finds business from a lady running a rice porridge stand. As he sets up his equipment, she settles onto a pink plastic stool and stares at him intently, as if trying to solve a puzzle.

Out on the main streets of the High-Tech Zone, Quanxi and his kind are now totally out of place, but even in the old villages they're fast becoming anomalies, and no one is quite sure what to make of them. The speculation surrounding them is fueled by more than just the fact that they are petty entrepreneurs—there are, after all, lots of those still wandering about. Rather, it's their refusal to take even one step toward the modern nation China is becoming that makes them so intriguing to others.

Quanxi does little to dispel the mystique, playing his part to the fullest with his peasant garb and loaded-down bicycle that looks more like a bag lady's cache than a working man's toolbox. Sure, he says, he could clean up his act. He could wear nicer clothes, get rid of the straw hat, and arrange his equipment

Wang Quanxi's equipment-laden bicycle.

neatly, but if he did that then everyone would want something from him. No one's going to try to steal his stuff or hit him up for cash when he looks like this. And besides, it would be ridiculous to do such a grimy job with anything other than raggedy gear and dumpster-dive apparel. "This way fits with people's sense of beauty," he says.

He's halfway through with the knife when the porridge stand boss finally decides that she's figured him out. "He doesn't count as a real migrant worker," she says, checking the bobby pins in her well-plastered updo. "He counts as someone with nothing to do. He's out here for fun and only comes to the city when there's nothing to do back in his village. He doesn't rely on this income to live."

Contrary to what the porridge stand boss and her kind might think, Quanxi doesn't know anyone who's out on the streets just for fun. He and his village mates surely are not. While it might be possible to survive on their farming incomes, it is not possible to come even close to prospering, so they see their work here not as a pastime but as a necessity.

Finding jobs in the city is a possibility—and a necessity—created by the country's shift away from communal agriculture in the late 1970s. The reforms that followed led to a shortage of arable land per person and an enormous surplus of rural labor, which in turn left peasants suddenly searching for ways to earn additional money. At the same time cities began rapidly industrializing, and the rural-urban income disparity widened dramatically. Newly freed to choose how to allocate their own time and labor, millions of farmers rushed into the cities and snapped up whatever financial opportunities they could.

Quanxi would have run right out with them, but with four little kids and farming practices that had yet to enter the mechanized age, his wife needed help at home. That didn't mean they could rely solely on farming, it just meant that he couldn't find outside work too far away. In the end he fell back on the only thing he knew: working at the brick factory in the same exhausting job he'd done for so many years, only now he got paid in cash.

It wasn't until later, when the kids were closer to junior high age and able to help with the chores, that he finally made it out of the village. He spent an afternoon constructing his bench and collecting all the sharpening gear he would need and headed out the next day with three other local men. They took the bus to the provincial capital and shook it down for every dull knife they could find.

Over time, Quanxi hit all the major cities in the area and eventually made it all the way to Xi'an. Business turned out to be pretty good, so he decided to stay put. The only problem was that he was now more than seven hours away from his village and couldn't go back home very easily. Of course he always, without fail, headed home at planting and harvesting time, when the workload on the farm was at its peak, but other than that the only contact he had with his family was his monthly trip to the bank to wire them money.

Whether or not he missed his wife and kids and whether or not they missed him were questions that never even figured into his equation; the family needed more money, and working in the city was the best way he knew to provide it. "There was no question of emotions or not. There was no other choice," he says. "There was no choice when I had to stay, and there was no choice when I had to leave. That's just the way it was."

Not only did Quanxi's knife sharpening income get all four kids through school, but it also enabled him and his wife to upgrade to an eight-room house. They didn't need such a big place, but this way they figured they'd have enough space to accommodate their kids' future spouses and children as well. But things didn't exactly go according to plan. Their oldest son and his wife lived with them for a few years but eventually transitioned into a three-roomer of their own. Their second son moved to the county seat, their third son joined the military, and their fourth child, a girl, got married and moved in with her in-laws. Now all those extra rooms in the house serve as storage space for their farm equipment—most of which was also paid for one blunt knife at a time.

Last year Quanxi's oldest son picked up part-time work building houses and fell and crushed his knee on the job. Shortly thereafter their daughter-in-law headed off for the city to earn money for his medical treatments, leaving Quanxi's wife to take care of their incapacitated son and his three daughters as well as both families' farmland and animals. For his part, Quanxi tightened his already miniscule budget and started sending more money home each month than ever before.

In addition to that, their second son recently bought a parcel of urban land and is planning to build a four-story home in which to live, run a convenience store, and rent out rooms to migrants. He doesn't have the 100,000 yuan needed to cover the construction costs, so Quanxi has been pushing him to build in the village instead. But their son insists that his future really is in the city, and so Quanxi has agreed to help in whatever small way he can.

"I can't not put in some money," he says. "Countryside parents have a big burden. We've got to take care of our kids for our entire lives." Never mind that his own parents didn't contribute much money for his wedding and that he had to lug hundreds of kilos of coal across the countryside to build his own home at his own expense. His parents lived through the bitterest of China's bitter days, and it's impossible to compare their lives to his, just as it's impossible to compare his life to his children's. He can't, after all, expect his kids to live like they're in the Stone Age just because their father still does.

Wang Quanxi has never had a wish. He's never had time for dreams or goals or sentiments. But if he ever did go so far as to have a longing, if he ever actually allowed himself to hope for the impossible, it would have been to own his own wholesale fruit operation. Back when he first came to Xi'an, in the 1980s, the country's economy was just starting to take off and wholesale fruit was becoming a big deal. But, alas, not only was he incapable of reading, but he also didn't understand adding. He could count money but couldn't calculate a bill or read a scale. Without those business fundamentals, he knew he'd never survive. "If I knew how to do all that, when I came to Xi'an I'd have started my own business. I'm sure I could have made a fortune." Then, in an uncharacteristic display of emotion, he adds: "Then I'd have been able to bring my kids here with me too. There'd have been no need for us to separate."

Deeming himself incapable of the closest thing he's ever had to a dream, he dropped whatever inclination he might have had to do something bigger and better and contented himself with his knife sharpening. Though he notices lost opportunities on a micro-level, and most certainly notices the two or three yuan here and there that people short him, he doesn't spend any time pondering lost opportunities on the macro-level. What he would have really liked to do, what he's missed out on in life, these are all very modern thoughts that he's not about to waste time exploring. "What's to give up?" he asks. "Every day I make money, eat, and sleep. What else is there?"

By the time Quanxi leaves the porridge stand, it's nearing 1:00 p.m., so he plunks down in the shade for a break. He never bothers with lunch, nor does he have any real place to take an afternoon nap, but there's no use roaming around in the heat when all the restaurants are still full and most other potential customers are either eating or sleeping. He watches a heated game of Chinese chess taking place in the alleyway for awhile and then takes out the sander and examines the blade. It's shamefully dull, so he spends the rest of his downtime back in the saddle sharpening it to perfection.

Though it's still early when he heads back toward the café, he's pleasantly surprised to find that the lunch rush has already subsided. They don't have four sets like they'd promised this morning, but they do agree to give him 15 kuai for three cutting boards. While Quanxi sets up, three teenage kitchen workers in matching yellow smocks roll the boards out to him.

The first one goes quickly, but the second board ends up having lots of nails in it back from the days when it was still just a tree. They're wreaking havoc on his newly sharpened sanding blade, so Quanxi starts yanking them out with a pair of pliers. This attracts even more attention than usual, and soon a crowd gathers around, helping him search for hidden nail heads burrowed into the board's natural-bark perimeter. When he finally moves on to the last board, it proves to be so hard and dry that it ruins his sander blade, leaving him no choice but to get out the bench and sharpen it again.

By the time he's finished, he's been working for nearly two hours straight. He stands up and pounds his lower back with his fists. A middle-age onlooker in a maroon shirt asks if his back is sore.

"Oh yeah," Quanxi replies.

One of the teenage servers brings out a 100-yuan bill and hands it to him, asking if he has change. Quanxi snickers. "How am I going to have change for a 100?"

The cook disappears into the restaurant and then brings out 12 yuan.

"We said 15 kuai," Quanxi reminds him.

They argue for a few moments before the maroon-shirted man starts scolding the young cook. "You see how tired he is! Give him another 3 kuai."

The cook goes back inside, only to come out with the 100-yuan bill again. "You should have said something earlier," he tells Quanxi. "The boss is gone and now we only have a 100, or 12."

Quanxi turns away, clearly annoyed. To work this long and hard for only 12 kuai, and to have wasted so much time resharpening the sanding blade on top of it all, is an insult, even to him. "You made him work until he ruined his back," the guy in the maroon shirt complains, still interceding on his behalf. But Quanxi doesn't stay around to keep arguing. He just pockets the 12 yuan, packs up, and moves on, leaving a pile of sawdust against the café's fake picket fence.

Though this kind of constant bickering and beguiling wears on Quanxi, he knows that many migrants go through much worse. While the government doesn't stop people like him by requiring business licenses or permits, it doesn't protect them from labor law abuses either. At least as a knife sharpener, Quanxi just gets shorted a few yuan here and there. For some, especially those working in factories or construction sites, it's not unusual to get cheated out of months of pay or to have to wait until year's end to collect a single paycheck.

Quanxi has enjoyed the benefits and endured the difficulties of the government's laissez-faire approach to rural migrants for twenty years, but those days are now drawing to a close. With 300 million migrants expected to descend on the cities over the next two decades, ignoring their trials is no longer an effective development strategy. Rather, assimilating them into urban society now compromises one of the country's most critical challenges.

But Quanxi knows nothing about the conundrum people like him pose to the country's leadership, and as he leaves the café behind he's not thinking about any of this. Instead, his anger dissipates as he reminds himself that the jackpot of the day—if not the month—still lies before him. With that in mind, he heads back toward the fancy restaurant where his day began, eager to get started on the whopping six knives and boards that await him.

When he arrives he once again he climbs the back stairway and stands in the kitchen doorway until someone notices him. The head cook catches sight of him and simply waves Quanxi away: they don't need his services today after all. Quanxi cranes to get a look at their chopping blocks, and sure enough, they are all flat and smooth as can be. Obviously some other knife sharpener must have stopped by earlier in the afternoon and they just let that guy do it instead. They've got no sense of loyalty to him at all, Quanxi broods, even though he tries to come by every three months—or at least as regularly as his sixth sense will allow.

It would help a lot if he owned a cell phone, but he isn't willing to spare the money to buy one. Besides, he wouldn't know how to use it; without being able to read, he couldn't operate the menu or navigate the address book. No doubt there are numerous other means of organizing and innovating that would improve his business, but at this stage in his life he'd rather just rely on the grit and determination that have served him thus far.

Quanxi is so busy dwelling on the lost opportunity that he starts wandering the streets, forgetting even to turn on his bullhorn. He perks up when he scores three knives from a dumpling restaurant, and doesn't even flinch when the boss bickers him down from his usual 2-kuai standard. Before long a woman in her mid-twenties stops to watch him whisk the blades back and forth over the grinding stone. When Quanxi pauses to wipe a trickle of sweat from his face, she asks the dumpling boss how much he's paying to have his cutlery fine-tuned.

"1.5 kuai."

"1.5 per knife?" she exclaims. "I thought it was at least 5 kuai! Oh, if it's like that, then he's really got a tough life." She does a quick calculation in her head and clacks out her sympathy. "If it's like that, he probably just makes 400 per month, and this is so tiring for him."

When Quanxi finally returns to his place in Gan Jia Zhai late that night, he's been out for almost fourteen hours, walked nearly sixteen kilometers, and has more than 50 yuan in his pocket, which makes it an exceptionally good day in his book. He parks his bike in the building's entryway, removes the sander and other valuables, and lugs them up the stairs to his tiny cavern of a room. The place has no semblance of being a home; instead, it is merely a cubicle in which to store stuff, himself included. The only real piece of furniture in it is a metal-frame bed with a wooden board for a mattress. Everything else—and there isn't much—finds a place on the floor.

For all the speculation on the street about his secret riches or downright destitution, the truth is somewhere in between. He's heard of knife sharpeners who bring in 1,200 yuan a month, but he's never made more than 1,000—and even that's a rarity. Most months he makes about 800 yuan, which is at least 200 more than the teenage servers make at local restaurants but at least 400 less than cooks in their twenties earn. Even that's not really a fair comparison: those kids are employees who get free room and board, don't have to do a lot of manual labor, and have long stretches of time every day in which to relax. At sixty-plus, Quanxi has none of those benefits.

The key to saving money for Quanxi, like so many of China's migrant workers, is to live like he's utterly poverty stricken. He's never once thought of living above his means, or even at his means; instead, he tries to stay as far below them as possible. In lieu of free room, he rents this place for 50 yuan a month, and in lieu of free board, he survives off another 50 yuan, eating steamed bread in large quantities and veggies, meat, and everything else sparingly. His other necessities come to about 100 yuan, which means he spends a total of around 200 yuan per month—even less than people throw down for a good pot of tea in the High-Tech Zone these days.

Still, 200 yuan a month seems steep to Quanxi, and it especially burns him up to hand over so much for nothing more than a place to sleep and house his stuff. For years he paid a mere 10 yuan a month to live in a room with ten other knife sharpeners, but when that place got torn down, he settled here with two roommates. A few months ago they had a big blowup and the other two moved out, leaving him to pay the entire monthly rent himself.

Quanxi plans to ditch the room when he heads back home for planting season in a few weeks, which means he'll also have to ditch all his sharpening equipment; though his motley gear perfectly complements his low-tech enterprise, it's certainly not worth 50 yuan a month just to store while he's gone. Though he's lugged most of the stuff around for longer than he can remember, it won't be hard to part with any of it... but it will be a real hassle to replace it all when he gets back. But who knows, maybe he won't even come back at all. His second son could use some help building his new house, and with his oldest son still out of commission, Quanxi's own wife could certainly use some nonfinancial help from him as well.

But never mind all that. Right now he has more important things to think about: he hasn't eaten anything since breakfast, and now he is hungry. He grabs a couple of potatoes off the floor and picks up his own not-especially-sharp knife to see what he can scrounge together for dinner before he falls asleep.

Wang Quanxi has never brushed his teeth or enjoyed the comforts of indoor plumbing. He's never patronized a barber shop and can't fathom why people would waste money on something as useless as a massage. But if there is one thing that he does know, it's that he's witnessing the end of an era. And though he's made it through revolution, collectivization, starvation, reform, and privatization, now, in the twilight of his life, he's caught up in the biggest whirlwind of all—China's economic coming of age—and it's the one storm even he's not sure he can weather.

It's a realization that is not particularly disturbing to him. It's been a good, long run, and if his time is up, then his time is up. Also, it seems somehow appropriate; it's not that he alone is being forced to retire but, rather, that his entire profession—his entire way of life—is slowly retreating from the streets of China to be found again only in the pages of history. "What young person is willing to sharpen knives? They want to make big money. They're afraid they'll lose face, afraid others will laugh at them if they do this kind of work. But that doesn't bother us old guys," Quanxi says with a laugh. "Gradually this craft won't even exist anymore. No one wants to do the sharpening, and no one wants to get their knives sharpened anymore either. Now people just throw them away and get new ones."

everything becomes fleeting— replaceable

Back when he first ventured out of the village, peasants like him were flooding the urban landscape to find any opportunity they could. Back then the country was just starting to develop and city folks were still content eating from the Big Rice Pot and didn't give people like him any competition at all. But who could have foreseen the juggernaut that China's economy would become? As the old farming villages are torn down one by one and high-rise enclaves and skyscraper office buildings replace them, Quanxi and his counterparts have to make room for bigger and bolder entrepreneurs who are willing to jump through bureaucratic hoops and put in money to make money.

There will still be room for petty entrepreneurs in China for years to come, but those who want to survive will have to be big enough, at least, to be able to learn and grow and change with the times—and that Quanxi admittedly is not. And so it is that later the next morning when he's smoking beneath a tree in the High-Tech Zone and a police officer warns him to move on or have his gear confiscated, Quanxi's temper doesn't flare, he doesn't feel indignant, and he doesn't even flinch. "What's to be angry about?" he asks. "Pushing this kind of bike really does look bad."

Instead, he simply hefts his bike off the curb and crosses the busy street without even a sideways glance. A trail of newspaper ash follows him into the nearest village, where he soon finds another knife just waiting for his TLC. When he's finished, he jams the 2 kuai into his jacket and pats his growing wad with a hint of satisfaction. Ah, yes. For today, at least, his hard work still has some real, tangible, money-in-the-pocket value.

CHAPTER THREE

The Teenage Beauty Queens

When the girls of the High-Tech Zone branch of M. Perfumine enter the beauty chain's corporate auditorium, it looks more like a pep rally than a quarterly sales meeting. Though they arrive nearly an hour early, the place is already bulging with over a hundred of the cutest—and certainly most made up—fifteen-to-twenty-one-year-olds in all of Xi'an. Jia Huan and a few other M. Perfumine veterans saunter to their seats with the affected nonchalance of seasoned professionals, but Zhang Jing, who just recently joined the company, squeals with delight when she spots a hip young woman across the room. "She is so amazing," Zhang Jing gushes, explaining that this was one of her favorite teachers at the company's mandatory, month-long training program she recently completed. "She isn't even married yet and she's already made it to teacher-level."

Zhang Jing is about to rush over to greet her when the High-Tech Zone branch manager, a sweet-faced woman in her forties whom the girls affectionately call Big Sister Hong Li, huddles them together to practice their store's cheer before the evening's festivities get under way.

"What's our team motto?" Hong Li asks, leading the cadence.

"Excellence, excellence, excellence unlimited!" the High-Tech Zone store's nine beauty therapists reply back in unison.

"And what's our team song?"

"It's better to do than to say, and if you're going to do it, do it the best way."

Once she's sure the girls remember all the words, Big Sister Hong Li has them launch into a full-scale, full-volume rehearsal. Other stores start practicing their cheers, too, and before long pandemonium descends upon the arena as each team tries to out-shout the others.

The yells are quickly replaced with applause when the hostess for the evening finally glides across the stage decked out in a shimmering-gold evening gown. "*Meinü*," she bellows into the microphone, using the address of choice for M. Perfumine's young, entry-level therapists. "*Beauties*, are you ready?"

An earsplitting "Yes!" reverberates through the hall.

After a quick overview of the night's agenda, the hostess leads the audience in the chant: "I am the most beautiful, I am the most beautiful, I am the most beautiful, yeah!" "And what about our company?" she asks as the din dies down. "Does it have beauty, too?"

Another resounding "Yes!" echoes through the room.

Next the girls from each branch take a turn shouting out their salon's cheer. M. Perfumine's CEO arrives just as the last team finishes and the hostess immediately introduces her to the audience and asks, "Which store wants to show her your spirit?" All of the *meinü* leap to their feet and the entire round of cheers begins anew.

When the cheerleading session finally ends, everyone settles back in their seats for the first award of the evening, which will go to the new worker with the highest monthly commission. The top three earners are called on stage and an M. Perfumine teacher fixes a tiara on the winner's head and hands leather-bound notebooks to the two runners-up.

"So how did you do it?" the hostess asks the winning girl. "How did you get so many new customers so quickly?"

The girl blushes and shifts uncomfortably in the spotlight before finally stammering, "I'm kind of … enthusiastic … a little." She shuffles away with the other two girls, pulling off the tiara before she's even stepped down from the stage.

The hostess turns to the crowd with a smile. "Beauties, do you envy them? Do you want to be like them?" Jia Huan and a few of the other more seasoned girls roll their eyes, but Zhang Jing claps and stomps her feet; as a new employee herself, her goal is to be exactly like these girls.

One of the company's top leaders steps into the spotlight and has the crowd repeat the phrase "I'm young, I'm beautiful, I'm confident!" until they do so with the vigor becoming of M. Perfumine beauties. Then she beams down at the sea of shining faces before her. "Little Sisters, don't be dissatisfied if you don't make it up here tonight. As long as you have a goal, as long as you are willing to learn, you will grow with our company."

She opens her laptop and launches into a PowerPoint presentation. "We women need our own source of money," she begins. "If you have economic status, you have everything. Economic status determines your position in society and the position of your family." She looks out at the audience—composed almost exclusively of poor countryside girls with no more than a junior-high education—and begins outlining the company's recently improved bonus system. In all, she spends the next twenty minutes on a variety of topics all meant to encourage the *meinü* to take charge of their salaries by increasing their sales.

After she's finished, she parades another hesitant girl on stage and asks everyone to guess how much she made last month. The audience throws out some numbers and the leader nudges the blushing girl. "Go ahead," she urges, "tell them."

"I'm not too sure myself," the girl mumbles.

"We calculated it for you," the leader says, pausing for maximum effect: "2,370 yuan!" Whistles and wows fill the auditorium and even Jia Huan can't keep a look of wonderment from spreading across her face. The leader turns back to the room full of beauties and asks: "So, who determines your salary? You do! You can tell people right now that you are a boss at M. Perfumine. In fact, today's meeting is really more like a manager's meeting than anything."

As the pep talk wraps up, the hostess floats back to center stage and the awards ceremony starts in earnest. The High-Tech Zone branch cleans house, with Big Sister Hong Li pulling in several awards and most of the shop's beauty therapists earning at least one accolade. Jia Huan takes home three accommodations, which each earn her a traditional Chinese red envelope filled with money.

There's time for one last round of cheers before the meeting draws to a close. "I wish there was room for all the M. Perfumine beauties on stage tonight," the hostess says. "You're the best, right?"

"Yes!"

"The best, right?"

"Yes!"

"Repeat after me," she hollers. "I am the best! I can do it! I will find success!" Applause fills the room and the hostess reminds everyone about the big sales event to be held at the end of the year. "Who will be our princess then?" she asks.

ZhangJing bounces to her feet, joining in the roaring chorus of "Me! Me! Me!" that rumbles through the auditorium, but Jia Huan stays glued to her seat and says nothing; she's too busy counting the cash stuffed inside her three red envelopes.

The next morning, the nine beauties of M. Perfumine's High-Tech Zone location are back to work at their salon. They are as made up as they were at the sales meeting, only now they're dressed in identical white smocks and teal pants, with matching neck scarves, and ponytails cinched with fake-hair scrunchies. A few of the girls are already treating customers in the back rooms, while others chat in the tiny employee lounge.

Jia Huan and Ma Haiying, her best friend at the store, huddle out in the lobby, comparing notes on last night's disappointing red envelope take. An outspoken nineteen-year-old with a shock of red hair and an ever-present smudge of green eyeliner, Jia Huan can't understand why she brought in a measly 100 yuan in bonuses, given that she made more than double that at last quarter's meeting. Sixteen-year-old Haiying is equally perplexed as to why she received a mere 75 yuan this time around. Having already worked at M. Perfumine for more than a year, the teens are two of the High-Tech Zone branch's longest-standing employees. And yet they are mystified as to how some of the girls called up on stage last night could have made upward of 2,000 yuan in a single month. Despite their regular customer flow, neither of them has ever earned enough commission to bump their 600-yuan base salary over 1,000 yuan. Maybe, they joke, last night's event was rigged. "Never mind all that," Jia Huan says, forcing a smile. "It's perfect because I was out of money and now I've got some cash to spend again."

A towel-clad customer in her late thirties wanders out from one of the treatment rooms looking for the restroom. Zhang Jing, who's been hovering nearby listening to Jia Huan and Haiying talk, rushes to open the bathroom door for her. Having freshly arrived at the shop, Zhang Jing didn't earn any accolades at the sales meeting, but it still left her quite excited. "I feel so happy," she says. "I got put in the High-Tech Zone store, and our shop won lots of awards last night. This shop is always number one or two." At age twenty, Zhang Jing is one of the oldest therapists on staff, and though she has only two weeks of actual work under her belt, she is already emerging as one of the most focused. Unlike many of the girls, who arrive at age fifteen, fresh out of junior high, Zhang Jing attended a year and a half of vocational high school and held a variety of other jobs before coming here. And though none of her experience was related to the beauty industry, she's been around enough to know a good opportunity when she sees one.

What the job consists of, for the most part, is providing local women with facials, massages, and traditional Chinese medicine treatments like cupping and acupressure. After they complete an initial month of training, officially the beauties' main duty is to continue to master all these techniques. However, since their commission is tied to the number of treatments they do per month, it is clear that after grasping the basics their real responsibility is to keep filling the salon with women who are willing to pay to relax.

That would have been a nearly impossible task in this underdeveloped corner of the country a decade ago. But these days, thanks to a steady rise in urban disposable income, coupled with the perennially cheap labor of countryside kids, a great number of luxury services are available at prices even the middle class can afford. In fact, today the beauty and cosmetics industry has grown into the fourth largest consumption zone in China— behind only real estate, automobiles, and tourism. As such, the problem Zhang Jing and her colleagues face is not drumming up demand for their products and services; instead, with female-only salons like M. Perfumine now peppering the streets of Xi'an, their conundrum is simply how to find and retain potential customers.

In an attempt to accomplish just that, the beauties spend a fair amount of time on the street handing out certificates for free facials. Yesterday, Zhang Jing used this method to snag four new clients—an almost unheard of success rate that has her especially enthused about her prospects at M. Perfumine. Today, however, Zhang Jing sits down to calculate how many treatments she's done so far and finds that despite yesterday's windfall she's already fifteen behind for the month. Though she knows she shouldn't expect to meet the company's sixty-treatment standard during her first few months on the job, she's still a bit disheartened by how very far behind she's already fallen. And so when Jia Huan and Haiying ask if she'd like to join them for lunch, Zhang Jing declines, deciding to forgo food in favor of distributing free spa certificates.

Though M. Perfumine provides its beauties with regular training on managing their customer base, for most of them the best and easiest advice to follow is Big Sister Hong Li's constant admonition to really care about their clients. "In sales, the first thing you sell is yourself," she often tells them. "If the customer has no feelings for you, it's because you have no feelings for them. People really just are this kind of emotional animal." To culti- vate the necessary loyalty, Hong Li advises the girls to befriend their customers and share some sort of professional knowledge with them each time they come in so that they feel they're get- ting both prettier and wiser during their time at the salon.

[handwritten margin note: ironic. women are systematic machine-like. Artificial connection.]

And so when one of Jia Huan's old customers unexpectedly comes in one evening after several months' absence, Jia Huan remembers her disappointing red envelope take and is more determined than ever to regain the woman's allegiance. Jia Huan, while escorting her customer into a treatment room, starts by marveling over her client's new hairstyle, then her dress, and then her shoes. The woman is here for *jiugong*—a traditional Chinese therapy that amounts to an hour of deep massage and acupressure of the abdomen—so Jia Huan has her strip down to her bra and underwear and stretch out on the only available massage bed left in the crowded room. She gently wraps the woman's legs and chest in blankets, shines a heat lamp over her bare midriff, and begins pressing into it with small, rhythmic circles.

"According to Chinese medicine, if your stomach doesn't get good circulation, you'll get dark spots on your face," Jia Huan vol- unteers, searching for tidbits of professional advice to offer. She continues circling lightly for a few more minutes and then gradu- ally adds pressure until her entire hand seems to disappear into the woman's stomach. "Now your belly is really soft," she notes.

"It looks like you've really gained weight recently," the thera- pist who's giving a massage at the adjacent bed tells Jia Huan's customer. The lady nods and Jia Huan and the other therapist start telling her about another customer's recent weight loss

Jia Huan smiles after a long day at the salon.

success. "She just kept doing *jiugong* and eventually her stomach was gone," the *meinü* says. Then she turns to Big Sister Hong Li, who's staying late to help out in the busy room tonight, and asks: "How many times did she do it?"

"More than ten," answers Big Sister Hong Li. "You've got to keep at it to see results."

The room falls quiet as the therapists concentrate on their work and the customers concentrate on relaxing. When Jia Huan finishes up the *jiugong*, she suggests that her customer get a facial, too, since she's already here and still has plenty of money left on her membership card. The woman, who has been dozing on and off, is quick to agree. Jia Huan hurriedly gathers the necessary supplies, giving the other beauties a knowing wink as she goes.

She starts the facial by rubbing the back of an ox-bone comb across her client's scalp and then swabs the first round of cleanser onto her face. "Your pores are all open. They're really big," Jia Huan notes, again searching for ways to demonstrate her worth as a therapist. "When you get home, be sure to drink lots of water to get rid of the toxins."

An hour and a half later, Jia Huan finishes the facial and leaves her ultra-relaxed customer resting in the treatment room while she heads out to the lobby. Most of the other *meinü* have already gone back to the company-provided dorm they share in Gan Jia Zhai, but Haiying and one other beauty stayed behind to wait for Jia Huan; given the village's reputation for crime, Big Sister Hong Li doesn't let them go home alone at night. Since their room doesn't have running water, Haiying and the other girl took the opportunity to wash their hair in the salon's bathroom sink. As Jia Huan watches them towel-dry their long locks, Big Sister Hong Li asks, "Who wants their salary?"

"Me!" exclaims Jia Huan. "You're paying us today?"

"Yeah, today."

But before Hong Li can get the money together, Jia Huan's customer emerges from the back. Jia Huan takes her by the arm and leads her to a table where the two review her chart and discuss how much money she has left on her card. When they're finished, Jia Huan escorts her client to the door, making her promise to come back soon. As the woman leaves, Jia Huan wheels toward Big Sister Hong Li with a gleam in her eye. "Pay, pay, pay! How much do I get?"

Hong Li gets out the salary chart and finds Jia Huan's name. "780 yuan."

"780," Jia Huan echoes, her brows suddenly knitting together. "The last time you calculated for me, you said I was going to get over 800."

"That was a mistake," Hong Li says, skimming back through the records. A few months ago M. Perfumine revamped its commission system to encourage the *meinü* to be more proactive about customer service, but as a result they are now more confused than ever about what is owed them.

After collecting their money the three girls get ready to head home, but Hong Li can tell by their sudden silence that they don't think their salaries have been calculated correctly. As branch manager, Big Sister Hong Li isn't just the beauties' boss but their role model and surrogate mom as well, and since they are all so young and far from home, she feels compelled to take good care of them. And so, though it's already after 10:00 p.m., she asks the girls if they'd like to stay and add up their salaries for themselves. Jia Huan breaks into a wide grin and bounds back to the counter, where she and the other two beauties start pouring over the books with Big Sister Hong Li.

For Chinese women, a good figure is everything. At least that's how it seems to Jia Huan as she sits through an early morning bra-sizing workshop at M. Perfumine's headquarters, listening to the nuances of helping customers find a good fit. In addition to giving facials and massages, one of her major duties at the High-Tech Zone salon is to help clients realize just how much they need new undergarments.

Jia Huan is not especially interested in her appointed specialty; she'd much rather be in charge of something more exciting, like breast beautification. But when she arrived at the High-Tech Zone salon, another *meinü* was already established as the shop's official breast specialist. Then the girl in charge of sizing quit and Big Sister Hong Li chose Jia Huan to replace her.

That means every so often Jia Huan has to sit through a half-day session with the sizing representatives from all the other local branches to learn how to sell more of the company's body-shaping underclothes.

This morning's training started off easy enough with an hour-long motivational video about dog sledding. But since then M. Perfumine's master sizer, Teacher Li, has been presenting a complex series of slides detailing the intricacies of a woman's figure. Jia Huan finds them mostly incomprehensible but scrambles to copy them down word for word just the same. After a little more discussion, Teacher Li writes several numbers on the white board and asks the beauties which bra size a woman with these measurements should wear. Soon the board looks like a math exam, with hypothetical calculations scrawled everywhere. Eventually, Teacher Li gives the beauties a full set of body measurements and asks them to calculate appropriate sizes for an entire bra, corset, and panty set. The crinkle of pages fills the room as the girls leaf back through their binders searching for guidance, but Jia Huan ignores her copious notes and just sits with her head down so as not to attract attention.

"I don't understand sizing. I can't do it," she whispers. Most of these trainings concentrate on how to raise customer interest in the company's line of upscale underclothes, so today's focus on actually understanding the sizing process is throwing Jia Huan for a loop. Usually, whenever she successfully entices a client into trying something on, she simply calls Teacher Li to come to the store to do the real measurements and close the sale. She doesn't know how girls in charge of sizing at other branches operate, but last month Jia Huan helped sell seventeen three-piece sets this way.

When Teacher Li is satisfied with the beauties' grasp of the subject, she breaks them into groups of three, hands them a measuring tape, and tasks them to size each other. Jia Huan's partners immediately fawn over her hair, which she stayed up late last night kinking, while Jia Huan raves over how big a partner's breasts have become.

The trio hasn't even gotten started when Teacher Li calls them all back to their seats and asks them to think about how many sets they can sell in the next twelve days. Jia Huan has been around long enough to know what comes next, so she stands up and announces that she can sell ten. Everyone claps, and the teacher writes Jia Huan's name and branch location on the white board, with a big "10" circled behind it. Three other beauties also promise to sell ten, and after recording their information the teacher turns back to the audience. "Now who's willing to say eleven? Who is courageous enough to add one more?"

The room settles into an uncomfortable silence, which prompts one of the company's big bosses to step forward and ask a bit more sternly for someone to volunteer to sell eleven. Jia Huan puts her head down, afraid to get caught in the woman's steely glare. She tunes out the cajoling and spends the next twenty minutes trying to remember all the treatments she's done so far this month. She tunes back in when the big boss finally starts wrapping things up, reminding the *meinü* that the purpose of all this pledging is simply to help them immediately increase their undergarment sales. "If you don't fulfill your responsibilities, our brand can't fulfill its responsibilities," she assures them.

Therein lies one of the greatest ironies of China's rapidly expanding beauty industry: in order to survive, companies like

M. Perfumine are dependent on countryside girls to promote their beauty treatments, products, and undergarments, despite the fact that most of them had never even heard of face masks or push-up bras before they joined the company. And yet here they are, tasked to entice much older and wealthier urban women into heeding their beauty advice.

Though admittedly challenging, from the perspective of M. Perfumine's management, it's a symbiotic relationship in which the company expects a lot from the girls but gives back even more than it demands. Unlike so many other jobs that rely on countryside youth labor but offer only a dead end in return, at M. Perfumine the *meinü* have a chance to develop a set of skills on which to build their futures. Theoretically, any one of them has a chance to excel beyond an entry-level beauty thera-pist and become a branch manager, a teacher, or even a member of upper management. "We give them a goal, so they're not just here every day for this little bit of money," explains Big Sister Hong Li, a former business owner who did not work her way up the ranks but, rather, entered the company directly at manager-level. "They're here for a higher purpose." Beyond the promise of a job with a future, there's something else M. Perfumine is promising its beauties, though unspoken and infinitely more sub-tle. With talk of being their own bosses, controlling their own salaries, and taking charge of their own promotions, the com-pany is promising the girls a way to become more than just another migrant who ultimately has to return to the country-side; it's promising the girls a ticket to a permanently better life.

Although Jia Huan feels anxious over the potential business she's lost during the morning's training, she doesn't set right off for the High-Tech Zone salon when the training ends shortly

[handwritten margin note: Contrasts w/ knife sharpener.]

before noon. Instead, she takes a bus to the other side of town where there's a self-serve photo booth that she frequents. There, twenty wallet-size pictures cost just 10 yuan, and she doesn't want to miss the chance to capture her new kinky-hair look.

As soon as she sits down on the bus, she pulls out a tiny mirror, wipes away a smudge of mascara, and redraws the green lines framing her eyes. Then she takes out the company's new brochure for body-shaping underclothes and examines it carefully. Though she's not impressed with the training or particularly interested in her appointed specialty, that doesn't mean she's not buying into the benefits of the product itself. Never mind that a three-piece set costs upward of 9,000 yuan, or $1,400—even more than her parents make farming in a year. To Jia Huan it's worth it, most definitely worth it, and she'd plunk down the money for a set, too, if ever she could scrape together such a sum.

Once she gets to the photo place, she checks herself over in the mirror, straightening the ruffles on her white shirt and smoothing her half-length jean jacket before slipping into the little booth for a ten-minute modeling shoot. Ever since she can remember, she's loved photos—loved looking at them, loved taking them, loved being in them—and has always dreamed of being a photographer. But photography was not an easy sell with her parents, who didn't have money to waste on a training program that wouldn't necessarily get her established in a stable profession. "My mom doesn't pay attention. She doesn't know what I like," Jia Huan shrugs as she steps out of the booth and waits for her pictures to be processed. "I told her, but she wouldn't let me study photography. So I ended up going into the beauty business instead."

Despite M. Perfumine's promise of a fair shot at a bright future, it's not so much the lure of good opportunity that brings the beauties here as it is simply a lack of other opportunities. In China there are only nine years of compulsory education; students who want to continue on after that don't simply need to be able to pay the fees—which can be prohibitive—but they must also pass a test to get into high school. In 2005 the rate of high school attendance across the country hovered at 58 percent, but that figure is deceiving: in urban areas, more than 80 percent of students went to high school, but only 51 percent of rural youth did so. By the end of 2010, total high school enrollment had risen to 82 percent, but the gulf between urban and rural educational opportunities still remains.

It's difficult to underestimate just how crucial this turning point is. Attending academic high school is generally the only way to enter the university system, so for those who, at age fifteen, do not pass the entrance exam, the door to future higher education is virtually closed. In recent years the government has started providing rural kids with subsidies to attend vocational high schools, but for many of them the end of junior high school signals the beginning of their employed life.

For her part, Jia Huan never even got a chance to take the high school entrance exam. Near the end of junior high, she got into a serious bicycle accident that kept her hospitalized for weeks. By the time she recovered, she'd missed the exam, which is only offered once a year. Her mother wanted her to repeat the last year of junior high so that she could take it the following year, and initially Jia Huan agreed. But then a relative asked her to help out at his hostel in Xi'an. Though she was nervous about heading off to the city all alone, anything sounded better than drudging through another year of school just to try and prolong her less-than-stellar academic career. Her mom acquiesced, so Jia Huan spent a year cleaning the hostel before an aunt invited her to work as a beauty therapist at her newly opened salon. Jia Huan knew nothing about the industry other than it promised, somehow, to make women more attractive. Her aunt gave her informal on-the-job training, but months into it she still felt lost. "I felt so stupid. I also didn't really like it," Jia Huan says, and then pauses and gives a crooked smile. "Actually, even now, I don't like it all that much."

Even so, she feels indebted to her aunt for giving her a future beyond changing sheets and scrubbing floors, so on a day off in early spring Jia Huan treks across town to visit her. On the way she stops to get her hair dyed and curled into flowing ringlets that leave her thrilled. She bounces into her aunt's salon, eager to show off her new do, but finds her aunt busy applying a coat of permanent color to a customer's lips. Jia Huan settles a bit glumly in front of the TV out in the lobby but perks up when her aunt's landlady comes in.

"You've got wrinkles," Jia Huan greets the woman, a friend from back when she worked here before.

"I'm old," retorts the landlady, who looks to be about fifty.

"You should do something about it, don't let yourself go downhill."

"I'm not afraid of getting old."

"Everyone else is afraid," Jia Huan snorts. "How can you not be?"

"I'm already up to my neck in dirt," she says with a grin. "Just a little bit more and I'll be totally buried in the ground."

They continue bantering until Jia Huan catches sight of her newly styled hair in a nearby mirror and quickly loses interest in the conversation. She gathers her curls into a variety of hairstyles, smiling and winking at herself after each one as if on her own one-woman photo shoot. Though she's always liked photography, part of Jia Huan's newfound interest in taking pictures of herself stems from the outward transformation she's undergone in the last few years. It's so dramatic that many of her neighbors back in the village don't even recognize her anymore; since becoming a beauty therapist, she's started wearing makeup and more provocative clothing, dyed her hair, extended and curled her eyelashes, removed moles from her face, and had her eyelids permanently creased to give her a more Western flair.

It was during her quest to get her eyelids done that a friend of a friend introduced her to Big Sister Hong Li. The two of them chatted about their experiences in the beauty industry for a while and then Hong Li advised her to think carefully about her current job. "You've already been at your aunt's place for one year, but when I ask you questions I feel that you don't understand anything about this industry," Hong Li told her. "You need a future."

Two weeks later, Jia Huan left her aunt's salon to see what kind of a future M. Perfumine could provide, and she found herself yet again on the steep side of the learning curve. "When I first came to the High-Tech Zone salon, I felt that I didn't understand anything, as if I'd never studied any of it before," she says. "I felt like I was so stupid ... again."

Jia Huan has wanted to take Haiying and another coworker named Meng Wei back home with her for a long time now, but the beauties only get two days off a month, staggered, so that there's never more than one of them missing from the salon at a given time. In May they finally finagle time off together and giggle as they pile into a single seat on an overcrowded bus. Two hours and several buses later they arrive in the town closest to Jia Huan's village, where they hire a motorized rickshaw for the bumpy ride out to the countryside. As they jostle through the fields, they talk about all the foods they miss from home. And so when Jia Huan's mother greets them at the roadside with a bowl of homegrown strawberries, the girls swarm around her, jumping up and down with excitement.

Within seconds the bowl is empty and Jia Huan declares that they should take a photo together. Her mother refuses. "You are all beautiful," she says, "and I'm so plain." And, indeed, the difference is obvious. The girls are fully made up for the occasion. Jia Huan wears low-rider jean shorts and a light-blue shirt that stops right at her waist, exposing the tops of her pantyhose every time she moves. Her mother, on the other hand, wears a simple striped T-shirt and khaki pants. She doesn't wear a speck of makeup and her salt-and-pepper hair is growing out of a dye job—pushed on her by Jia Huan—that triggered an allergic reaction that's left her face and scalp broken out for more than a month now. When Jia Huan finally convinces her mom to take a picture with them, they stand in front of the house next to two big mushroom-shaped stacks of wheat stalks. On one side is Jia Huan's grandmother sitting on a stool cutting twigs with a small ax, and on the other side is the back wall of the family latrine.

As soon as the photo op is finished, Jia Huan's father ushers them into the house, where a feast of rice porridge, steamed bread, spicy cucumbers, and pickled garlic tops awaits them. The three girls devour the meal and then crowd around the mirror to freshen up before going out for a stroll around the village. "I don't understand what she does in that salon," says Jia Huan's mother as she watches the girls remake themselves. "She

Jia Huan, Ma Haiying, and Meng Wei visit Jia Huan's village.

says it's taking care of people's skin, but I don't understand. We villagers don't just put any old thing on our faces. You could never start that kind of business in the village. No one would go. We wouldn't know what it's for."

But though she's decidedly unimpressed with the beauty industry as a service, she thinks it's proven to be a winner as a job for her daughter. "The beauty industry is good for Jia Huan. As a girl, what else is she going to do? She has no skills. The hostel work was bad for her. There, all she could do was menial labor, and that's no kind of future." Besides, she's been impressed with the changes she's seen since Jia Huan started working at M. Perfumine. "Now she treats people with courtesy, speaks with confidence, and has a different way of thinking. Now she doesn't come home often; she doesn't like the countryside."

She says this last bit not with hurt or anger but, rather, with a hint of pride; while China's skyrocketing consumerism and prosperity over the past decade have made urbanites increasingly self-assured, for those who remain in the comparatively unchanged countryside there is a growing feeling of abasement. As Jia Huan wobbles off down the dirt lane in her high heels, her mother nods in approval. "Farmers all wear very simple clothes. The fact that she looks like this means she's already not a farmer."

While she's proud that her daughter is shedding her rural roots, she's also worried. The problem, she explains, is that getting out of the village is not the same as staying out of the village. "Here most kids go out to work. No one wants to stay and be a farmer anymore. But when they get to the right age, many of them will come back to the village to have kids, and maybe stay here to be farmers." She then pauses, sighing as her daughter disappears in the distance. "Nothing's sure yet for Jia Huan."

When the girls return a few hours later, Jia Huan leafs through the family photo albums with her friends. Pretty soon, Haiying and Meng Wei drift off to sleep in the afternoon heat. The house is quiet, so Jia Huan heads outside to look for everyone. She locates her mother in a tiny shack, which serves as the family's kitchen, and then she goes to find her younger brother. She passes by the little cabin that the family lived in for most of her life and heads toward two caves carved into the steep hillside out back. Jia Huan's father grew up in these grottoes, and the family still uses them to escape the summer heat and winter chill.

Jia Huan locates her brother at a table in the back of one of the caves, trying to stretch a ball of dough into noodles. His grades are so dismal that he has virtually no hope of making it into high school, so last summer Jia Huan paid for him to attend a summer cooking course. Next year she'll send him to a half-year culinary training program in the hope that this can be his way out of the village.

After watching him show off his burgeoning culinary skills for a while, Jia Huan reclines on a bed near the cave entrance and puts her feet up on the sill of the room's lone window, legs crossed at the knees in her best magazine fashion pose. She leafs through some photos of herself, stacking her favorite ones on her stomach and noting how much she's changed since she started working in the beauty industry. "Now I'm better. Not because I'm older, but because this industry changed me. I wasn't refined before. I was very ordinary, nothing special. Now look"—she stamps a fire-engine-red stiletto on the cave's windowsill for emphasis—"I'm very different. At the very least, now I can make people on the street look twice."

But though her time in the beauty industry has clearly had a big impact on her appearance, her thoughts, and her life course, she still can't bring herself to get excited by it. "There's nothing I really dislike about it, I just have a very lukewarm feeling toward it. I don't really like it, but I don't really hate it either." Jia Huan has thought a lot about studying photography for a year or two and switching jobs, but aside from the money she put aside for her brother's cooking course, she's been too busy accumulating the accoutrements of proper city-lady living to store up any savings.

Regardless of what she ultimately ends up doing in the future, her goal is still the same. "I want to make something of myself," she says. "Then in Xi'an I'll have a small car and buy a house." This is where Jia Huan and her counterparts represent a new breed of migrants. Whereas other, slightly older migrants still have the mind-set to endure, endure, and endure some more, for those who grew up during the country's rapid economic growth of the 1990s, eating bitterness is not a highly held value. They're willing to work hard, but not without expectations for their future—or at least hopes of someday fully integrating into modern society.

The problem is that they are not sure how to go about attaining these dreams. The easiest route would have been to go to university and become proper white-collar workers, but that door has long since closed. And though M. Perfumine keeps a picture of a rosy future dangling in front of them, Jia Huan, like most of her colleagues, doubts that the company can actually deliver. Instead, they see marrying up as their best shot at securing themselves a permanent berth in the city. "I don't want to go back to the countryside. Now I'm used to city life, but we'll have to see," Jia Huan says as she leaves the cave to go check on her friends. "If fate is on my side, I'll marry into Xi'an."

The beauties' metamorphosis from lowly countryside girls into full-fledged head-turners didn't happen overnight, nor did it happen by accident. The folks at M. Perfumine are not naive enough to think that putting a jar of whitening cream in the beauties' hands is enough to complete the transformation, nor is requiring a smear of lipstick on the job going to do the trick. Instead, each branch manager is tasked to systematically train her *meinü* in the ways of their more cosmopolitan clientele.

"Here the employees are not very cultured, so we have to guide them on how to be a person in every sense," says Big Sister Hong Li. She talks to the girls about everything—from how to dress and speak properly to how to maintain healthy relationships with their parents. And when it comes to matters directly related to their work, the guidance gets more detailed yet. "For even the smallest things, we always tell them what to say. They're all very young, so we have to."

Big Sister Hong Li generally holds weekly staff meetings to review the fundamentals of becoming true M. Perfumine beauties. But one mid-May morning she gathers the beauty therapists together not for further edification but to share some very special news: in just five days, Ceri Silk, the foreign expert who represents M. Perfumine's high-end product line and is featured prominently on many of its marketing posters, will come to the High-Tech Zone salon to give free customer consultations. This is an opportunity of a lifetime, Big Sister Hong Li assures them, and she has promised upper management that she'll get at least seventy customers to attend the event or she'll step down from her position. "Is everyone willing to support my job?" she asks the girls assembled before her.

"We're willing!" they exclaim in unison.

She asks the beauties to scan through their customer lists to determine how many people they can persuade to come. She starts with the salon's most experienced therapist, who volunteers to bring in six people. Hong Li gives her an incredulous look and the girl raises her pledge to ten. "You've got the most customers of all. So many people know your service and like you," Big Sister Hong Li scolds.

"Okay, fifteen," the beauty mumbles.

Apparently satisfied, Hong Li turns to Haiying, who offers five.

"Five is not enough. Can you do ten?" When Haiying doesn't respond, Big Sister Hong Li compromises at eight. But when Jia Huan says eight, too, Hong Li simply laughs. "Even Haiying pledged eight and she's got fewer clients than you."

"I can't pledge more, I'm not sure," Jia Huan whines.

"I'll put you down for ten. In a bit I'll show you how you'll do it."

When Zhang Jing says she can promise five customers, Big Sister Hong Li lights up for the first time of the morning. "See, Zhang Jing just got here, but she's only pledging five less than all of you," Hong Li says, reminding them that a chance with an international expert like this is worth at least a million dollars.

"Now from Zhang Jing I can see several things," she continues. "She's been here a very short time but already has several customers who really acknowledge her. You can say she's professional, but she's not as professional as the rest of you. And you can say she's experienced, but she doesn't have as much experience as the rest of you. But she's still attracting customers."

Indeed, Zhang Jing is one of those naturals, one of those rare girls with deep thoughts and a go-getter spirit that make her easy to train. Most of the beauties are willing to follow Big Sister Hong Li's lead; some just need more attention than others. And yet despite the time and energy required to groom its entry-level staff, it's worth the investment for M. Perfumine. If the company hired sophisticated city girls, it would have to pay more and deal with greater job turnover. "In the city, kids' options are broader. They can study, they can do other things," explains Hong Li. "Young countryside girls are more stable because they're not used to city life. If they were to switch to another industry now, it would all be strange to them." When they arrive they're young, alone, undereducated, and largely without skills. Once they've settled in at M. Perfumine, where else are they really going to go?

The next day, preparations for the Ceri Silk event are in full swing at the High-Tech Zone salon, with a whole team of M.

Perfumine teachers on site to give the place a makeover. Meanwhile, a Pygmalion-like training session is under way in the lobby as Teacher Ding, a plainly dressed young woman in charge of special activities, coaches Jia Huan and Zhang Jing on how to most effectively invite customers to attend the event. After making a few phone calls under Teacher Ding's heavy scrutiny, Jia Huan escapes into the employee lounge, where several of the other beauties are making their phone calls unsupervised.

Teacher Ding follows closely behind her. "You've got to speed it up a little," she tells Jia Huan. "At this rate, you won't finish all your calls today. Then what are we going to do?" She coaxes Jia Huan back to the lobby, puts the phone in her hand, and points to the next customer on the list. Jia Huan grimaces and dials the number. "I've got really great news to tell you," she begins, summoning up her enthusiasm. "On the fifteenth, we're having a special event. We've invited a foreign expert. It's a very hard chance to come by." She explains the details and then pauses while her customer talks for a while. "Really?" Jia Huan says excitedly. "No kidding! You've definitely got to come then... See you then!"

Jia Huan hangs up and turns triumphantly to Teacher Ding. But rather than congratulate her, the teacher simply says, "You've got a little problem in the way you talk."

Zhang Jing nods in agreement. "You're stammering and saying uh, uh, uh."

"That's right," says Teacher Ding. "Next call."

"I've still got to call?"

"You've still got to call."

After Jia Huan finishes another successful invite, Teacher Ding says her problem is that she's too soft on important words like "foreign expert." Jia Huan's stomach growls and she wanders into the break room again, followed by Teacher Ding and Zhang Jing. "I'm hungry," Jia Huan announces. "Beauties, we've got to eat something."

"Finish calling, then eat," says Teacher Ding sternly.

"Finish?"

"Finish!"

Jia Huan makes another call, but as soon as Teacher Ding steps out to use the restroom, she empties a package of numb and spicy ramen noodles into a bowl and douses them with hot water. Upon her return, Teacher Ding sinks silently onto a footstool, ready to once again pin down Jia Huan as soon as she finishes her meal. But before Jia Huan is even halfway through her noodles, one of her customers shows up. She skips off to give the woman a facial, smiling at Teacher Ding as she goes. Several other therapists slip out of the lounge before Teacher Ding sets her sights on them, leaving just Zhang Jing and a therapist named Taoling in the room. Zhang Jing asks Teacher Ding to tell them how she became a teacher at M. Perfumine. When Teacher Ding admits that she has a mere three-year history with the company—two years as a beauty therapist and now one year as a teacher—the *meinü* nudge each other excitedly.

"Wow," Taoling exclaims. "You've done amazingly well!"

"Only two years and you were able to move up to teacher-level," Zhang Jing says with a look of awe.

"And you're so young, too, but you seem so old and mature," Taoling adds.

And, indeed, it is hard to believe that Teacher Ding is the same age as Jia Huan—not even twenty. But unlike all these girls, Teacher Ding is not from the countryside. She grew up in Xi'an but chose to forgo high school in favor of a three-year vocational course in hotel management. When that proved too boring, she dropped out and became a beauty therapist here, quickly standing out from her less urbane countryside colleagues.

It's unusual for someone with only two years of experience to make it to teacher-level, but last year the company expanded its education department and promoted a number of outstanding therapists, Teacher Ding among them. When Zhang Jing and Taoling start moping about their own chances of moving ahead so swiftly, Teacher Ding assures them that sooner or later their time will come. "At M. Perfumine, everyone's equal. If you do well, you will move up."

When Big Sister Hong Li really wants to impress upon her beauties what promising futures they have at M. Perfumine, she tells them the story of Songling, an early High-Tech Zone therapist who was so hopelessly backwoods when she arrived that she couldn't even give a one-sentence self-introduction at her first employee meeting. Big Sister Hong Li thought she was a lost cause, but after working at M. Perfumine for a few years, she blossomed into an elegant young woman who ultimately found a really good husband with a university degree. "If she hadn't chosen this job, she'd still be back in the village, married to a local boy," Hong Li often tells her beauties. "Every day would be just the same as when she grew up. But now when she goes home to her village, everyone there really treats her like she's somebody."

At the High-Tech Zone branch of M. Perfumine, Songling's Cinderella story is so extolled that newcomers sometimes suspect it's merely a legend. The point that seems lost on Big Sister Hong Li, however, is that Songling never actually achieved big success at M. Perfumine. She didn't work her way up the ranks from therapist to manager or teacher and establish herself in a

[handwritten marginal note: (if not economic success, many rich personal opportunity to do so at least)]

long-term career path. Instead, she worked as an entry-level employee for several years—improving greatly under Big Sister Hong Li's careful tutelage, no doubt—but when the opportunity arose, she quit her job and married a city boy.

By hiring countryside girls with low education and few opportunities, the industry may be getting more stable employees, but it is also largely getting employees who don't believe. It's not that the beauties don't believe in the company's products and services—like Jia Huan, they would all gladly purchase them if they had that kind of spare cash—and it's not even that they don't believe in M. Perfumine's promises of where they could someday end up. The real problem is that despite the changes they've seen in themselves, most of the girls don't believe they have what it takes to climb the corporate ladder.

"I never really think about being a boss because I know I don't have enough ability or knowledge," says Haiying. From the time she was in primary school, she'd already planned everything out: she'd finish junior high and then make the six-hour journey to Xi'an to find work. But now that reality has caught up with her life plans, she can't envision a future for herself here. Unfortunately, she doesn't know where else to look either. "We're all like this," she grumbles. "Totally ignorant."

"This job is not long term," says Jia Huan. "It's a job for young people. When you're older, you can't keep doing it—almost nobody does." The only practical way to stay in the industry beyond the age of thirty is to become a teacher or a manager. But, like Haiying, Jia Huan doesn't imagine her future lies in that direction. "I can't do it. I don't have any confidence for it. I see those teachers are all so capable." Although Jia Huan does believe in the merits of the marriage option, even if she is lucky

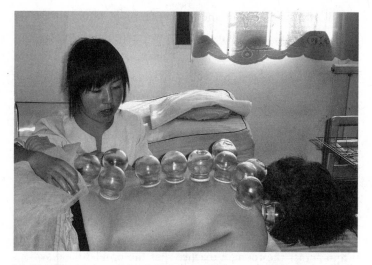

Ma Haiying gives a traditional Chinese medicine treatment at the salon.

enough to find an urban husband she doesn't want that to be her only avenue for success. "I don't want to depend on my husband," she says. "I want to have a really good career of my own."

She has no idea what that may be. If she ever scrapes together enough for a photography course, she'll probably take it, but for now she'd rather spend her salary on shoes and clothes than save it for something like that. As long as M. Perfumine is keeping money in her pocket, she might as well just stick with it. Who knows, Jia Huan says, someday she might end up excelling at this job and become an even bigger success story than the legendary Songling.

After five days of frantic provisioning, the afternoon of the Ceri Silk event finally arrives. The High-Tech Zone's nine beauty therapists are all perfectly made up and ready for action and a small army of M. Perfumine teachers is on hand to help ensure success. When the first customer shows up promptly at 3:00 p.m., the beauties chime "Welcome dear customer" and bow in unison. Since Ceri Silk herself has yet to arrive, they direct the woman into one of the treatment rooms, where two teachers happen to be waiting with laminated summaries of the day's super-special deals.

Within an hour, every corner of the salon bulges with customers. Most of them have a teacher or a *meinü* glued to their side expounding on the merits of M. Perfumine's various products. Jia Huan has been talking with one of her regular customers for quite some time, but with so many people crowded into the tiny space, both she and her client keep getting distracted. From across the room, a teacher sees the problem and swoops in, putting a hand on both their shoulders. "How's it going?" she asks.

"Jia Huan's explaining this to me," the customer says, nodding toward a promotional poster taped to the wall.

"Let me take you through it," the teacher says. She speaks with enough force and conviction to hold the woman's attention, despite the ruckus around them, and soon Jia Huan's customer is at the cash counter adding another 1,000 yuan to her membership card.

It's nearly 5:00 p.m. when Ceri Silk finally arrives. The customers teem into one of the treatment rooms to hear her speak. "Whatever your skin concerns are, we have a product for you," the renowned foreign expert begins. She talks for less than five minutes before opening it up to the audience for questions; in another ten minutes the meeting disperses into a product-ordering frenzy. Ceri is whisked into the employee lounge, which will serve as her makeshift office for the rest of the afternoon, and customers start lining up for private consultations.

A brief lull eventually falls over the salon and the beauties retreat into a back room to contact customers who have not yet shown up. A teacher named Lili sits on one of the massage beds and listens to them make their calls. Unlike many M. Perfumine teachers, who are either college graduates or from the city, Teacher Lili is one of the few countryside girls who actually did work her way up from an entry-level therapist to a teacher. Now, at age twenty-six, she makes as much as 3,000 yuan a month, including bonuses. And though she chose to forgo the marriage option in favor of marrying a guy from her own remote village, she still feels firmly, and permanently, established in Xi'an.

This is particularly encouraging to Zhang Jing, who settles in next to Teacher Lili in the hope of culling some advice from her; although Zhang Jing is quickly earning a reputation for being the most determined therapist on staff, even she could use some encouragement. "In China, if you don't have a good education, you're never going to be as good as others," she says. "If you don't have a degree and you're not especially pretty, who wants you? So you've got to rely on your own abilities to survive."

By 8:00 p.m., Ceri Silk leaves and the last few customers clear out of the salon. The teachers hold a brief meeting to congratulate the *meinü* on the day's success; though the exact figures aren't available yet, more than eighty customers showed up and purchases definitely exceeded expectations. That will certainly mean bragging rights for the High-Tech Zone's nine beauty therapists at the next quarterly sales meeting, but at the moment they are too tired and hungry to care. As they crowd into an empty room to change out of their uniforms before going out to dinner, Jia Huan finds a cucumber that she'd stashed away earlier. She waves it back and forth, taunting her ravenous coworkers. Zhang Jing and Haiying lunge for it, but Jia Huan ducks out of the way and a playful chase ensues. Eventually Jia Huan snaps it into pieces and passes them around for everyone to share.

Whether or not this job really is as good for rural girls as M. Perfumine claims, and whether or not the beauties believe they have a future here or are in it just for the paycheck, few of them doubt that it is better than most of their alternatives. Here at least they work in a clean environment with heating and air conditioning. They don't have to do a lot of hard physical labor and are surrounded by girls their own age and a boss who cares for them. Despite their grand dreams for the future, as poorly educated countryside youth short on skills and career options, that just might be enough.

CHAPTER FOUR

The Ever-Floating Floater

Zhang Erhua sleeps in a cardboard-lined metal box perched above a mountain of old newspaper. When he wakes up in the morning, he leaps from his bed, slides surfer-style down the towering paper mound, and his ten-second commute is finished. His boss hands him a steaming bowl of noodles, which he slurps down with loud, lip-smacking enthusiasm. Then he rakes his fingers through his wildly tousled hair, tucks a cigarette behind each ear, and pronounces himself ready for work.

There's not all that much to do just yet, though, so to pass the time, twenty-eight-year-old Erhua hurls himself into the paper heap and rummages for something to read. He stumbles upon his electric razor, which he quickly zigzags over his chin. Then, with a cigarette burning in one hand and the razor whirring in the other, he throws his arms around his coworker and roommate up in the box, fifty-eight-year-old Wei Laifu, dragging the older man backward until they both collapse into the newspapers with a laugh. Their boss, thirty-one-year-old Liang

Hongxia, sniggers at them as she cleans her nails with a jagged shard of glass.

Things aren't always so relaxed in this open-air recycling operation, but Hongxia's husband went back to the village for a few days, and everyone's motivation seems to have gone with him. Eventually, though, business picks up, as three-wheel bicyclers start rolling in, looking to exchange whatever recyclables they've scavenged for some good old-fashioned cash. Unlike Erhua and Laifu, these recyclers don't work for Hongxia and her husband—they are simply independent operators who make it their business to rid the High-Tech Zone and its environs of its more lucrative trash. As such, Erhua and the others don't jump up from their busy state of repose to greet them; instead, they simply watch the recyclers struggle to balance their paper, cardboard, glass, plastic, iron, or copper on the outfit's severely undersized scale. Only after everything is properly weighed do Erhua and Laifu swing into action, dragging the goods to their proper piles around the 150-square-meter enclosure in which they work, live, and play.

They've been plugging away for less than an hour when the operation's star collector rides in, three-wheeler piled high with shoeboxes and milk jugs. On good days he brings in up to 50 yuan worth of recyclables an hour. He'd be making a killing if it weren't for the fact that he and the other bicyclers have to pay for most of what they collect: with so many of them out hunting for recyclables, people don't just give the stuff away—at least not in any substantial quantity. To score this load, he paid out nearly 35 yuan, and now Hongxia hands him just 10 yuan more than that, for a profit of less than $2. He squirrels the newly acquired bills into his wallet and then rides off, already scouring the alleyway for more castoffs.

"China's very poor," observes Hongxia's mother, who recently came from the village to help her daughter out for a while. "China's very poor, and we are very poor."

Laifu nods in agreement, while Hongxia takes a quick survey of the cash left in her fanny pack. "In this country all we talk about now is money," she says drily. "We don't talk about anything else."

Erhua—who has scurried up the paper mound and catapulted himself into the box he and Laifu call home—lights a cigarette and listens with amusement to the conversation below. He's been all over the country and worked all kinds of jobs, and no matter where he goes everyone seems to thrive on talk of how poor they are; it's pervasive enough to be an unofficial migrant mantra of sorts.

On the one hand, it is understandable. After all, they've all left behind their families, friends, and homes in pursuit of a better life, and none of them would be out here at all if they weren't in need of money. But, on the other hand, it seems to Erhua that people need to let themselves think beyond money's narrow confines sometimes. People need to have time to move and laugh and live a little—otherwise, what's it all for? "You can't live without money, but as long as you've got some, that's enough," he says. He pauses and holds his cigarette thoughtfully, as if reviewing his life experiences before concluding: "Besides, too much money makes it easy for a person to turn bad."

China has no formal recycling program. The only thing even close to curbside pickup is the legion of recyclers patrolling the street corners on hot summer days, asking beverage-toting pedestrians to surrender their nearly empty bottles. In recent years many cities have installed bins to separate recyclable and nonrecyclable materials, but so far few people differentiate between the two. Undaunted, recyclers pick their way through the trash cans, and the garbage dumps too.

It's no surprise, then, that recyclables arrive at Hongxia's place quite dirty. They get even dirtier piled up behind walls that are so cheap and slipshod that whole sections are simply stacked bricks without any mortar at all. A thin plastic awning arches high above the paper and cardboard mountains to protect them from the elements, but it's hardly adequate. By the time Hongxia accumulates a big enough load to haul off to the plant where everything is actually recycled, she invariably gets fined for turning over goods that are deemed too dirty.

But while the recyclables might not be clean enough for the folks at the recycling plant, Hongxia and her crew have no qualms about utilizing them. During this afternoon's post-lunch lull, Laifu lounges on a stack of cardboard, Hongxia sprawls out on half a lawn chair, and her mother balances on an overturned paint can. Meanwhile, Erhua stretches out in his usual roost amidst the newspapers, eyeing a rusty barrel that arrived this morning. It's the industrial-use kind that likely stored chemicals before savvy street vendors reincarnated it into a stove for baking sweet potatoes. Erhua picks himself out of the papers and rushes toward it, leaping into the air and delivering a Kung Fu-style kick that knocks it over with a loud thud. A cloud of powdery white ash rises up out of the old stove and engulfs him. He doubles over and coughs with such theatrics that soon everyone is laughing.

Erhua is, to put it mildly, a bit rash and uncalculated. Several times a day, for no apparent reason, he wraps his arms around someone's neck and pulls them into one of the recycling piles, hooting and hollering all the while like a high schooler from the winning football team. He'd be an intolerable oddity in more stoic Chinese circles, but here his shenanigans are usually a welcome way to make the day go by more quickly. And despite all his antics—or perhaps because of them—he's the best employee Hongxia and her husband have ever had. Erhua has worked here four times already, each time for just a couple months to help them out of a bind. They would love to have him stay on indefinitely, but that's proven impossible. It's not just that few people— Erhua included—are willing to work day after day in this filthy environment and sleep night after night suspended above it. The real problem is that although all migrants are members of what is commonly referred to as China's floating population, for Erhua the term is almost a literal description.

Though the word sounds fairly innocuous in English, in Chinese *liudong,* or "floating," connotes itinerant, unstable, shiftless, and even dangerous. Peasants who float into the city are often seen as lowering the quality of city life. Whereas in other nations a person from the countryside can move to an urban area and gradually integrate into the local population, in China that is all but impossible thanks to its antiquated *hukou,* or "household registration system." Back in the 1950s the government instituted the system, which designates all citizens as either urban or rural, depending on their parents' residential status at the time of their birth, as a means to stop farmers from fleeing rural areas after collectivization began. Those wishing to venture beyond the confines of their place of residence needed to first obtain official approvals and carry supporting documents with them as they traveled.

Over time, restrictions eased, and today the *hukou* system no longer prevents rural-urban migration, but it still presents would-be migrants with significant challenges. Under the *hukou* system, all citizens are entitled to free services, such as education and health care, but only in the location in which their *hukou* is registered. That means migrants frequently are unable to access city services, including affordable health care and education for their children. For those with a rural *hukou*, obtaining official permission to remain in the city still requires numerous certificates, which can be both costly and time-consuming. As a result, most migrants live and work without legal documentation, which in turn makes them susceptible to mistreatment. And since it is generally extremely difficult to transfer from a rural to an urban *hukou*, the system ensures that all but the most successful of migrants are forever seen as outsiders who are temporarily "floating" in the nation's cities.

Despite the label and its associated stereotypes, however, not all members of the floating population are interminably transient. Some, like Hongxia and her husband, find what could be called a career path and stay in the city for years or even decades, and yet they are still considered floaters because their *hukou* is registered back in the village. Others, like the three-wheeling recyclers, go back to the countryside several times a year to help with planting and harvesting but generally stick to the same line of work each time they return to the city. Still others, like Laifu, come just once to fulfill some special financial need—in this case, his son's upcoming wedding—and then resume their agrarian lifestyle.

Then there are those like Erhua, who embody the term to the fullest, floating from place to place and job to job with no apparent pattern. Over the past nine years he's had more jobs in more cities around China than he can remember—running the spectrum from welding bed frames to assembling electronics to crafting ramen noodles. In the last year alone he's worked in a leather factory in southern China, remodeled houses in central China, and, now, for the past month, he's been shepherding recyclables here in the western part of the country. "I don't like to work outside my village for too long," explains Erhua. "If I do it for too long, my heart gets tired."

Whenever that happens, he simply quits his job and hightails it back to his home in the countryside. He spends a few days or weeks or months there helping his parents in the fields, riding around on his motorcycle, and playing with the farm dogs. Then, when he runs out of money or just gets bored, he starts looking for city work again.

How long he stays at a given job depends on how well he gets along with the boss and how long he can stand the conditions. Usually that's not too long; whereas other migrants seem to have no problem accepting their limited options and throwing themselves into anything that makes money, Erhua is searching for something he can really put his heart into. Until now he has yet to find a suitable vocation, and so he keeps wandering, floating back and forth and contributing to the economy and his own personal prosperity in whatever way he can, whenever he feels like it.

Though some people might think he's lazy, unmotivated, and shortsighted, Erhua doesn't see himself as any of these things. He's just as willing and able to eat bitterness as the next guy; he's just not willing to focus his life exclusively on the pursuit of wealth. "I'm not in it just for money, like most people are," he says. "Money isn't all powerful. You've got to live comfortably too."

When the dust from the old barrel finally settles, Erhua knocks out the brick and coal chunks and starts pummeling it with a sledgehammer. Then he shovels the ashes into a wheelbarrow,

Zhang Erhua walks behind the recycling center.

singing an old folk song as he works. While living in a box above a heap of trash is far from what is typically considered living comfortably, contentment for Erhua comes in choosing what he wants to do when he wants to do it rather than letting financial concerns dictate his every move. More than stability or a steady income, that, to Erhua, is real comfort.

There's a reason Erhua so dislikes the money-at-all-costs mentality pervading this level of society: not only does it cause people to lose sight of the world around them, but too often it gives rise to a petty ruthlessness in which one's quest for getting ahead is put above moral considerations, including others' health, safety, and livelihood. In recent years, reports of tainted Chinese milk, pet food, drywall, and a host of other product-safety issues have highlighted the dangerous extremes to which this money-first mind-set leads.

In the recycling universe, the mentality manifests itself most frequently as simple attempts to cheat the system. Some three-wheel bicyclists hide rocks and sand in their recyclables to try to bolster their income without having to find so many goods. Owners of ma-and-pa recycling outfits employ similar tactics by watering down their cardboard to make it heavier, and thus more valuable, when they turn around and sell it to the recycling plant. Hongxia and her husband weren't initially inclined to cheat in this way, but the practice ultimately became so prevalent that the recycling plant began fining everyone, regardless of whether their cardboard was actually wet. After that, hosing down the cardboard became standard operating procedure.

And so each afternoon Erhua and Laifu spend a couple hours turning the cardboard heap into a slippery, soggy mess. Today Laifu scrambles to the top of the pile and starts dousing it with water, while Erhua searches the recycling pit for stray cardboard. He spots the shoe boxes the star recycler brought in earlier and drags them over to the cardboard mountain. Rather than simply tossing them up to Laifu, however, he punts them in the air, erupting into a victory cheer each time one hits its mark.

If Erhua had grown up in another time and place he may very well have been labeled with attention deficit disorder, but in rural China he was just considered intolerably naughty. He never could sit still long enough to like school: he didn't even start first grade until he was nine, and he quit after sixth grade, at age fourteen. When he couldn't sit still at home either, his family found him a job finishing home interiors with a family friend in Gan Jia Zhai, a six-hour train ride away from their village in neighboring Henan province.

It was 1993 and Erhua made the equivalent of a mere $12 plus room and board per month, but for a boy who'd never had money of his own, it seemed like a fortune—a fortune he spent visiting local tourist sites, hanging out downtown, and playing cards with his buddies. "At that time I was so young, I only knew how to play. I never even thought about saving money," he says. Though he enjoyed his downtime, the work itself was anything but fun; a typical day lasted at least eleven intense hours and frequently dragged on well into the night too.

It was during this time that Erhua and his new friends tried giving each other tattoos, and the botched attempts decorating his forearms still serve as a reminder of those days. The only tattoo that really turned out is the character for "endure" imprinted on his wrist. Taking it as a sign of sorts, Erhua tried to bear through each sweat-drenched day, but it wasn't easy for such a rambunctious teen. He had no particular problem with his boss or his work; he was simply too restless to be restrained by someone else's salary, schedule, and expectations.

And so, with a yearlong, cursory introduction to the industry under his belt, fifteen-year-old Erhua quit his job and went into business for himself. He rounded up two employees, ages sixteen and seventeen, and promised them a full 300 yuan a month, since they had significantly more experience than he did. Then he rented a room for the three of them to live in and started drumming up business. "It didn't matter to me whether I did well or not, I just didn't want to work for someone else," he says. "Working for yourself is definitely still tiring, but it feels different. You feel that it's all yours."

His enterprise started off surprisingly well. Construction of the High-Tech Zone had just begun and along with it came a corresponding house-building boom in Gan Jia Zhai, which made finding contracting jobs easy, even for an inexperienced teenager. Collecting money after he finished a job, however, turned out to be far more difficult. Over time, the outstanding payments started adding up and eventually, with more than 10,000 yuan still owed to him, he no longer had the cash flow to pay his own employees. Though they continued working for him with no compensation other than his promise to reimburse them, after several months of unsuccessfully trying to recover his money, Erhua borrowed some cash to pay back his employees and then closed his doors for good. "No matter how things worked out, I definitely had to pay them," he says.

Maintaining such integrity was quite an accomplishment for an inexperienced youngster who was getting stiffed by many of the adults for whom he worked. Part of the reason he had such a hard time getting paid was that he was young, timid, and afraid to confront people, but part of it was simply a symptom of the emerging man-eat-man capitalist culture that overlooked stepping on others to get ahead; bilking him was just another way for people to add to their own bank accounts. "A lot of businesspeople started small and grew big quickly, but that's not me. A bunch of people from our village did that, and now some of them even have millions. But they made their money by not paying their workers. If they were honest, they couldn't have taken off that fast," Erhua says. "There are so many big bosses around now who have black hearts."

In total, Erhua's enterprise lasted three years, making his teenage foray into entrepreneurship his longest-standing work experience to date. In 1997 he left for northern China to help his brother, who ran a stall in a wholesale market in Tianjin. He worked there for two years—his second longest job ever—and would have remained even longer if his girlfriend hadn't suddenly broken up with him, taking his interest in staying put along with her. After that he headed to Anhui province to try his hand at welding and has been floating ever since, never able to find something worthy of his extended attention again. Even here, in Hongxia's recycling pit, Erhua is so restless that he can't sit near the newspaper pile without rummaging through it like a madman or douse down the cardboard mountain without turning it into punting practice.

Erhua and Laifu are still drenching the cardboard when the star collector rides back into the pit with another load of recyclables. Glad for the diversion, Erhua slips away from the task at hand and watches him pile goods on the scale. After Hongxia pays the star collector, he tosses them each a stick of gum and launches into a story about his kids back in the village.

With that, Erhua slides down into the collector's now-empty bicycle cart and drifts out of the conversation. Part of what enables him to enjoy such freedom of movement is that he's not yet married and has no major life responsibilities. People like the star collector who are out here with the express purpose of sending money back to their families tend to be floaters of the less mobile type: they don't have the luxury of hopping from job to job. But Erhua just has his own life to support. He doesn't even need to think about taking care of his parents, as they get regular subsidies from his older brother—a floater of the more stable and successful kind. Erhua knows that someday, when he has a family of his own, he probably will have to start thinking more seriously about saving for all the expenses that accompany married life. His parents and siblings are eager for that day to arrive, but for now he's content to just keep floating.

Regardless of whether or not they're married or have other financial responsibilities, one thing that allows rural people like Erhua the freedom to leave their villages and venture city-ward in search of work is the parcel of land they are each allotted at birth. When collective agriculture came to an end in the late 1970s, peasants no longer enjoyed the assurances of eating from the Big Rice Pot. Instead, under the newly implemented household responsibility system, every man, woman, and child with a rural *hukou* received a parcel of land. The farmland wasn't theirs exactly—they lost it if they let it go fallow and it returned to the village when they died—but as long as they kept planting and breathing, they could call it their own.

While urbanites were still assured of free food rations and long-term job security, this allotment of freebie land was seen as an equivalent form of security for the rural population. And indeed, even today this lifelong parcel ensures that rural migrants have a plan B to fall back on if by chance things in the city don't go as planned; as long as someone tends their land while they're gone, they can rest assured that it will be there waiting for them when they decide to return home.

Ironically, however, while the land may be what enables people like Erhua to head city-ward, it is also largely what necessitates the move in the first place. With more than 800 million rural *hukou* holders across the country, by the time all the arable land is divvied up, each person receives an average plot size of just one *mu*, or one-sixth of an acre. Even for a Chinese family of four, that translates into an area of land 673 times smaller than an average American farm. Thus, in the end, land given to rural *hukou* holders is really more of a sustenance insurance plan than a viable livelihood. Those looking to do much more than keep their family fed have to either find some sort of business in the village or send at least one family member out to join the swelling ranks of the floating population.

Like everything else in modern China, land policies, too, are changing, and in some places the younger generation of rural *hukou* holders is no longer automatically receiving a free allotment of land. But no matter how dramatically the rural landscape may change in the coming decades, as Erhua sees it his life will forever be intimately tied to the land. "If you're born in the countryside, you're always going to be a peasant," he says simply. Even if he hasn't done any earnest work back on the farm since he left home at age fourteen, thanks to that tiny stretch of soil he can call his own, he knows that someday, when he's too old and broken to do city labor anymore, he will live off his land again. For China's farmers, this isn't seen as a perk but as the most basic of entitlements and the only real form of social security they have.

Strangers are always drifting in and out of the recycling pit, meandering in to size up the metal scraps, weigh themselves on the scale, browse through the old newspapers, or even just lounge around on the ever-changing array of makeshift furniture. Erhua and crew don't seem mind—it's difficult, after all, to have a closed-door mentality when living and working in an open-air setting. And so, when a passerby wanders in one morning and lets his toddler loose in the iron pile, none of them even blink. A few minutes later, Erhua pulls himself out of his paper pile nest and starts playing with the little girl, who has already collected a handful of nails. He playfully directs her to throw them at Hongxia, and Hongxia reciprocates by showing the child how to slap Erhua's hand.

Recently Hongxia has been stepping up her requests for Erhua to stay long term, but so far he's only committed to stick around until Spring Festival. He wasn't too keen on coming here in the first place, but Hongxia's husband is his *laoxiang*, or "hometown mate," and an old childhood friend on top of it, so Erhua couldn't refuse; for villagers who head to the city, such hometown connections are precious resources that need to be carefully preserved. Though Erhua has none of the money-in-the-bank stability of most urbanites, thanks to the extensive network of hometown mates he's cultivated over the years, at the very least he can almost always find a job when he wants one. More often than not, some *laoxiang* offers him a job before he's even ready to start working again.

Given the sometimes brutal environment permeating migrant life in places like Gan Jia Zhai, where a mishmash of people from every corner of the country takes refuge, seeking out those from a common geographical location is more than just an egocentric or a parochial tendency: it's a survival instinct. By utilizing an informal *laoxiang* network, those on the hiring side feel they are getting more reliable workers, while those seeking jobs feel more confident that they will be treated well and paid regularly. In lieu of strictly and consistently enforced labor laws to govern this level of society, the *laoxiang* network serves as a sort of makeshift safety net where everyone looks out for their own.

The system has become so integral to the inner workings of China's cities that entire markets are often run by entrepreneurs from a single village, entire streets are canvassed by peddlers from a single county, and entire industries are sometimes dominated by people from a single province. Gan Jia Zhai has sixteen recycling outfits like Hongxia's, and all of them are run by people from their same corner of Henan province. The result of all this *laoxiang* back-scratching, Hongxia says, is that their hometown is now thriving on the financial front. "Now the villagers all have a lot of money. They all have cell phones, motorcycles, vehicles—everything," she says. "In our area, anything under 100,000 yuan (approximately $15,625) is small potatoes now."

It's true that conditions in some parts of the countryside are changing at a rapid rate, thanks in large part to the influx of cash sent back home by those who've already left. But the ironic thing for Erhua is that despite all the money focus of those driven city-ward, despite all the conniving and wheedling to get ahead, he doesn't see many migrants attaining a significantly better life. In fact, in terms of living standards, they are often much worse off in places like Gan Jia Zhai than they were in the countryside. Back in the village most peasants now enjoy a host of modern appurtenances, but in the city migrants' living spaces are too cramped and their stays too uncertain to proffer up the money for such luxuries. And whereas in the countryside they at least had a plentiful supply of fresh air and sunshine and movement, in the city they're cooped up like prisoners of their own lifestyles.

Hongxia is a perfect example: she's lived in Xi'an for nearly a decade and has never been downtown, much less to the Terra Cotta Warriors or any other local historic sites. Sometimes months can pass without her stepping out of Gan Jia Zhai, even though the High-Tech Zone is just half a block away. And in all this time she's never hired anyone who wasn't a hometown mate, nor has she befriended anyone else either.

Though Erhua, too, gets bound up in the particulars of a given job, and though he may get immersed in the world of whatever factory or market he works at, at least for him it's usually just in couple-month spurts. Then he takes time to enjoy himself before heading back out to the isolation of the migrant world again.

A truckload of scrap wood arrives later that afternoon, but the recycling pit is so packed that there's nowhere to put it. Erhua and Laifu decide to clear some space by moving a sack of miscellaneous junk up onto a wall behind the cardboard mountain. Hongxia urges them to be careful; there are actually two parallel walls there and she doesn't want it to get stuck in between them. As Laifu balances the bag of junk up on the ledge, Erhua pokes it with a stick and, sure enough, the sack falls into the narrow opening.

Laifu shimmies in between the walls to try to dislodge it, while Erhua neatly stacks a heap of tires to make more room for the scrap wood. The only problem is that he inadvertently piles them in front of the passageway between the two walls, thus trapping Laifu into the crawl space. Rather than simply moving the tires, Erhua scales the cardboard mountain and spends the next five minutes trying to heave his roommate up and over the wall. Hongxia tries to look stern as she watches from her broken swivel chair, but she still ends up laughing at her two bumbling employees.

Though Erhua doesn't love working here or sleeping in the cold, drafty box, he does appreciate having a boss who usually shrugs off his escapades. At other places, goof-ups much smaller than this could lead to serious problems—and he's definitely had his fair share of boss issues in the past. That's one of the reasons he'd really like to work for himself again, if possible. Over the years he's dabbled in a variety of different business ventures, but until now none of them have lasted anywhere near as long as his first juvenile venture into the world of the self-employed.

His most recent entrepreneurial attempt came last summer when he opened a small restaurant in Tianjin. At the beginning, the location seemed perfect—right next to a school, a military base, and a construction site. The problem was that he started in

Wei Laifu at the recycling center.

July, when students weren't in school, and only realized after he had already opened that people weren't allowed off the military base—which left construction workers as his only remaining customer base. Still, that might have been enough, but then in August the construction manager ran off with the investment money and the site closed down. The construction workers ended up going home unpaid and empty-handed, and a few weeks later, with no customers left to sustain him, so did Erhua.

When Erhua opened his restaurant, he didn't go through the *laoxiang* network like most migrants would have, but even if he had, it wouldn't have saved him—similar to his experience as a teenage entrepreneur, his business failed in part because of the unscrupulous behavior of those around him. But though Erhua resents the havoc these "black hearts" can wreak, he can't bring himself to blame his failures on them. For him, this type of unethical conduct is so common as to be just another facet of doing business that any entrepreneur should be ready and able to cope with. Though he knows he can be a bit too playful and scattered, in the end he's convinced that the real reason for his repeated failures comes down to fate. "In business you've got to rely on luck. That's what most of us do. If your luck is good, you make money. It's just like gambling. It's the same principle."

A few days later, Hongxia's husband returns from the village, and Laifu's youngest son, who's decided to find a job in the city for a few months, tags along with him. Although the nineteen-year-old has never done anything other than farmwork in his life, that doesn't seem to daunt him. In fact, as he sits on an old metal bed frame that someone just dropped off and talks about his plans, his attitude sums up the quintessential floater mentality: "I came to play and I came to work. I'm only staying until Spring Festival, so any old job I can find is okay." With so many of their *laoxiang* living in Gan Jia Zhai, he's fairly confident he'll have a job by afternoon.

Now that her husband is back, Hongxia takes an uncharacteristic leave of absence to run some errands. With this changing of the guard, the place takes on a new tone. Erhua and Laifu no longer roam around waiting for recyclables to roll in. Instead, they move outside behind the recycling pit to work on the part of the operation that Hongxia's husband oversees: bagging beer bottles. Three big stacks of bagged bottles line the brick wall, and there's still an enormous pile of bottles left for them to deal with before Hongxia's husband hauls the entire load off to the recycling plant.

From inside the walls of the recycling center, the place is its own universe. The rubbish heaps, the iron scraps, the box bed, and the parade of nameless wanderers all seem right in place.

But from back here, where chickens run past the military-style tent that Hongxia's mother sleeps in at night, while gleaming new High-Tech Zone apartment high-rises loom large in the background, it is clear that they are living on the cusp between two dramatically different worlds.

When Erhua came to Gan Jia Zhai in 1993, what is now the High-Tech Zone was mostly all still farmland. And although Erhua himself contributed to the development of the area, he had no idea that the place ultimately would become one of the premier locations in all of western China. Though he's not as sequestered as Hongxia and most other migrants, and though he regularly leaves the recycling pit and Gan Jia Zhai and notices all the glamorous changes taking place right next door, he still doesn't have much of an opinion about the area's dramatic transformation. "I don't think there's anything good or bad about it for people like us. There's no advantage or disadvantage. Mainly it's just good for them"—he waves a hand toward the towering buildings behind him—"It's bringing glory to the ancient city of Xi'an."

The real change that Erhua has noticed—the change that is affecting everyone, regardless of whether they live in the most glorious palaces or the darkest recycling pits—is the one taking place in people's hearts. "Before people were better than they are now. Before people here treated others extremely well," says Erhua, recalling how, when he first came to Gan Jai Zhai as an out-of-his-element fourteen-year-old, it was the kindness of the local people that helped him survive. It might also have been their greed that caused his first company to fail, but even so the place was much better back then than it is today, he says. "We were so young and out working already, and the people here treated us like their sons. But no one cares about these types of kids anymore. Now people don't have much for feelings. Now they only have feelings for money." As he talks, Erhua absently crushes pieces of broken glass beneath his foot. He's not just referring to those who do anything to get ahead—he's talking about an entire shift in culture and country that's sweeping everyone into its vortex. "Now everywhere has changed to be very complex. Now it's so hard to understand what people are thinking about. Beijing, Tianjin—everywhere was different before. Everywhere was better."

That makes things harder not just for the kids who come to the city looking for work but for people like him as well. He would like to operate his own business again, but in such an unstable environment, who knows if and when fate will ever be on his side? Regardless of whether or not he finds the elusive key to success, right now his dream is still to open another restaurant. It's not that he feels particularly inclined toward the food industry but simply that he sees it as easier than most other endeavors. After all, there are not a whole lot of risks or start-up costs involved—at least not for the bare-bones type of diner he'll open again. He's already got enough money saved to launch another restaurant, but after that his money will be gone. So for once he's trying to be rational, biding his time at temporary jobs until just the right opportunity presents itself. Who knows, if all goes well, maybe he'll find that this is a calling that he can really devote himself to and finally stay put for an extended period of time.

But all that is in the future, and Erhua is not big on planning ahead. Right now he doesn't even know where he'll be or what he'll be doing in another month or two. All he knows is that he's here now and even if someone offers him a better job, he won't take it, and even if his heart tells him it's time to go home, he won't follow it. Instead, he'll take the advice of his only legible tattoo—he'll endure. He's promised Hongxia and her husband he'll stay until the upcoming Spring Festival, and if nothing else he prides himself on being a man of his word. Though China is changing around him, though people may not be as warm or as welcoming as before, for Erhua, the floater extraordinaire, a person has to draw the line somewhere. Otherwise, if he starts letting go of his ideals, he'll become just another anonymous "black heart" joining the country's crazy chase after money.

CHAPTER FIVE

The Landless Landlords

With less than two weeks before his home of twenty years was to be demolished, Wang Tao did what few other men in his position might have the nerve to do: he disappeared. It wasn't the first time he'd gone MIA; it was a common enough occurrence that his wife and three grown children didn't even notice at first.

In fact, several days pass before it finally dawns on his twenty-four-year-old daughter Wang Jing that something is missing. "Hey, I haven't seen my dad in three or four days," she notices. "Ma, where did dad run off to?"

"To Canton," replies her mother, forty-eight-year-old Zhang Liping, referring to the capital of Guangdong province some twenty-seven hours away by train.

"Canton?"

Ma shrugs. "Yesterday he called me and said he was in Canton."

"He must have taken off because he's afraid people in the village will try to suck him into playing mahjong again," Wang Jing concludes, musing about why her father would suddenly trek off across the country when they still need to find a new home, pack two decades of belongings, and relocate, all in the next week or so. "Maybe he went to Canton to get straightened up and doesn't want people bothering him."

Liping has nothing to say on the topic, so she simply picks up the mop and starts wiping down the tile floor for the second time this afternoon.

"Ma, when are we going to move, anyway?" Wang Jing asks.

Liping lets out a long sigh. "Your dad will take care of it," she says finally. Though Wang Tao's disappearance is adding drama to the family's pending move, Liping and the three children aren't acting like people about to be evicted either. Part of the reason is that they aren't totally convinced that the move will actually take place. Threats and rumors have come and gone for years now, but none have ever panned out. This time, however, even the Wangs have to admit that a reprieve is unlikely, given that their little corner of Gan Jia Zhai just happens to be blocking an extension of the main road through the High-Tech Zone.

Several weeks ago, village leaders dictated April 25 as D-day, but now that the deadline is just nine days away, Liping is hoping to stay put until May. Though that's likely to draw the ire of village leaders, in Gan Jia Zhai she and her husband have famously thick skin.

From outside, a neighbor hollers that one of their blankets has blown into the bustling marketplace in front of their home. Wang Jing scurries out, gathers it up, and then sprints three flights up the home's narrow, open-air staircase to the rooftop, where they hang their laundry to dry. Wang Jing reappears in the second-floor room that serves both as her parents' bedroom and the family's living room and starts flipping channels on an ancient yet surprisingly large TV set. She stops on one of her mom's favorite shows, a Chinese *Idol* of sorts, and pretty soon Liping sets her mop in the corner and settles down next to her daughter.

"Ma," Wang Jing says, cracking a sunflower seed between her teeth, "if dad really called you from Canton, he'd have to pay huge roaming fees." Knowing that her father is not sentimental enough to burn through money just to phone home, Wang Jing can only conclude that he wasn't actually calling from so far away.

"Never mind," Liping replies without a hint of emotion. "No matter where he is, he's up to no good."

Wang Tao finally does reappear later that same afternoon, proceeded up the stairs by a deep, gut-busting cough that years of late nights in smoky gaming halls have rendered permanent. As he traipses into the living room, sunglasses on and cigarette clamped between his lips, he looks as worn down as his lungs sound. "Went to try out my hand at Cantonese gambling," he announces in a flat and mechanical voice.

"For God's sake," Liping murmurs. She shakes her head without looking up and that, without further fanfare, is the extent of their reunion. Wang Tao ambles aimlessly around the room before tossing a bag of snack food at his daughter. "Here. I brought this for you. Cantonese specialty."

Wang Jing takes one look and exclaims, "Cantonese specialty? Nonsense! These are local fried seeds!"

Wang Tao laughs and Wang Jing gives out a playfully miffed sniffle, clearly curious as to where her father has been. But Liping is still glued to the TV and shows no sign of interest at all, so Wang Tao plunks down on the bed—which in the daytime doubles as a second couch—and starts watching too. He eats two bananas and drinks tea directly from the spout of a small teapot, coughing and wheezing all the while.

About a half hour later, Wang Tao confesses that he hasn't been to Canton after all, but that he actually went with a friend to the nearby city of Yangling to play mahjong. He played for four days straight and has the same amount of money in his pocket now that he started with. The fact that he was not in Canton is not much of a surprise to his wife and daughter, nor is the fact that he was out gambling and came back without any winnings.

"He's turned mahjong into a real career," Liping mocks, talking to him, as she and the three children are prone to do, in the third person, as if he were not even there.

"Last year I lost the equivalent of a small car," Wang Tao groans. "My back is aching. My head is aching. My legs are aching."

"But still he won't stop," Wang Jing says.

"Not until he brings the money that he's lost back home," Liping adds.

"That's when I'll stop," he agrees.

"Man," Wang Jing sighs. "It's been like this for twenty years."

Wang Tao simply grins at his daughter and lights another cigarette. Then he leans back against a stack of neatly folded blankets, covers his eyes with one hand, and immediately falls asleep. He needs all the rest he can get: after all, there are only a few hours left before the first round of the evening starts at the mahjong parlor down the street.

Wang Tao wasn't always like this. He used to be a respectable man—or at least far more respectable than he is now. It used to be that he could work hard when the situation demanded and keep food on the table and clothes on the kids. He didn't chain smoke, travel in packs with other degenerate men, or go missing for days at a time. Come to think of it, one could almost say that Wang Tao used to be something of a family man.

When he and Liping got married, back in 1981, Gan Jia Zhai was still practicing collective farming and Wang Tao had no money to escort his new bride home in a car or a carriage, as was the tradition. So he did the next best thing. He shined up his old wheelbarrow and pushed her to the tiny earthen home they were to share with his parents. It sounds fantastically provincial nowadays, Wang Tao realizes, but at the time it was a touching expression of love—a romantic gesture of a devoted husband and a clear sign of a potentially capable father.

Indeed, once upon a time he was nothing like the man who now hacks back home at all hours of the day and night; he was a fun-loving but hardworking peasant who spent his days breaking his back in the fields and his nights sound asleep in his bed. But, alas, that was a much simpler time, before mahjong took over and all the qualities of diligence, resourcefulness, and family unity that the Chinese have prided themselves on for centuries went flying out the window—values still remembered and yet utterly beyond his reach.

The story of how and why Wang Tao started playing the game depends on which day he's telling it. In one version, he took up mahjong to keep his mind sharp, in another version it was simply a way to spend time with friends, and in yet another version it was sheer curiosity that led him to try the tile-clacking pastime that had recently returned to the mainland after being banned by the Communist Party in 1949. Liping's version is different yet, but no matter who's telling the story, they both agree that he would never have gotten so hooked on the game, *could* never have gotten so utterly embroiled in it, if their lives had still been tied to the land.

It all started when collectivized farming ended about a year after they got married. Rather than working together with an entire production team on communal land, each family received one *mu* (approximately one-sixth of an acre) per person to farm and one plot per household on which to build a homestead. Wang Tao and Liping diligently nurtured their newly acquired land and snapped up whatever odd jobs they could find to bolster their income. Six years later, in 1988, they finally scraped together enough to move out of his parents' place and build a modest home of their own.

Soon thereafter they heard whisperings that a massive development project was to be built on Gan Jia Zhai's farmland. The rumors were confirmed in 1992, when construction began on the High-Tech Zone—one of only twenty-six in the country at that time, and the only one in the underdeveloped West. That year, the government bought up all the farmland from three of Gan Jia Zhai's six production teams, entities that, though significantly weaker than they had been during collectivization, still oversaw the distribution of land to their members. A year later, the government bought a portion of the land held by the production team to which Wang Tao and Liping belonged. In exchange, each person—man, woman, and child—received 7,000 yuan. That put the total payout for their family, which now included daughters Wang Jing and Wang Mei and son Wang Kai, at 35,000 yuan.

At a time when wealth wasn't measured in millions but in ten thousands, it was rather like winning the lottery. "Back then we farmers didn't have money. We were barely able to put food on the table," Liping says. "So to put that much money in the bank was pretty phenomenal."

And that was just the first wave—the money given to them for a mere portion of their land. After redistributing the remaining farmland, each person in the production team still had about one-tenth of an acre, land that would, no doubt, eventually be bought up at a similarly phenomenal price. "They just gave you the money and you could do whatever you wanted after that," says Liping. It was that sudden explosion of free money and free time that signaled the beginning of the end for Wang Tao. Though he'd already played mahjong casually for several years, now, without much land to cultivate or the need to work for money, the game grew into a full-time occupation. Before long, he and many other formerly hardworking farmers were addicted, spending days and sometimes even weeks on end in the gaming halls that seemed to spring up around the village overnight. A host of other vices quickly followed suit, and a blanket of torpor settled over their lives; within a few years of the loss of their land, Gan Jia Zhai's social fabric had clearly started to fray, and Wang Tao's intentions of being a good family man, like Wang Tao himself, had all but disappeared.

Wang Tao has tried giving up mahjong before—tried many, many times before. His failure, he says, is because the game has become one with his mind and left him with no alternate path in life. Someday he hopes to break the addiction, but for now it's too strong to be interrupted by something as trivial as the pending loss of the family's home or the urgent need to find a new place to live.

So six days before the official move-out date arrives, Wang Tao's afternoon is spent, like most others, at the mahjong parlor. The family's two youngest children, twenty-three-year-old Wang Mei and nineteen-year-old Wang Kai, are both at work. Though Wang Jing is supposed to be job hunting and Liping is supposed to be packing, they are instead huddled around the coffee table eating fruit and seeds and halfheartedly watching TV.

"My life now is just eating and sleeping," Liping says. "If there's nothing to do, I watch TV. If there's nothing to do, I sing a song. When I wake up the next day, it's more of the same." She inspects the rhinestones on the front of her scoop-necked fuchsia shirt and then wipes an invisible smudge off her stylishly see-through mesh boots. Though she typically has nowhere to go and nothing more to do than repeatedly mop the floor, she is always impeccably dressed; it helps her feel good, especially when she remembers the days when she worked so hard but still wore nothing but homely clothes.

"Having money really is better," she says, tugging at the pearls laced around her neck.

"Yeah," Wang Jing scoffs, "who's willing to be poor?"

"Everyone's willing to wear nice clothes and eat good food."

"We definitely wouldn't want to be farmers again," Wang Jing says. "Now only in economically undeveloped places are people willing to do hard work. Once a place develops, people aren't willing to do physical labor anymore."

These days most of Gan Jia Zhai's manual labor is done by outsiders—migrants who still have to work hard just to save a few yuan. Nowadays there's only one thing that the financially stable villagers of Gan Jia Zhai are still willing to do: collect rent payments. That's possible because, like most other Chinese villages, Gan Jia Zhai was designed with the farmhouses clustered together, away from the fields. So while the High-Tech Zone gobbled up Gan Jia Zhai's farmland and turned out a steady stream of new buildings where crops had once been, the farmers' homes were left untouched. When migrants started pouring in to find work building up the new area, Gan Jia Zhai's villagers, quick to spot an opportunity, began leasing out spare rooms to those looking for a cheap place to stay. As demand continued to rise, they began adding on to their homes to make room for more renters.

In 1997 the Wangs tore down the front of the house they'd built just a decade before and put up in its stead a sprawling two-story compound that extended across their entire lot. Gone forever were the gated entryway and the courtyard—two traditional staples of civilized countryside living—as it was now floor space, not land, that was worth money. The Wangs' floor plan included seven rooms on the first floor with storefront access—valuable commodities that quickly filled up with eateries and other small businesses. Over time, the footpath in front of their home grew into a thoroughfare for Gan Jia Zhai renters heading in and out of the High-Tech Zone. Peddlers of every sort flocked in, and rent prices soared. The Wangs added a third story to their home and let out even more rooms to individual boarders, leaving their own family of five a mere four rooms on the second floor in which to live and bringing their total rental income up to 10,000 yuan per month. "Our fate has been good," Liping admits. "Even some city residents envy us here."

And, indeed, from an economic standpoint, most local, white-collar city residents do have much to envy. Even for well-trained professionals in the High-Tech Zone, a typical salary isn't more than 4,000 yuan a month for a minimum of forty hours a week, high stress, and a congested commute, while the unskilled, poorly educated farmers-turned-landlords of Gan Jia Zhai bring in more than twice that much without much effort at all. And then there's that substantial nest egg that they have safely nestled away: on top of their initial payout, in 2000 the government bought the remaining portion of their land for a whopping sum of 60,000 yuan per person. For their family of five, that means a grand total of 335,000 yuan, or about $52,350, in savings that they have never dipped into, not even once.

That, Liping is quick to point out, is because she collects all the rent, pays all the bills, and, most importantly, keeps Wang Tao away from the family fortune. In order to do that, she built a little shack onto the corner of their building to serve as a fast-food joint. The shack is Wang Tao's to oversee; he collects that rent and is free to spend it as he pleases, which, invariably, means it ends up on the mahjong table.

"I can't let him randomly collect all the rent," Liping says. "He can only get the money from that one."

"Otherwise he'd gamble it all away and what would happen to us?" asks Wang Jing.

Just as the Wangs are not alone in their struggles with idleness and addiction, their efforts to keep a place for themselves in a rapidly changing China are also not unique to their family, or even the whole of their village. Similar issues have emerged across the country as expanding metropolitan areas gobble up the nation's farmland, leaving in their wake pockets of run-down farmhouses stranded amidst a sea of prosperity—a social phenomenon so common that such areas are given a name: "city-villages."

The farmers who lose their land in this process typically expand their homes to accommodate renters, thus staking out a lucrative new livelihood for themselves while also providing an essential low-cost housing option to migrants who would otherwise be unable to afford urban living. But since it is clear from the beginning that the city-villages themselves will fall victim to urbanization sooner or later, they tend to rebuild their homes cheaply and haphazardly—without regard for aesthetics, safety, or sanitation—and then pack them to overcapacity with a steady flow of workers from around the nation, those workers who, though industrious, remain largely anonymous and highly transient.

The resulting mix is more often than not an atmosphere of suspicion, a dramatic spike in crime, and an ever-widening gulf between life in the city-villages and the cities that surround them. Even so, their homes are still the most valuable source of income the former farmers will probably ever have and thus are not something they're willing to relinquish easily. Liping has heard stories about peasants who gave up their homes too easily and were compensated with nothing more than a high-rise apartment, but she's also heard plenty about the farmers from eastern China who are all driving around in BMWs now. Her hope, obviously, is to follow more closely in the latter's footsteps.

A few days ago, village leaders posted notices urging everyone to leave as soon as possible, and it was enough to scare many families' boarders away, but not the Wangs'. "My tenants aren't afraid," Liping boasts. "I told them that it's still early. I told them we'll leave at the very end." Despite the recently posted notices, and despite the fact that three of her seven storefront renters have in fact already moved out, Liping seems more resolved than ever to stay put. "We don't listen to people's nonsense. We'll be the last ones to move. They say we've got to go before the twenty-fifth, but in reality they're always pushing the deadline back. There are still lots of problems they haven't solved."

"There's a conflict in the village," Wang Jing says.

"They gave us a notice, but we don't agree with it," says one of her friends, whose family is also slated to move. "When they put up a notice we agree with, we'll all go."

"That's right," Wang Jing says. "They still haven't found the *right* direction."

The only really *right* direction as far as they're concerned would be to call the whole thing off; let them keep their homes with their lucrative storefront rentals and forget all about moving. Though it's an option that's frequently tossed around in Gan Jia Zhai, it's one that most of them don't really believe to be possible. Not only is Gan Jia Zhai's oasis of old-style living now completely circumscribed by new luxury developments, but with the Wangs' section of the village blocking the High-Tech Zone's main street, people currently have to drive all the way around the village just to get to their destination. Already a two-story-high row of billboards shields drivers from the unsightliness of their corner of the village, but it is clearly just a temporary fix. In the end, even Liping and Wang Tao begrudgingly admit that there really is no other choice but to rip down their homes and lay a new road in their place.

For now, only about a quarter of Gan Jia Zhai is to be demolished, but the rest of it doesn't have much time left either. The whole village has already been signed over to the High-Tech Zone, and within three or four years, it will exist only in the villagers' memories—and their yet-untouched savings accounts. To compensate the villagers for the loss of their homes, they will be relocated to a new complex, where each family will get a three-story, 360-square-meter unit with three storefront rental spaces on the ground floor.

But construction on that hasn't even started yet, and so, in lieu of being able to take what the villagers see as the only *right* direction, local officials decided to have those who are being uprooted by the new road move in with those whose homes will not be torn down right now. Though it's just a temporary arrangement until the new complex is finished, the policy has everyone up in arms. Both the families who have to move and the families who will be moved in with will receive a so-called "transition supplement" to compensate them for their loss of rental income, but it will be a mere living wage, which means it won't even come close to what families in the Wangs' thriving portion of the village are used to making each month.

Liping and family intend to milk every last moment of time from the ongoing conflict and still hold a glimmer of hope that maybe it will never get resolved and they'll be able to stay put indefinitely. For several days it looks like the plan just might work, but then, on April 22—just three days before the official move-out date—Wang Tao's mother rushes into the kitchen where Liping is preparing lunch and bubbles over with the latest news: word is that the original plan stands and village leaders really will take their keys on the twenty-fifth after all. Grandma, who lives a few houses down from them and has already secured herself a place on the other side of the village, urges Liping to get Wang Tao to hurry up and find someone willing to take in their family of five before it's too late.

At age seventy, Grandma is an ardent Buddhist and a leader of sorts at the village temple. She's been especially busy in recent days because the mayor's wife just died. Last night Grandma led a special prayer session for the woman's soul, but now she's disturbed by the fact that there won't be time to recite the third and final round of scripture at the mayor's house; the mayor, it turns out, lives in this section of the village and is getting uprooted too.

Lunch is ready and Liping sets piping-hot plates of egg and tomato, home-style tofu, and numb-and-spicy cucumbers on the coffee table and then goes to the next room to get Wang Jing and her best friend, Lina. As they sit down to eat, Grandma looks at her watch and suddenly stands up. It's later than she thought and she won't be able to stay after all, she says. There's a study class in a few minutes, and they won't start until she arrives. As she leaves, she reminds Liping to brew up a batch of Chinese medicine for her. Given the demands at the temple, she has no time to do it herself these days.

"My grandma is too pious," says Wang Jing, shaking her head as Grandma disappears down the stairway.

"After our land got bought up, Grandma also had nothing to do. Only after she started looking for something to fill her time did she begin believing in Buddha," Liping says, as the three of them dip their chopsticks into the meal spread before them. "Now many people in this village have turned to Buddhism, and many others have turned to gambling."

After they finish eating, Wang Jing and Lina clear away the lunch dishes while Liping prepares to wash them—not an easy task, given their lack of running water. "I'm going to miss this place," she sighs, as she draws water from a jug on the countertop. "I'm definitely going to miss this place." She pauses, flashes a mischievous grin, and then adds: "Of course, the thing I'm going to miss most is the storefront rentals."

They all laugh, but underneath the joke is a sober reality. For ten years their main source of income has been their rentals—especially their lucrative storefront properties—and now suddenly they will have none. Their days of pulling in five digits a month are almost over, and that has them all a bit unsettled.

Zhang Liping in the living room of her soon-to-be demolished home.

"We won't have any source of income after this," Lina complains.

"Economics is the foundation of everything," Liping says. "Even if you want to make friends, economics is still the foundation. Friends come over, they eat fruit and seeds, watch TV, and listen to music. All that takes money."

Liping finishes with the dishes and then reaches for the mop while Wang Jing bustles around the room, getting ready to go out shopping with her friend. As the two of them head out, Lina mentions that she's going out of town for a few days and won't be back until the twenty-ninth. "Will you still be here then?" she asks Liping.

"I hope we're still here," Liping answers earnestly, her resolve to stay put suddenly wavering in the wake of Grandma's earlier announcement.

"Oh come on, let's just hurry up and move already," Wang Jing whines, stepping out into the narrow stairwell. "My heart is aching. The place I've called home for the last twenty years is going to be gone soon." Wang Jing, it seems, may actually have some nostalgia for the place that goes beyond money.

All of Gan Jia Zhai has running water—it was, in fact, one of the earlier villages to boast such a luxury—but a plumbing problem in the Wang's house prevents water from making it up to the family's quarters on the second floor. To remedy this, Wang Tao snaked a hose up through an open kitchen window and into an enormous orange plastic jug. As the water can only be turned on and off from outside, they fill the jug up and then ladle water out of it for several days before it needs to be refilled again. This afternoon, water is running low, and since everyone else is out of the house, Wang Jing starts refilling it herself. But it takes so long to fill such a big container that she goes into the living room to watch a little TV while she waits. By the time she remembers to go back and check, water is flooding the bare cement kitchen floor. She races outside to turn off the water and then hurries back into the kitchen, sweeping the ankle-deep water into a drain below the defunct sink.

When she's finally done cleaning up the mess, she grabs an apple from the fruit bowl and collapses onto the couch. After they leave this place, at least they won't have to worry about mishaps like that again, she says. Already it's five days past the move-out deadline, but so far the family has still managed to stay put. "Most other people are all moved out now, but not us," Wang Jing says. They are thinking of moving in with some relatives who live on the other side of the village, but until now Wang Tao has yet to work out the details with them. "You've got to live in their house for at least two years, so you definitely need to get their full agreement."

Wang Jing turns her attention back to her TV show, which, to her dismay, keeps dissolving into fuzz. "That's because the wire is so old," she explains. "We've been using the same wire since we moved here. When we finally move into the new housing complex, we'll have a new wire, a good wire. Then everything will be good."

"When we get to the new housing complex, then everything will be good" is one of the family's favorite sayings these days; it's also indicative of one of its biggest ironies. On the one hand, the Wangs are clinging to their old place and their old ways of life as tightly as they can. But on the other hand, they've long been anticipating their new life, and that can only begin after they abandon their city-village and finally settle into the new complex a few years from now. Then they'll get new furniture and new appliances. They'll have a refrigerator that serves as more than just a shelving unit and have no more worries about running water. In the new house, they'll even go all out and install a hot water heater.

Aside from all this, the best part of moving, at least from Wang Jing's perspective, is that once they settle in the new complex they will officially become urban, rather than rural, *hukou* holders, which will make her future job searches much easier. "If you try to find a job with a rural *hukou*, people look down on you. They think, 'Your life and your thoughts are not as good as us city people,'" Wang Jing says. "In China, the good side of being a farmer is that people know you're industrious, but the bad side is that people think you don't have any culture and that you don't understand a lot."

As a vocational college graduate, Wang Jing could have taken the education option and obtained an urban *hukou* back while she was in school, but then she would have forfeited her allotment of land and the family would have lost out on 60,000 yuan when the High-Tech Zone bought it from them a few years later. In her university class, only two rural *hukou* holders didn't change over to a city residence—Wang Jing and a girl from another village that, like Gan Jia Zhai, was soon to give money in exchange for their land. Another of Wang Jing's classmates didn't know that was about to happen in her village, so she gave up her rural *hukou* and missed out on a big payout the very next year.

The TV snaps out of a long fuzzy spell just as Wang Jing's cell phone rings. It's a call from a training center where she interviewed last week. They want her to teach English to little kids, but she doesn't want to do it; she'd rather wait and find an opening at a university. Never mind that her rural *hukou* makes it harder to snag a good job. Having grown up a city villager, not a villager, and as a soon-to-be-urbanite whose family has a large chunk of change in the bank, Wang Jing can afford to be a bit picky.

It isn't until the third of May that the Wangs start acting, to some small degree, like they're about to make a life-changing move. It's not that Wang Tao has finally found them a place to stay, or that Liping has started packing—neither has. But since the last of their seven storefront renters vacated yesterday, Wang Tao spent this morning scrounging around for anything of value left on the first floor. There was nothing obvious, like a desk or a lamp or a chair, but there were windowpanes and light fixtures and pipes and all sorts of scrap metal—all of which he sold to the flock of recyclers now circling the area on their bicycles like vultures, just waiting for the next family to go.

When Wang Tao removed the old electric meter he must have messed something up, because suddenly the whole house lost electricity. Now he's spent the last hour out on the second-floor landing, sweating as he holds up a flashlight for the electrician. "He has to take care of these things," Liping says with a hint of a satisfaction as her husband scrambles into the candle-lit living room looking for a screwdriver. "Water, electricity—he has to do these types of things. He can't leave me to take care of everything in the house."

While Wang Tao is uncharacteristically occupied, one of his favorite gambling buddies comes in with half a watermelon tucked under his arm. Like Wang Tao, his eyes seem perpetually glazed by late nights and lack of regular sleep and his mouth almost always houses a cigarette. He crowds around the coffee table with Liping and Wang Jing, slurping down the juicy melon. The electricity comes on a few minutes later and almost immediately Wang Tao is back lounging on the bed, all trace of diligence gone. He stubs out his cigarette in one of the watermelon rinds and takes a piece for himself.

When the melon is totally finished, Wang Tao's gaming buddy cleans off the table. As he sits back down on the wooden couch, two slats fall out of it.

"Better fix that," Liping advises. "We still need to use that couch until we move into the new complex."

"Hey," Wang Tao protests. "They still might not tear this place down." Wang Jing snickers and even Liping chuckles. Now, with so many of their neighbors already moved out and their own house growing increasingly empty, it's no longer a matter of *if* they'll move but simply *when* they'll move.

Later that afternoon, Wang Tao dons his mirrored sunglasses and slips out of the house. Once he sets foot on the road—a drastically quieter road than he's used to—he breaks into a smile.

"This is my turf," he says. "I know this village. I was born and raised here, and I almost never leave it."

He doesn't waste time exchanging pleasantries with anyone he runs into but instead heads directly for the nearest mahjong parlor, which his own uncle started up a few years back. As he approaches, there is no billboard, no flashing lights, not even a single sign enticing people to come in and gamble. The mahjong parlor, in fact, bears no resemblance to a decked-out Western-style casino; it is simply a home where the game mahjong also happens to be played for money. The only indication of what's going on inside is the distinctive clacking of tiles audible from nearly a block away.

As Wang Tao enters the house, he passes by the first couple of rooms, which are overflowing with players and onlookers. He pokes his head into a slightly larger but equally crowded bedroom, where he finds his uncle talking about world affairs to whoever isn't focusing too hard on the game to listen. "America shouldn't fight," he's saying. "Here we love peace."

"Here we love to play mahjong," Wang Tao corrects him, as he carves out a bit of standing room for himself.

The centerpiece of this room is an automatic table that shuffles the tiles and then spits them out in four neat stacks, one in front of each player. The table can also roll dice when needed and manage the players' chips so that they don't have to be bothered to do anything but play. Sporting a variety of flashing lights and sound effects, it seems more like it belongs in Atlantic City than crammed next to a rickety bed covered with a hand-spun red-and-white-checkered spread. "You can say that we've gone from poor to rich," Wang Tao says. "All this"—he gestures toward the contraption in front of him—"is what communism has brought." It might sound like sarcasm from someone else, but from Wang Tao it is a sincere form of praise.

He watches a bit longer but the feeling just isn't hitting him here, so he meanders back out onto the street. With his silver shades, black T-shirt, black cargo pants, black plastic sandals, and white cell phone strapped around his forearm, he has a bit of a comical air about him that makes it clear that he is not a typical villager. Even way back in high school, he was known as the class clown, and in some circles he's still seen as something of the village fool; but in the circle that matters to him, he's a mahjong force to be reckoned with. His losses may have surpassed his winnings in recent years, but here he is, nonetheless, ready to throw 1,000 kuai out on the table twice or even thrice a day.

Wang Tao wanders on autopilot to another of his favorite mahjong parlors. Like his uncle's place, this one, too, is simply a home and is entirely unpretentious. He deposits himself at the playing table in the large front room and lights a cigarette. This place is deserted for the moment and even the boss—one of Wang Tao's oldest and best friends—is nowhere to be found. About ten minutes later the boss's wife appears with a bowl of noodles for Wang Tao. In city villages like Gan Jia Zhai, mahjong is much more than a game—it's an entire way of life. It has none of the glamour of a place like Vegas, but neither does it have the anonymity; these are Wang Tao's classmates and neighbors and relatives. He comes because he likes to gamble, but he also comes to eat, talk, hang out, and relax among friends. For a farmer with no land and no alternative formal occupation to fill the empty hours, what else is there to do?

Five days later, the exodus out of the Wangs' corner of the village is almost complete; all of the shops and food shacks have closed and even the recyclers have moved on to find more fertile territory. In the daytime there are still enough people milling around to give the impression that the neighborhood is semioperational, but once the sun sets, it's clear just how deserted it has become. Besides the lights streaming out of the Wangs' second floor and one other home of holdouts, the other buildings are dark and eerily hollow looking, picked clean of every last pane of glass and scrap of wood of value.

Up the street, a man is cutting down one of the only trees left in all of Gan Jia Zhai. It's a difficult task, and soon a crowd gathers, with many onlookers defending the man's decision to chop down his tree for cash.

"That tree is personal property," an old woman says.

"That's right," a young man standing next to her agrees. "And it's worth good money."

"The High-Tech Zone doesn't have any use for that tree," the woman adds. "It's his tree."

For anyone still harboring doubts, watching the felling of the tree—likely the longest-standing structure in the area—drives home just how impermanent their lives here have become. A few days ago even Wang Tao finally got his act together and found the family a place to stay on the other side of the village. He still needs to get it cleaned and painted before they move in, but he's not in any great hurry. Staying put after everyone else has gone is starting to wear on Liping, though. Life on this side of the village is no longer convenient; this morning she had to walk several blocks just to find something as basic as steamed buns, which used to be available right outside her doorway. Her kids are up in arms that the Internet connection has been cut, and she's especially depressed that her good friends are no longer around to keep her company. "The High-Tech Zone's tearing the place apart, and that's put us all in a bad mood," she says.

"Well, thankfully, we're moving any day now," says her daughter Wang Mei, who's not home enough to keep up to speed with the family's latest plans.

"We'll see," Liping murmurs. They were supposed to start receiving the High-Tech Zone's so-called transition supplement starting in March, but it hasn't been deposited into their bank account yet. Although they know the money will come, Liping and Wang Tao have latched onto this as their newest—and most legitimate—reason to stay put. "As soon as they transfer the transition fee, we'll move. But now they're saying that might not happen until July, and that's still two months away."

"It's still better to move," Wang Mei sighs. "There's nothing here anymore."

Later that night Liping's close friend Zhang Ai stops in for a visit. She moved across the village last week and, like Liping, she's now bored, lonely, and frustrated. "This is the worst time ever. Our friends are all split up and our income is gone," Liping whines, and her pal is quick to agree. The only thing helping them through it is the promise of a new life in the modern housing complex a few years down the road. "When we get there, we'll be happy again. Then everything will be new."

Rather than stay in the house and fret, the two friends decide to go out for a stroll. They eventually end up at Zhang Ai's new residence—four depressing rooms in a building with bad lighting, funny smells, and a long line of tenants waiting to use the toilet. Liping has yet to see the place Wang Tao has secured for them, but she imagines it will be equally dismal, since only villagers with the worst houses in the worst locations are willing to take in people like them. And so it is that when the two women join Zhang Ai's husband and new landlord in the cramped living room, the atmosphere is just as moody and restless as it was back at Liping's place.

"We are profession-less people," Zhang Ai's husband complains. "Now we're out of work."

"We are farmers," adds the landlord, "without any culture."

"If you look at us from the outside, you'd think we have a better life now, but actually we're emptier than ever," Zhang Ai's husband broods.

"That's right," says Liping, descending into the pity party. "Before, when we had land, at least we could take care of our basic living on our own. We just had to buy soap and detergent and a few things like that. But now that we don't have any land, we have to buy everything."

"We're so pitiful," the landlord moans.

"And being pitiful is tiring," yawns Zhang Ai's husband.

Ever since their land got bought up, people in their village have been looking for some sort of formal occupation; some find Buddha, some find mahjong, but many others—like the four of them here—still haven't found anything. And that, they agree, is the most pitiful condition of all.

The next day a dust storm hits and a brooding yellow haze settles over the city. The wind howls through the deserted homes in Gan Jia Zhai with such ferocity that even Wang Tao doesn't dare step outside. Instead, he mopes around the house, watching TV with his wife and daughter. If their renters were still here, at least they'd have people to chat with, but now that there's no one around, nothing to do, and nowhere to go, boredom is consuming them.

One reason it's hard to deal with their overabundance of free time is that they used to have so much to do that they didn't have a moment to think, much less rest. After the days of collective farming ended, Wang Tao bought a tractor and transported loads for money. Liping worked at the village brick factory and ran a store in their home. A few years later, when Gan Jia Zhai started to attract increasing numbers of lonely migrants, Liping put a pool table and a karaoke machine out in front of the house and charged people to play or sing. When the weather got too cold to stay out on the street at night, she rented movies and charged people to sit in their living room and watch.

Liping kept running all her side businesses for several years after the first land payout, more out of habit than anything else. "Finally, I said to myself, 'Forget it. What do I need so much money for?'" And so when they added a third floor onto their house, she suppressed the inclination to open a film house up there and instead rented the space out to others and enjoyed having nothing in particular to do for a change. But on days like today, Liping can't help but remember fondly those bitterly busy days of old.

Last year, when the summer heat wave hit and people couldn't stand to stay inside—at least not in the non-air-conditioned homes of Gan Jia Zhai—Wang Tao suggested that they put the karaoke machine outside again to raise a little extra money. But Liping wanted no part of it; she knew that if she agreed, he'd set everything up and then disappear, leaving her to do all the work again. "That's just the kind of person he is. He can't stay put at home. The only place where he can stay put is the mahjong parlor."

Wang Tao illustrates Liping's point by wandering out onto the landing to assess the severity of the storm, clearly eager to escape after just a few hours stuck at home. Though Liping surrounds herself with friends to help pass the time, having a real partner to keep her company has been a struggle ever since she lost Wang Tao to mahjong.

It's easy for Liping to keep track of how long they've been drifting apart since Wang Tao first started experimenting with mahjong when their son was just a few weeks old, and this year the boy turns twenty. At the time she was confined to bed for a month, as is the postpartum tradition in China, and while she was unable to get up, Wang Tao brought in four tables and rounded up sixteen villagers to come try the new game. "From then on, he started to play more and more, until eventually he made it his main means of making money," Liping says.

"And now I'm Gan Jia Zhai's biggest gamer," Wang Tao boasts. "At those mahjong parlors, I'm very hot. I'm a key person. If I don't come around for a few days, they start calling me."

"If you didn't have money, who'd call you?" Liping retorts.

After fighting with Wang Tao about his gambling habit for seven or eight years, Liping eventually just let it go. She stopped needing—or even wanting—his help, his companionship, or his support. And yet, as difficult as those times were—and as lonely as these times still can be—she has never seriously considered divorce. "It's not just me who's living like this. My good girl-friends have all gone through it," she says. "In this village, most of the men are all like this."

Liping has never once watched her husband play mahjong, and she's certainly never tried the game herself: not only does she find it boring but the family would be finished if she somehow got hooked too. No, mahjong is Wang Tao's life now, and if she can't stop it, at least she can be sure not to have any part of it. "People say he's a good player, but I've never seen a single cent from him."

"My dad's very sincere, but he's not smart," Wang Jing adds. "And yet his life has been very lucky. He's very foolish but still has more money than people who have money."

Wang Tao nods his head in agreement, not the least offended by his wife and daughter's depiction of him. "I don't do a thing, but my life is better than most."

"Dumb people have dumb luck," Wang Jing sighs.

Being cooped up all day during the big storm apparently took its toll on Wang Tao; when the dust settled that evening, he went out to play and didn't come back again. At first Liping pays no attention, but when village officials start pressuring her to evacuate the house and the place Wang Tao had arranged for them to move into falls through, she gets anxious for her husband's speedy return. After three days, he waltzes back home, listens to Liping ramble on about the housing situation, and then promptly falls asleep. He wakes up just as Liping is putting dinner on the coffee table.

Wang Jing ladles porridge into a bowl and holds it out toward Wang Tao, who stretches, coughs, and drags himself slowly off the bed. They sit in silence for a while, eating and watching a show about China's liberation.

"Before we ate a lot, a lot of bitterness, but now life is good. Everything is good," Wang Tao says. He picks up a piece of flat bread with his chopsticks and examines it for a moment before continuing: "Now if you let me be the county mayor, I wouldn't do it. I'm very content with my life. It's carefree and easy. If I want to eat at home, I eat at home. If I want to eat out, I eat out. If I want to gamble, I gamble, and if I don't want to, I don't."

"Living the life of a pig," Wang Jing sneers.

"China has a billion people. Nine hundred million of them gamble and the other 100 million are stand-ins," Wang Tao tells her matter-of-factly. And though he knows that it is not quite that pervasive, it is especially common in city villages, and almost everyone he knows in Gan Jia Zhai gambles. "If it's not mahjong, it's cards, and if it's not cards, it's mahjong."

"It's a waste of life," Wang Jing says.

"There's already no hope for me. Now it's a high-tech society, and I'm not capable of doing anything else." He pauses and then adds, "I'm not interested in doing anything else either." Well, actually, he can think of one thing that he'd like to do right now: go out for a good foot massage. After three days of nonstop gaming, sitting here is making him anxious, and he could use a little relaxation. After dinner is finished, he starts getting ready to go back out.

"Can't stay put again," Wang Jing scolds.

"A person has to be satisfied."

"This is not called satisfied," Liping says. "This is called depraved."

"What can I do?" Wang Tao asks, shrugging his shoulders to emphasize his helplessness. "My heart has already flown away." He grabs his phone off the bed and puts on his mirrored sunglasses just as one of Liping's friends steps into the living room. She takes one look at him and says to Liping, "He looks like someone from the mafia."

"He looks like a criminal," says Liping, frowning as her husband darts down the stairs two at a time.

Wang Tao walks to the corner where the big tree used to stand and then turns left, heading through the High-Tech Zone toward

Shajingcun, a nearby city-village that houses his favorite foot massage parlor. He stops to chat with a mechanic he knows, and as he stands there, his best gambling buddy zips by on a motor-bike. "Treat me to a foot wash," Wang Tao commands. "You're a boss, you have a career. I'm just an idler."

His buddy is an easy sell, and within minutes they're lounging in oversize reclining chairs, reviewing the menu of different liquids in which to soak their feet. Wang Tao opts for the traditional Chinese medicine bath, and his buddy goes with a milk soak. As Wang Tao slips his feet into a steaming wooden tub, he closes his eyes and breathes deeply. When he thinks about how dramatically his life has changed over the past few decades, it's hard for him to believe everything has happened in just one lifetime—and even harder to believe that the eager and addiction-free young man who cruised through those bitter days of old without a hitch somehow turned into the person Wang Tao is today.

Back when he finished high school, in 1977, his parents had taken more than their allotted food rations to feed their five kids and thus had run up a big debt with their production team. To help the family get back in the red, the team leader assigned Wang Tao to a very special job: scooping the shit out of the school latrines and hauling it in a wheelbarrow back to the fields to be used as fertilizer. It was a 2.5-kilometer walk one way, and he made six round-trips a day. The work was exceedingly hard and smelly, but whereas people assigned to normal farm work only made eight points a day, he made six points per trip, which came to a total of thirty-six points per day. Making such an enormous amount at a time when his parents needed his help made him a very happy shit-hauler indeed. Never for a minute did he feel burdened or tired or disgusted by his special job, though

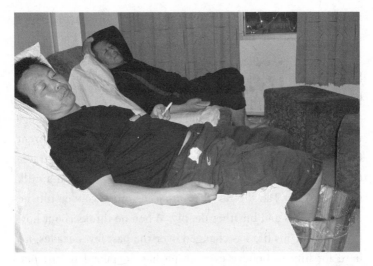

Wang Tao and his gambling buddy enjoy a foot wash.

today he shifts uncomfortably in his seat just thinking about it. "Back then it would never cross your mind to feel unsatisfied. Only after the reforms started did people's minds open up to capitalist ideas and start wanting more," he says. "At that time, we couldn't imagine that we'd be able to get our feet washed in the future. This kind of thing all came afterwards."

A year later Gan Jia Zhai's six production teams bought a tractor together, and he was reassigned to driving duty. He didn't make anything near what he had before, but by then he'd already paid off his parents' debt and felt like the king of the world. He drove the tractor for the next three years before communal farming ended and there was suddenly no need for a collective tractor. Wang Tao borrowed money from everyone he could, bought the village's tractor, and started charging farmers to haul their loads. "Then mahjong arrived, and that's the rest of my life history," he jokes, as a young girl dries his feet and launches into a massage. "From *chiku* to this."

To hear him tell it, he only seriously delved into the mahjong universe in order to drum up more tractor business. After construction of the High-Tech Zone began, his tractor didn't stop for a whole year. To keep up with the demand, he upgraded to a better machine and hired someone else to actually do the driving, while he turned his attention to finding even more business. He met lots of construction bosses while playing mahjong, and only after establishing gaming relationships with them did he secure the opportunity to work for them as well.

By 1998, with a hefty rental income pouring in, Wang Tao sold his tractor and lost the desire to do anything but play. "Before my aspirations were so big," he says, with a glint in his eye. "I wanted to bring Tiananmen to our door, but it wouldn't budge. I wanted to have ten wives, but I only got this one." But his biggest dream of all, to have a son and keep the family line going, is the one wish he managed to achieve. "If Wang Jing were a boy, I'd have spent the last five years guiding her. But girls don't need my guidance. Now my son is turning twenty and I want to guide him, but my strength is already gone."

If there's one thing Wang Tao has tried to teach his son, one thing he's made sure to summon up his waning energy and impress upon all three of his children, it's that they should stay far, far away from gambling. "It's the most terrible, rotten thing of all," he says, suddenly turning serious.

He's long lost count of how many times he's tried to free himself from the addiction. Early on he realized that quitting was impossible in Gan Jia Zhai, what with him being so famous and in demand at all the mahjong parlors. So whenever he got serious about stopping, he always headed out of town. Once he went to a retreat center, but there, right next to the cafeteria, was a gambling hall. Another time he holed up in a hotel outside Xi'an, but as he was checking in the manager said they were one person short for mahjong and asked if he played. He even tried heading up into the mountains but found people there were playing as well, and what choice did he have but to join them?

For now, at least, he's quit trying to quit. "Now I'm incurable. I'm no different than an opium addict. Only if they cut off my hands will I be able to stop gambling," he laments. Though the custom in this part of China is usually to honor the dead by putting fruit by their remains, when he dies they'll do things differently, he says. "When I go, they'll put mahjong tiles next to my ashes."

The next day is Mother's Day, one of the many Western holidays that have come into vogue in China in recent years. For the occasion, all five members of the Wang family gather at a nearby restaurant; though they technically all sleep under one roof, it's the first time they've spent all together in months. A hostess stands at the front door distributing complimentary red carnations to all mothers, and Wang Tao snatches one from her and shoves it toward his wife.

While Liping and the three children scour the menu, Wang Tao, who just ate at the gaming hall and isn't hungry, watches diners at the next table play a loud drinking game. Wang Tao rarely drinks—he needs to keep his mind sharp to make money on the mahjong table—so he suggests that the family play a water round of the game instead. Unsurprisingly, there are no takers. "Come on," he urges. "Let's see if your brains are fast or not."

"When it comes to things like this, your brain is definitely the fastest," Liping says.

Wang Tao roams around the restaurant while the rest of the family eats, talking with the waitresses and scouting other tables for interesting-looking dishes. He finally sits back down and starts singing in falsetto.

"Your brain's got a problem," Liping complains.

"I'm happy," Wang Tao shrugs. He calls the waitress over and asks for an empty beer bottle. Then he puts Liping's carnation in it, sets it next to her, and smiles as if he's accomplished all that he set out to do for the day.

"So, when are we moving out?" Wang Mei asks.

"The end of this month," Wang Jing answers.

"June," Liping says.

"We're not moving until the very end," Wang Tao says. "The High-Tech Zone's transition money still hasn't come in yet."

"As soon as we get that money, we'll leave immediately," Liping adds.

"Otherwise, if we go before the money arrives, we'll starve to death," Wang Jing says. "We're the 'nail' tenants. We're the hardest to pull out."

"That's right," Liping and Wang Tao agree.

After they finish eating, their son Wang Kai slips away to meet a friend while the rest of the family huddles together on the sidewalk, deciding what to do next. They're just a block from the High-Tech Zone's expansive Electric City shopping area, which is already teeming with people dancing in the plaza. Though Liping is no longer the dance enthusiast she once was, anything is better than heading back to the isolation of their home. And who knows, maybe her daughters will waltz across the men of their dreams out there. She turns to Wang Tao and asks if he'd like to join them.

"Well, I guess I'd better get back to work," he says with a trademark smirk that leaves no doubt about the type of occupation he's talking about.

As his wife and daughters cross the street, Wang Tao turns in the other direction and heads back toward Gan Jia Zhai. Looming in the distance he can see the row of huge billboards that hides the village from sight. Usually as he looks out from his own home all he can see are the signs' metal backsides, but from here in the High-Tech Zone he can read one sign's enormous characters with perfect clarity: Be a Civilized City Person, Uphold the New Urban Morality. That, Wang Tao figures as he ducks behind the billboards and into the darkness that their section of the city-village has now become, is something he can do from the inside of a mahjong parlor as well as anywhere.

CHAPTER SIX

The Nowhere Nanny

Xiao Shi stands in the doorway of the spare bedroom, hands on her hips, assessing the place like a general preparing for battle. Then, with a dry rag in one hand and damp cloth in the other, she sets about ridding the room of dust. She scrubs from floor to ceiling in a precise order—not because she's compulsive about cleaning, but simply because, after years as a live-in housekeeper and nanny, she's developed a regimen that allows her to sanitize the house on autopilot.

While she combats the disorder downstairs, the lady of the house, Cui Yanwen, is upstairs playing a computer game. Yesterday Cui's four-year-old daughter stayed home from kindergarten with a sore throat, so Xiao Shi spent the day taking care of her rather than doing the housework. Today the girl is back in school and Xiao Shi is back to her usual routine, but the place is, to her trained eye, intolerably messy.

Xiao Shi moves on to the bookcase, dusting under the knick-knacks and then carefully setting them back in their original positions. She has to be careful: Cui's twelve-year-old son studies here and he gets upset if she doesn't put things back exactly as he had them. That's not an easy task, considering the random assortment of junk crammed into the room. In addition to the boy's countless action figures and Matchbox cars, there's a massage chair that no one uses anymore, a kids' karaoke machine that's never been taken out of the box, and a scooter that has yet to roll across a sidewalk—and that's all just in one small corner. Xiao Shi doesn't know how other rich folks in Xi'an live—she supposes that they, too, might have huge houses crammed with more merchandise than they can possibly use—but at the very least, it's like nothing she's ever seen back in her village. There, most houses have only a few rooms and even fewer closets, and the only thing that tends to pile up is farm equipment.

At noon, Xiao Shi retires her rags and heads into the kitchen, mulling over what to prepare for lunch. She decides on noodles, as they're a quick fix that will get her back to her housework faster than other dishes. She pours flour into a big steel bowl, adds water, and starts kneading the two together with practiced agility. "Handmade noodles taste better, but a lot of people can't make them," she says. Then her lips tug into a hint of a smile and she corrects herself: "A lot of *city* people can't make them."

She's just starting to roll out the dough when Cui bounces into the kitchen in a pair of tight-fitting exercise pants and announces that she's going out and will eat when she gets back. Xiao Shi sighs with relief: at least Cui will have lunch today. Sometimes Cui sleeps until noon and wakes up with no interest in what Xiao Shi has already prepared. Other times she decides to eat out after Xiao Shi has already started cooking. Though Xiao Shi hates to waste food, unless her boss tells her otherwise, she's compelled to make something.

When Cui returns, almost two hours later, Xiao Shi has long since finished lunch and is in the middle of sweeping the living room. She hustles into the kitchen to reheat the noodles. Cui takes a bite and then shows Xiao Shi a blemish that she's had on her hand for nearly a month. "Now that I'm getting older, my skin is not the same as it was before," she complains to Xiao Shi, who, at thirty-eight, is just two years older than Cui. "Before, if I got a pimple one day, it was gone the next. Now it takes a long time to recover."

"Hmmm," Xiao Shi murmurs as she starts wiping down the royal-blue kitchen cabinets. Though she's anxious to get back to the rest of the house and has no real interest in Cui's aging skin, she's learned to look at her boss's mood and adjust her schedule accordingly. When Cui isn't happy, Xiao Shi is sure to disappear into another room. But on days like today, when her boss is in the mood to chat, Xiao Shi finds plenty of work to keep her nearby—busy, yet still available.

After eating, Cui trots back upstairs, leaving Xiao Shi free to return to the living room. She dons an oversized pair of pink rubber gloves and squats down to scrub the floor by hand. She's been at it less than fifteen minutes when Cui hurries back downstairs, her sweats now exchanged for a black-and-white checked mini-dress. She inspects herself in the full-length mirror near the door, flinging her long curled locks over her shoulder and turning sideways to inspect her trim waist. Though the two women are nearly the same age, Xiao Shi's short, unstyled hair and lack of pretension give the impression that she's from an entirely different generation than her glamorous lady boss.

Cui heads out to meet some friends and Xiao Shi turns back to the floor, simultaneously wiping it and waddling forward in a fluid motion made possible by years of repetition. Before Xiao Shi started working here, she assured Cui that housekeeping was no problem for her, but after a few days on the job she found she could do nothing right. She'd never mopped before—after all, in the countryside, homes have concrete floors that simply need a good sweeping now and then—and though she'd cooked for her own family for years, it wasn't the city-style food Cui's family liked. Her hygiene standards and child-care skills proved equally inept. After a month of constant failure, Xiao Shi nearly called it quits. "I didn't have the confidence to keep going. It was too hard and I wanted to give up," she says. "But then I thought that lots of other people can do this job, so I should be able to do it too. It's not like they have some special talent—everyone's got to learn."

So she stuck with it. The first three months here felt like three years, but after that she started growing into her responsibilities and adjusting to the ways of city life. A year later, Cui gave birth to her daughter Shuanger, and though that added a whole new dimension to her daily duties, by then she felt capable enough to handle anything.

Over the years she's tried to resign several times to pursue higher-paying jobs, but Cui is always quick to give her a raise and keep her on board. Two years ago, Cui and her husband bought a vacation villa about an hour outside of Xi'an and hired Xiao Shi's husband to serve as its caretaker. Since then, Xiao Shi hasn't tried to leave again. Nowadays Cui frequently tells her how fortunate she is to have a double-income household with kids who are already in school and no other major life responsibilities dragging her down. "You guys are so lucky. You can save a little money and you don't really have anything else to worry about," Cui says. "Not like us. We've got lots of pressure."

irony/perspective

And indeed, despite their money and their comfortable lifestyle, Xiao Shi doesn't envy them at all. "They really do have a lot of stress. It's not easy to manage a house like this. They don't have to worry about things like cleaning and buying vegetables, but they still have to deal with all the big things." That includes the family's frequent travels, two homes and two cars, and all the kids' fancy clothes and gadgets as well. On top of that, Cui's husband owns a fertilizer factory where he provides several hundred employees with room, board, and job security. "Me, when I put my head on my pillow at night, I fall right asleep," Xiao Shi says. "Not them. They've got too much pressure. Recently things have been better, but sometimes they can't even sleep."

The next morning starts off like any other, with Xiao Shi up by 6:00 a.m. to cook breakfast before waking the kids and getting them ready for school. After shooing Cui's son out the door, she puts Shuanger on the back of her bike and pedals her across the High-Tech Zone to kindergarten. By the time Xiao Shi gets home, Cui's husband has already left for work while Cui is just waking up. About an hour later Cui goes out for the day. All alone in the big house, Xiao Shi totes the radio into the living room and cranks up the volume. Then she bustles through her cleaning routine with a little dance in her step, even skipping lunch so she can get ahead on the housework.

By mid-afternoon, both upstairs and downstairs are sparkling and Xiao Shi turns her attention to the laundry. She unfolds an ironing board in what is technically her bedroom, though in reality it's more Shuanger's. The girl has slept with Xiao Shi since she was eight months old, and though she has her own spacious room upstairs, most nights she still insists on sleeping in here with her nanny. As such, her storybooks and sippy cups clutter the nightstand, her clothes spill out of the closet, and her Winnie the Pooh posters adorn the walls.

There are, in fact, no signs of Xiao Shi in this room at all—not even a photo of her own two daughters, whom she hasn't seen in more than three months now. While she's spent the last five years in Xi'an taking care of Cui's family, her own girls have stayed in the village with relatives. During the upcoming week-long Labor Day holiday, she's really hoping to visit them—their village is, after all, little more than an hour's bus ride away—but whether or not she can make the journey will depend on Cui's plans. If Cui and her husband take their kids out of town, then Xiao Shi will be free to go back home. But if they remain in Xi'an, she'll have to stay and take care of them instead. Her guess is that they'll drive out to their vacation villa, in which case it'll just depend on whether or not Cui is in the mood to invite her daughters to join them there or not. Though the holiday is less than two weeks away, Xiao Shi has learned over the years to wait for Cui and her husband to broach such subjects; if she asks them now, she will force their hand, and they won't be happy no matter what they decide.

This ability to read people and push her own needs aside has helped Xiao Shi survive as a nanny. Lots of people in her village think she's crazy to do this job, think it's like being a slave, both physically and emotionally, twenty-four hours a day. Xiao Shi can't deny that it is much more grueling than farming back home, where long stretches of downtime punctuate the busy spurts. And even for the toughest of migrant jobs, after ten or twelve or fourteen hours on duty, there's usually the reward of going home for the night. As a live-in nanny, that concept doesn't exist. Xiao Shi works from the moment she wakes up until the moment she falls asleep—and with Shuanger by her side, sometimes throughout the night as well.

But over the years Xiao Shi has come to see lots of positives to this occupation as well. Most rural migrants are stuck living on the outskirts of society in places like Gan Jia Zhai, but here in Cui's High-Tech Zone home, Xiao Shi has access to every conceivable convenience. Her only contact with the city-village is an occasional stop she'll make there to buy cheap vegetables. She has no expenses to speak of—Cui even provides her toiletries—and she gets to travel with the family regularly, flying around the country and frequenting some of its best hotels and restaurants. Yes, Xiao Shi says with a sheepish smile, it took some time to warm up to it, but she likes this job even if it requires more tact and perseverance than others. "There are opportunities for growth here," she says. "No farmer lives like this."

always discussing this. varied.

Sometimes it's hard for her to believe that she is indeed living like this, especially given the abysmal situation she and her husband, Zhang Rui, found themselves in right after they got married. Back then they grew sweet potatoes and wheat and lived with his parents in complete poverty. Though Zhang Rui took on extra work, every month he handed his entire paycheck over to his mother, who in turn used it to pay off one of her other sons' lingering debts. Most of the time Xiao Shi had no money whatsoever, except for the occasional spare change her own mother secretly slipped her. Though plenty of people told her that she shouldn't tolerate the situation, her mother-in-law, or *popo*, was so fierce that no one dared confront her.

But though Xiao Shi was raised in better financial circumstances, she could live with the destitution. What proved harder to bear, however, was the unspoken anger directed at her after she gave birth to her first child; like so many rural Chinese, her in-laws had hoped for a boy. Such pressure is so prevalent in the countryside that China's one-child policy permits rural women who have a girl the first time around to try once more. During Xiao Shi's next pregnancy, all the local superstitions pointed to a son, so she wasn't prepared for the firestorm that erupted when she delivered yet another daughter.

Her *popo* promptly arranged to give the baby away—a popular means of subverting the one-child policy and getting yet another chance to have a boy. Xiao Shi and her husband vehemently opposed the decision, but her mother-in-law, who ruled the family with absolute authority, would not budge. Three times *popo* took the girl to childless families; three times the families had just accepted someone else's female castaway. Chagrined, Xiao Shi's mother-in-law consulted a local fortune-teller, who pronounced the babe too strong-willed to be discarded. Uneducated and highly superstitious, *popo* relented, and Xiao Shi got her daughter back. Even now Xiao Shi feels lucky that things turned out so well; if her sister-in-law hadn't already produced a grandson a couple years earlier, even the fortune-teller wouldn't have been able to convince *popo*. "That's just the way the countryside is," Xiao Shi says with a shrug. "It's just like being in a feudal society."

Since then, she's never gone through anything quite so agonizing again, though those first couple months working for Cui were pretty emotionally taxing too. In recent years things have gotten better and better, and nowadays she feels thoroughly content with her life; as long as her daughters are respectful, in good health, and doing well in school, there's not much more she could ask for.

Her older daughter, who's currently in seventh grade, is earning especially high marks this year, so it looks like she will make it into high school and probably college as well. For Xiao Shi it's a prospect that is exciting and yet nerve-racking at the same time. Last year one of her nieces tested into university and the girl's parents, who had no savings, had to tap all their friends and relatives just to scrape together the first year's tuition—which amounted to more than the family's entire yearly income. Avoiding a situation like that is precisely why Xiao Shi and her husband are out working rather than living back in the village with their kids. "Don't think your parents have gone to the city to forget about you," she reminds her daughters every time she sees them. "We're in the city to create opportunities for you."

Xiao Shi's tranquility is broken a week later when Shuanger comes down with a high fever. It subsides by morning, but the girl is still complaining of a headache, so Xiao Shi reluctantly keeps her home from school. She wouldn't mind so much, but today Cui is returning from a six-day trip, and Xiao Shi hates for her to come home to a sick child. "She will definitely blame me," Xiao Shi says. "She'll say Shuanger's sick because I didn't take good care of her. If the kids don't get sick, everyone thinks my cooking and cleaning are fine. But as soon as one of them gets sick, they think it's my fault."

Yesterday Xiao Shi's own father fell ill and Cui's husband had one of his drivers take her back to the village to go get him. While she was there, she picked up her daughters, who'd just gotten out of school for the week-long holiday. She left her father and older daughter at a relative's place on the other side of Xi'an but brought her younger daughter, nine-year-old Zhang Yuan, back to Cui's house with her. Though she never officially got Cui's permission, she's quite certain her boss won't mind; after all, the girl can help entertain Shuanger during the break.

Since city schools don't let out for the holiday until tomorrow, today would have been Xiao Shi's only chance to spend some time alone with her daughter. But with Shuanger home sick, the four-year-old is now running the show, leading Zhang Yuan around the house to admire her impressive array of toys. Eventually they make their way to the kitchen, where Xiao Shi is just starting to think about lunch. For no apparent reason, Shuanger throws a storybook on the floor. It breaks apart and the pages scatter across the room.

"Pick it up," Xiao Shi demands.

"No, you pick it up," the four-year-old sasses back.

Such an attitude would earn her own daughters a swift slap back home, but here Xiao Shi just sighs as the child runs out of the kitchen. She turns toward her daughter, who is watching from out in the hallway. "Quick, come over here and pick this up for mama," she says. Without a word, Zhang Yuan scoops up the book pages and hands them to her.

Xiao Shi is still pondering what to cook when Shuanger starts crying to go outside. It's too windy, so Xiao Shi placates her with one of her favorite DVDs instead. Before Xiao Shi even makes it back to the kitchen, Shuanger is screeching that she can't hear the TV; Zhang Yuan, it seems, is cracking sunflower seeds too loudly. Xiao Shi calls her daughter out of the room, but a few minutes later Shuanger hollers again, upset now because she doesn't want to watch all alone. Xiao Shi sends her daughter back into the living room with strict instructions not to make so much noise this time. "From morning to night, Shuanger is always yelling. Even if my daughter wasn't here, she'd be yelling," Xiao Shi says. From her perspective, it's clearly a problem of upbringing. The girl sees how Cui relies on Xiao Shi to do everything for her, and now it's become her habit too. Xiao Shi tried being strict with Shuanger, but Cui didn't like that, so in the end she just gave up.

The two girls resettle in front of the TV. Xiao Shi is pulling out the ingredients to make a steamed noodle specialty called *liangpi* when the doorbell rings; it's the driver, who took Xiao Shi to pick up her family yesterday, stopping by with a bag of books that her older daughter forgot in the car. Xiao Shi takes the parcel into the kitchen and leafs through it. She stumbles across her daughter's diary, and since it's the kind that has to be turned in to her teacher every day, she decides to glance through it.

On the opening page her daughter writes about how so many of her classmates feel aggravated, and how she wants to give them a part of her own happiness. Moved by her daughter's magnanimity, Xiao Shi puts the notebook down, face beaming. "Look at my baby. Look how well she writes. Whenever I think of her, no matter how tired I might be here, I always feel happy. But whenever I think of Shuanger, always getting sick like this, I get a headache."

Xiao Shi turns her attention back to making *liangpi*. After she's mixed everything together, she flips open the diary again and is treated this time to an exposition on how much her daughter misses her. "This is the first time for me to know how she's feeling," Xiao Shi declares. "I always knew she missed me, but I didn't know it was so deep." She props up the diary on the counter so that she can keep reading while she stirs the runny *liangpi* dough with a chopstick. It's not long before her smile disintegrates. "Now I'm finding out that my daughter isn't satisfied with me anymore. She says she hates me." She continues reading, laughing nervously as she goes. "Here she asks, 'Why did I have to be born into this kind of a family?'"

Xiao Shi prepares steamed noodles.

Out in the hallway, Shuanger starts fussing again. Zhang Yuan slides into the kitchen looking for an escape, but Xiao Shi wheels around and hollers: "Don't come in here! Go out there and keep her quiet. She's giving me a headache." The girl slinks out and Xiao Shi turns immediately back to the diary. Her older daughter's anger, it seems, stems from the fact that Xiao Shi made her switch junior high schools this year. Her daughter strongly opposed the decision, but Xiao Shi felt there was no other choice. Since the student dorms were full, the school had put her daughter off-campus in an apartment with several other junior high schoolers. Her daughter, of course, liked this arrangement, as she got to roam free without any adult supervision. But though it's a common situation at countryside schools, Xiao Shi was afraid it wasn't healthy for her fourteen-year-old.

Her daughter now lives with a distant relative who teaches at the new school. Not only is this auntie very strict with her, but the school is also academically much tougher than the last one. In the diary her daughter repeatedly asks why this school gives so much homework. "But every year this school has students test into the best universities in the country!" Xiao Shi snaps at the book, indignant that her smart daughter even has to ask such an obvious question. "Countryside kids can only make it if they really study hard and test into university. Otherwise, they have to stay at home in the village."

Zhang Yuan tiptoes into the kitchen and closes the door behind her. Xiao Shi orders her out, but the girl shakes her head, speaking out for the first time of the day: "I don't want to play with Shuanger anymore." Xiao Shi nods her concession and then finishes the last few pages of the diary—all filled with more anger directed squarely at her.

It's almost 2:00 p.m. by the time the diary-delayed lunch is ready. Zhang Yuan dives into her *liangpi*, but Shuanger won't touch it, no matter how much Xiao Shi coaxes. Instead the girl pulls a package of ramen noodles out of the cupboard. "You know you can't eat that stuff when you're sick!" Xiao Shi scolds. Shuanger throws the package on the floor and huffs out of the kitchen. Though Xiao Shi is usually quick to blame the girl's bad behavior on bad parenting, after reading her own daughter's diary she feels like she, too, has failed as a parent.

She can't control herself and snatches the book off the counter again, skimming through it a second time to make sure she didn't miss anything important. She realizes now that this is not the diary intended for her daughter's teacher. This is her daughter's personal diary full of private thoughts—but it's too late to stop reading now. Though Cui will be here in a couple hours and the house is a mess and Shuanger is running wild, Xiao Shi stands in the kitchen, glued to the pages revealing her daughter's innermost feelings. With worries about her daughter's anger, Shuanger's health, and Cui's unhappy return bombarding her from every side, tonight, for once, Xiao Shi will be the one who can't sleep.

A few days later, Xiao Shi stands beside her husband in the spacious kitchen at Cui's vacation villa, skewering squares of mutton to grill later that night. As they work, they talk mostly about work: how to choose ripe fruit, how to fry chicken, how to best roll out dough. Before Zhang Rui became the custodian here, he'd never cooked much. But since Cui's family only comes on the weekends—and sometimes not even for a month or more at a time—he's had more than enough free time to teach himself.

Cui peeks her head into the kitchen to ask about dinner plans. Xiao Shi squeezes her husband's shoulder. "He's going to show off his new noodle dish for you tonight," she boasts.

Cui studies the reunited couple with a sly grin. "Look at Xiao Shi," she teases, "blooming like a flower."

It's true, Xiao Shi is definitely more animated than usual at the vacation home—for her, being here is like a mini-vacation and a family reunion rolled into one. It's especially nice to have Zhang Yuan with them this time, but Xiao Shi is still disappointed that her older daughter wasn't able to join them as well.

At first Cui said they weren't coming to the villa over the holiday break. Then, last night, she and her husband suddenly loaded everyone into the SUV and drove out after all, which didn't give Xiao Shi any time to go pick up her daughter.

Since stumbling across the diary, Xiao Shi has been rehashing her decision to come out to work and leave her kids behind. After all, if she was still back home, her girls would live with her, not at school or with relatives, and this kind of thing would probably never have happened. And even though her older daughter ranked near the top of her class last semester, Xiao Shi has no doubt that her studies could be even better—*would* be even better—if she had her mother by her side to help her stay focused.

Even so, Xiao Shi knows her decision to leave was right. She tried several different ways to make extra money back home before resorting to this. After those first few impoverished years of marriage, she and Zhang Rui opened a convenience store in her grandfather's home on the village's main road. They borrowed 8,000 yuan for a small truck with which to haul in supplies, and by the time they repaid that debt, so many similar shops had opened that there was little profit left to be made. After that they started driving the sweet potatoes they'd grown to a county where they didn't grow so well. It was a grueling four-hour trek in their little open-cab vehicle, and one that had to be made in the dead of night since such automobiles were not legally allowed on the highway. But selling their yams for a higher price than they could get locally made it all worth it. Unfortunately, over time, many farmers started buying vehicles and hauling their sweet potatoes out that way too.

When the family started to struggle financially yet again, Zhang Rui took a part-time construction job in a nearby village, but with their oldest now in school, even that wasn't enough. Xiao Shi realized she'd reached a crossroads: she could stay back home, raise her daughters, and have no money, or she could go to the city to earn money for their futures and not raise them. It wasn't possible, she concluded, to do both. Convinced that the second option would ultimately prove best for her children, she headed to Xi'an to work as Cui's live-in nanny and left her own two daughters back home—the oldest handed off to Xiao Shi's mother and the youngest sent to stay with *popo*, the very woman who'd tried to give her away just a few years earlier.

It may be an almost unthinkable choice from a Western standpoint, but it's an all-too-familiar dilemma facing Chinese farmers in search of more than the countryside can offer. Going to the city as a whole family is difficult, as most available jobs offer only dorm-style accommodations, demand long and erratic hours, and provide unreliable paychecks. Thus it is that a large portion of China's married migrants has decided that their best chance for success lies in parting ways. Leaving their kids behind is merely another kind of bitterness to be eaten on the path of progress, and they tend to approach it with unsentimental matter-of-factness: living apart allows them more options in the city, and more options mean more money.

"Now we've got four family members, and we live in four different places," Zhang Rui laughs. "But there's no other way. Farmers are short on money, and we've got to do this just to get by. Our parents, our kids—we've got to take care of everybody. We're out here working for our family's sake." Such flexibility wouldn't be possible, of course, if it wasn't for China's traditional multigenerational family unit, which allows working-age parents to leave their kids with grandparents or other family members without feeling guilty; chasing after a change of fortune is not, after all, a motive to be second-guessed. Besides, those who go out tend to send a substantial portion of their earnings back to those who remain in the village, thus helping to raise local living standards in their absence. In many impoverished areas, these remittances are such a vital source of rural income that local government officials encourage each family to send at least one member to the city for off-farm work, as it is one of the most expedient means of lifting the entire household out of poverty.

In rural China, the dispersed family model has become so common that many villages are now ghost towns of sorts; the only ones who remain are old people and young children. "Our life is very ordinary," Zhang Rui says. "Everyone's living like this." Then he glances around the villa's extravagant kitchen and corrects himself; living apart might be typical for migrant families, but the opulence he and his wife are surrounded by most certainly is not.

As dusk approaches, Cui's husband calls Zhang Rui out to the deck to roast some meat for the family. While he's gone, Xiao Shi washes and chops the vegetables for his special noodle dish. But when forty-five minutes have passed and he still hasn't returned, she starts fretting about getting dinner finished on time. Flustered, she pounds a lump of dough against the cutting board; this is Zhang Rui's specialty, and she wasn't intending to cook tonight.

He breezes back into the kitchen a bit later and Xiao Shi immediately perks up. "I love this place," she says, peering out the window into the darkness as he takes over dinner preparations. Though it is beautiful and single-unit homes like this with their own lawn and deck and gazebo and fish pond are almost unheard of in space-cramped Chinese cities, Xiao Shi is fond of the place simply because she doesn't have so much to do here. All she has to do is help Zhang Rui out in the kitchen and keep an eye on Shuanger—though that alone can be a full-time endeavor sometimes.

A few minutes later Zhang Yuan skips in and, without a word, starts tracing a line with her finger across the countertops. Xiao Shi appreciates that her daughter is infinitely easier and less time-consuming to manage than Shuanger, but sometimes the girl's penchant for silence irritates her. "She doesn't like to talk," Xiao Shi complains to her husband, who simply smiles and rumples his daughter's hair as she cruises past.

Back when his mother wanted to give their infant daughter away, Zhang Rui tried to dissuade her by arguing that girls are actually better than boys. Girls treat their elders better and are far more obedient, he pointed out. In his own family there are three boys and one girl, and only his sister really takes good care of their parents. His mother didn't buy it and still wanted to trade her granddaughter in for another shot at a grandson, but Zhang Rui really talked from his heart that day and felt vindicated when she ultimately came to love Zhang Yuan most of all. His mother grew so attached to Zhang Yuan during the years she looked after the girl that when the older woman fell sick a few years ago and realized she didn't have long to live, she was most disturbed by the thought that no one else would care for her precious granddaughter as well as she had. She sent Zhang Yuan to stay with her aunt's family for a trial run, and her heart was put at ease only after the girl reported back that they had treated her well.

More than anything, Xiao Shi's grace through the whole saga reinforced Zhang Rui's conviction that, from every aspect, girls really are better than boys. From the beginning Xiao Shi proved understanding of his mom's ignorance and never held a grudge against her for hoarding their money or trying to discard their daughter. Later, after they'd borrowed 20,000 yuan from Cui to build a new home back in the village, his mother suddenly declared that it was an unlucky year to undertake such a project. To keep the peace, Xiao Shi agreed to put it on hold until the following year, but in the meantime his mother's health declined and Xiao Shi didn't hesitate to spend the construction money on her medical treatments and ultimately her funeral. After that, there was not enough left to build even half a house, so Xiao Shi simply let the plan go.

Then, and now, his wife continues to do what Zhang Rui himself cannot. On a usual day here at the villa all he has to do is clean a bit, take care of the yard, and feed himself—probably less work than Xiao Shi does in an hour or two back at Cui's home in Xi'an. Though he, too, is working for their daughters' futures, he doesn't know if he could stick with it if he had to do what Xiao Shi does every day. "My wife can really *chiku*," Zhang Rui says. "She herself is willing to eat bitterness."

Zhang Rui's special noodles aren't ready until well past the family's usual mealtime, but they turn out to be a big hit nonetheless. When everyone has eaten their fill, Cui and Xiao Shi take the kids out for a stroll. Cui's son runs ahead and Shuanger swings between her mother and her nanny as they walk. Zhang Yuan catches Xiao Shi's other hand and flashes her a smile.

As they weave their way through the cluster of expensive villas, they come to a section of the road where the streetlights are off. Shuanger pulls back, not willing to venture into the darkness until they turn on the flashlight, but Cui urges her onward, telling her to enjoy the bright stars for a while instead. "This is

Shuanger's first time walking on a dark road," Cui tells the others. "Back in the village we kids only had dark roads. We used the stars to guide us."

Cui loves to tell her kids about her days growing up in the countryside, which always amuses Xiao Shi. Like Xiao Shi's girls, as a child Cui was left in the countryside while her parents worked in Xi'an. But she was only six when they brought her to live with them in the city, and though Cui still likes to talk like a village insider, now she can't even tell weeds from wheat.

Nothing about Cui resembles a village girl anymore, but those first few formative years spent in the countryside have probably enabled Xiao Shi to live with her for so long. Though Xiao Shi still has to be careful not to upset her boss—must, as she puts it, "have eyes in the back of her butt"—overall, Cui treats her well and even tries to make her feel like part of their family. She frequently thanks Xiao Shi for her help in raising Shuanger and has even promised her a retirement pension someday. When Xiao Shi first asked to borrow money to build a house back in the village, Cui didn't hesitate to offer up as much as she needed, and she repeatedly assured her that there was no hurry to pay it back; it was Xiao Shi who insisted on having a big chunk deducted from her salary every month until the debt was repaid. Though that meant a financially tight couple of years again, somehow knowing that it was her choice this time made it much easier to deal with—and made her more appreciative of her boss than ever before.

The next morning finds them in the kitchen once again: Zhang Rui mops the floor while Xiao Shi steams egg custard and Shuanger and Zhang Yuan play with a ball of dough. After the custard is finished, Xiao Shi pours soy sauce, vinegar, and chili paste on top of it. Shuanger wants to mix it all together, but Xiao Shi explains that this dish is not meant to be stirred—just scooped into smaller bowls and eaten directly. Unconvinced, Shuanger snatches a spoon and starts slashing into the eggs. When Zhang Rui sees what she's doing, he gives a yell fierce enough to send his own two kids cowering into a corner, but Shuanger simply hits his backside and laughs. "I'll spank you, I'll spank you," she taunts.

After breakfast, Cui decides to take Shuanger for her first excursion into the mountains. She anticipates that it won't be easy and brings Xiao Shi and Zhang Yuan along for backup. Zhang Yuan runs ahead as soon as they reach the trailhead and Shuanger starts whining shortly thereafter: her legs are tired, the path is too steep, and her pink Crocs have sand in them. Xiao Shi empties out the girl's shoes and pours water over her feet, but as soon as they start moving again she launches into a fresh round of complaints. Xiao Shi slings Shuanger onto her back and carries her up the rocky path, but the girl keeps fussing. When Xiao Shi catches sight of Zhang Yuan coming back down the trail toward them, she tries to quiet Shuanger by saying: "Oh, look at how much Zhang Yuan envies you. I've never once carried her like this."

Although lots of peasant kids stay back in the countryside while their parents work in the city, Xiao Shi realizes it is a bit strange to leave her own kids behind only to take care of someone else's. It feels even stranger to admit that she doesn't miss her daughters all that much when she's in Xi'an but misses Shuanger something fierce whenever she's gone for a few days. From time to time she asks her girls if they're angry with her about the situation, and they always say no. At first it was a hard adjustment for them to make, but over time they, too, warmed up to Xiao

Shi's new occupation. When Xiao Shi travels with Cui's family by airplane—a feat that few, if any, villagers ever accomplish—her daughters proudly boast about their mom's amazing adventures. They happily wear the designer castoffs that Cui and her friends give them and love the bragging rights that a trip to the unfathomably upscale villa earns them among their friends. This summer Xiao Shi is thinking of sending the girls to camp in Beijing for a week, and though her purpose is to let them start seeing the world like city kids do, it's an opportunity that should make them real superstars back home.

All this mingling of city ideas and opportunities with their traditional rural lifestyle has not only pleased her daughters but also earned Xiao Shi new respect in the village. At first she was just another migrant, and people even looked down on her because she worked as a nanny. They started to rethink this assessment as they heard about her travels and watched her bring home an impressive array of clothes and gifts for her family and friends. But it wasn't really until her mother-in-law died and Xiao Shi paid for the entire funeral (since Zhang Rui's own siblings had nothing to contribute) that she was deemed a person of real capacity. The clincher wasn't simply that she foot the bill; what really impressed everyone was that, despite her hefty financial contribution, she was still down-to-earth enough to cook and care for all the guests who flooded in during those sad days. "Now in my hometown, I count as someone with really strong abilities. When I'm not around, everyone's buzzing about how well I'm doing."

Along with this recognition of her capacity comes an assumption that she earns a lot of money in the city. To her, this is one of the biggest compliments of all, given that she and Zhang Rui never did build themselves a house—which is not only seen as a key indicator of prosperity in village life but also as an important form of security for the future. Obviously people don't know that the funds she used for the funeral actually came from Cui and took years to pay back, or that her salary is actually pretty low and until recently she's never managed to save much. And while she's never tried to pretend that she has a lot of money, neither does she disabuse the notion that her family is now financially fit. "Anyhow, we're way better off than the people who are still back in the village. Now we're doing better and better," she says with a laugh. Then she lowers her lashes and adds: "I guess it sounds a little arrogant to say it like that."

By the time they return from the mountain, Shuanger is fast asleep in her nanny's arms. Xiao Shi lays the girl in her bed and then settles back into the kitchen to help Zhang Rui prepare lunch. They confer for a moment and decide to make *liangpi*, the spicy steamed noodle dish that Cui's family loves. Xiao Shi begins mixing up a batch of dough while Zhang Rui pulls out the requisite steamer trays and cheesecloth. As they work, Xiao Shi shares with her husband highlights of the morning's hike. She takes special care to tell him how Shuanger pinched their daughter but that rather than running or retaliating Zhang Yuan just cried and let the four-year-old keep pinching. Zhang Rui looks over at his daughter, who is playing with a ball of dough again, and tells her with mock seriousness to fight back next time Shuanger does something like that. "Whack her," he says, letting out a series of air jabs. Zhang Yuan smiles and then giggles as her father continues sparring with an invisible opponent.

As Xiao Shi watches the two of them interact, she wishes once more that her older daughter could have joined them for this rare snippet of family time. She knows that some migrants do bring their kids to the city with them so that the family can stay united, but that's not an option she and Zhang Rui ever seriously considered. If all four of them had come to Xi'an together, she and Zhang Rui would have had to do business for themselves— they couldn't, after all, have their girls stay at Cui's house or in some other type of workers' dormitory. But after their dismal entrepreneurial experiences back home, setting up shop in the city seemed too risky.

Besides, neither of them was convinced that the urban environment was the best place for their girls to grow up—a belief that living with Cui's family has only reinforced. "Countryside kids are quiet and well-behaved," Zhang Rui explains. "The conditions aren't the same, the things they encounter aren't the same—nothing's the same. And the way of educating them is definitely not the same. When we talk to our kids, they have to listen. If they don't listen, we'll let them have it. City kids are all spoiled."

"City kids get whatever they want," Xiao Shi agrees.

"Village kids' behavior is definitely better," Zhang Rui says. "I think that this"—he nods at Zhang Yuan, who is now standing near the window playing quietly with a string—"is good."

Though leaving their kids behind is not easy—even in a culture where it is widely accepted—it may in fact be the better choice, at least as far as their education is concerned. As rural *hukou* holders there's no guarantee their girls could attend city schools. Some places refuse migrant kids outright, and others require so much documentation or additional fees as to make it virtually impossible. Even if Xiao Shi and Zhang Rui could get their daughters in, on their wages they realistically could only afford low-quality city schools or unofficial migrant schools. And even those would only be viable options through primary school, junior high at the latest; since high school and college entrance exams generally must be taken at the location where the *hukou* is registered, migrant kids are ultimately forced to go back to the countryside to finish their education anyway.

By keeping their daughters back home, Xiao Shi and Zhang Rui can afford to send them to the best schools in the area and can rest assured that they will be able to continue on their educational path without interruption. And in the countryside, at least their daughters are not surrounded by a flood of materialism that they can't partake in. As Xiao Shi sees it, if everyone around you is poor, then no one feels badly about it. If you happen to get a special outfit or a chance to take a trip somewhere, you feel infinitely lucky. But if her daughters really grew up in the city, they'd be surrounded by kids like Cui's son, whose sneakers alone cost almost twice Xiao Shi's monthly salary. Rather than feel like big shots because their mother has flown in an airplane, in the city they'd feel like losers because their parents were measly migrant workers who couldn't even provide them with their own ATM card.

After lunch, Cui's husband retires to the family room to watch TV. Cui and her son lounge in the adjacent living room, watching a movie on the family's new widescreen plasma set. The flick proves too boring for the boy and soon he drifts away. He wanders through the house until he locates Xiao Shi and the two girls huddled together in Zhang Rui's closet of a room, also watching TV. He surveys the tiny room with the tiny bed and the tiny television, apparently never having visited this part of the house. "You all sleep in here at night?" he asks Xiao Shi, a bit doubtful given its size.

"Yep," she replies.

"That's a bit of a throwback to the olden days, isn't it?"

"That's right," Xiao Shi says, unruffled by his hint of sarcasm. "When we were little we all slept on one big bed."

The boy squeezes in next to his sister, tentatively, as if giving the place a try, and then he leans forward to focus on the small screen in front of them. When Cui's kids get too demanding—beyond even the limits of what new city wealth deems appropriate—Cui frequently recounts the days when only one family in her entire village had a television. At night they'd put it outside so that everyone could crowd around for a look. "You ended up so far back from the TV that you had no idea what you were watching, but you still felt so happy," Cui tells them.

It is not a concept that her two kids have ever been able to fathom, nor is it a concept that many countryside kids can understand anymore either. But it is one that is not lost on Xiao Shi. As she sees it, the key to contentment is that despite the luxury in which she now lives, she doesn't want status, jewelry, or even her own credit card; she simply wants to make some extra money so she can afford to send her daughters to college when the time comes. She knows that if she lets China's shifting priorities get to her—if she doesn't keep her goals manageable and if she starts longing to attain that newly imported American Dream—then she won't be able to maintain her present peace of heart any longer. Instead, she, too, will feel like a loser for being a measly migrant worker.

The morning after they return from the villa, Xiao Shi drops Zhang Yuan at their relative's house, where her older daughter has been stranded for the whole week. She can't stay for long, so she doesn't say much and doesn't even mention the diary. Instead, she lets her husband, who will escort the girls back to their respective homes, deal with it. "Your mother is working so hard out here, and it's all for you," Zhang Rui tells the girl. "If you need something, she gives it to you. Don't hate her."

These last few nights Xiao Shi's been thinking that they really do need to build that house back in the village after all. When the funds they'd originally borrowed got gobbled up by *popo*'s medical bills, they decided a house wasn't all that important for their family. But this past week, with her older daughter left essentially homeless, Xiao Shi realized that without a house of their own, they have no choice but to stay with relatives or Cui's family when they have some time off. As it is, their chances to be together are limited. They don't want to miss out on an opportunity to catch up just because there's nowhere for them to go. If they build a house now, they'd need to borrow another 20,000 yuan just to cover construction costs, which means they'd be in debt again for years to come. Though Xiao Shi tries hard to rein in her desires and content herself with less, she suspects that this may be worth the expenditure.

But the decision depends, in part, on how well her older daughter scored on the recent midterm exams. Last year her grades weren't great—not terrible, but not excellent either—and so this year Xiao Shi had her repeat the seventh grade. Though not technically allowed, when her daughter switched to the new school Xiao Shi simply didn't inform them that the girl had already completed seventh grade elsewhere. The strategy seems to have worked: last semester her daughter placed ninth out of eight hundred kids in her grade. If she can keep up this kind of performance, then she really will be able to make it into university— even a famous university—in which case Xiao Shi and her husband should probably forget about the house and just keep stowing away their cash. If indeed her daughter tests all the way into university, then not only will Xiao Shi's years as a nanny have come to fruition, but they will also likely come to an end; when her daughter heads off to college, Xiao Shi plans to quit this job and follow her. "Wherever she goes, that's where I'm going too," Xiao Shi says. After all, at that point the girl will be in some urban area and Xiao Shi can make money by her side there just as well as anywhere. She might have missed out on her daughters' childhood years, but she definitely plans to be there to enjoy the fruits of her labors when the day comes.

Sometimes Xiao Shi finds it comical how parents' love for their children manifests itself in such diverse ways. She and her village-mates leave their kids behind for years, all out of love and hope for their future, while people like Cui demonstrate love by giving their kids carte blanche in the city's fanciest boutiques. Both stem from the same impulse, but the result is so radically different. "In China we say that wealth won't last more than three generations and neither will poverty," Xiao Shi explains. "Our two families are a prime example of this. Cui's husband worked hard and became rich. He knows how to eat bitterness, but his son has never had to *chiku*. He gets whatever he wants, but he doesn't love what he gets. If you don't eat bitterness when you're young, when you're older you definitely won't be able to eat it. If you waste money when you're young, when you're older you'll waste it even more. When you get down to Cui's son's son, there's no need to even talk about it."

"In our family, my mother-in-law was very poor," she continues. "We started out that way too, but we've worked hard, and gradually we're doing better. When our daughter goes to college, everything will be better. Who knows, maybe she'll even do something really big with her life."

Few people are as qualified as Xiao Shi to compare the two worlds, and over the years the biggest insight she's gained as she's traveled between them is that people simply can't compare themselves to others. Though Cui and her husband have access to anything they want, anytime they want it, they also have that much more to worry about. For her part, Xiao Shi is quite satisfied here at the crossroads, where she and her family can enjoy a taste of the high life without all the headaches and side effects that go along with it. Living it secondhand is enough, at least for her generation. But if she ever had to choose, if tomorrow someone, somehow, gave her an ultimatum, she would go back to the village, regardless of whether or not they ever do build that new house there. When it comes right down to it, despite all the perks that accompany city life, she's still most comfortable in the countryside. Though she knows a lot of people would think that's foolish talk—and though she doesn't expect or even want that to be enough for her own daughters—to her it makes perfect sense. There's a saying, she says, that perfectly explains it: A gold house or a silver house is still not as good as your own doghouse. It may not be much, but in her own doghouse at least she knows that most nights she can put her head on a pillow and fall right to sleep.

CHAPTER SEVEN

The Opportunity Spotter

When Hu Yazhen moved with her two young children into a Gan Jia Zhai room so dilapidated that she could count both the rats and the stars from her bed at night, she wasn't thinking about health or hygiene; she was thinking about money. She'd recently sent her husband off to join the building frenzy in Xi'an's newly launched High-Tech Zone while she stayed in the village with the kids. But though her husband found a decent-paying job—at least for a peasant accustomed to making nearly nothing—he kept coming back to visit them, sometimes missing up to ten days of work a month. While in other life circumstances it might have been interpreted as a sign of affection, to Yazhen it was a softheaded sentimentality that only hampered their progress as a family.

Six months later she went to Xi'an for a visit of her own. As she walked Gan Jia Zhai's dusty and windswept roads, she saw more than just an ordinary western Chinese settlement; she saw an up-and-coming city-village packed with opportunity. Though the rural migrants like her husband who were flooding the place weren't big spenders, she realized that they still had consumer needs of their own—needs that no one yet seemed to be fulfilling. This bit of foresight struck her as both a prime business prospect and an expedient solution to the problem of her lovesick husband.

The very next day she secured a place for the family to stay in Gan Jia Zhai. Then she bought a load of cheap sneakers, displayed them on a cloth spread street-side, and promptly went into business. Though holding an infant and trying to rein in a toddler, in thirteen hours on the street she still made over double her husband's daily wage—more than enough, in her mind, to compensate for the rodent-infested living quarters she'd rented. "Me, I'm the kind of person who just has to look at money and I get all happy," she says. "As long as money's involved, there's nothing I can't deal with."

Her endeavor proved so popular that the local laborers snapped up her wares in a matter of days. Within a month, she rented a room with street-front access, shoved a bed in the back to give the family a much-improved place to sleep at night, and opened one of the village's first real shops. Before long, she let her husband quit his construction job to become her full-time assistant; within a year, she sent her two young children to live in a boarding-style nursery school so she could focus wholly on making money.

Twelve years later, Yazhen's situation looks largely the same: she still runs the same dingy storefront in Gan Jia Zhai with her husband and still calls the bed tucked in the back home. Like most migrants, she still cooks in the building's hallway, still pays to use the public shower, and still tries to stow away every possible penny. Her kids, now teenagers, still live at school, and her time is still dedicated almost entirely to her business. The only visible difference in her life is that now she sells bedding rather than shoes—a switch she made about five years ago after getting fed up with footwear.

But though her outer life has remained largely unchanged over the years, these days the longtime entrepreneur finds her inner life increasingly turbulent. Her husband has long since ceased being of any real help at the shop, leaving her stranded there for endless hours each day. She is bored with mindless buying and selling, and she longs to leave the city-village behind and lead a "normal" city life, one where she at least has the luxury of her own bedroom and kitchen and bathroom. But most of all, Yazhen is just tired of working fourteen hours a day for more than a decade straight without a real vacation. "You can't just make money until you've got no life left," she says. "Your life is still the most important thing." And yet working her life away is precisely what she's continued to do, day in and day out, burning through her twenties and more than half of her thirties with no end in sight.

Yazhen gets a reprieve of sorts when she is invited to attend a big meeting in her home village in early November. Though it doesn't start until 7:00 p.m., she decides to make a day of it, leaving her husband to babysit the shop while she catches an early bus for the forty-five-minute ride back home. She bounces in her seat and swings her feet in the bus aisle like a giddy schoolgirl reveling in an unexpected snow day. By the time she arrives in the village, it's raining, but even that can't dampen her spirits. Instead she skips down the main road, enjoying the pavement for as long as she can before turning onto a dirt lane and facing a sea of mud puddles.

As she threads her way through the muck and up to the house where she grew up, her mother doesn't greet her with hugs or hellos but simply clucks at the nearly impassable road and calls out "The countryside is no good" before ushering her inside. Yazhen plops down in an armchair and sips a cup of steaming-hot water while wiping mud off her shoes and pants. Her mother launches into one of her favorite conversations, explaining how she would like to repaint the house's Communist-era white-and-green two-toned walls, but has to wait until after the road out front gets paved. "If you fix the house but not the road, what's the point?" she asks.

They chat until Yazhen is cleaned off and warmed up. They then grab fresh umbrellas and trudge through the mud to the new house Yazhen and her husband are building further down this same road. As they approach it, Yazhen admires its sparkling tile façade and grand double-door entrance and can't help but think that it looks like a jewel set between the sagging mud-brick homes beside it. With a full five bedrooms and an indoor kitchen and bath, the place has nearly as much space as the rest of the homes on the block combined.

It might seem like quite an accomplishment for a woman who spends upward of twenty-three hours a day confined in a 30-square-meter, mold-infested sheet shop, but beneath Yazhen's seemingly poverty-stricken lifestyle back in Gan Jia Zhai lies a very different reality. The truth is simply that she and her husband have lived so far below their means for so long that they've amassed more than enough savings to build this mansion, keep their kids in fancy boarding schools, and send a regular stream of money back to their own parents as well.

This ability to *chiku* even in the financial realm has enabled China to maintain the highest savings rate in the world. Though

Hu Yazhen in her sheet shop.

a typical Chinese family saves up to 30 percent of its disposable income, among the migrant class the expectation is often to save as close to 100 percent as possible. This is accomplished by living in the tiniest rooms in the shabbiest locales, eating the simplest food, and eschewing everything else as wanton extravagance. Such a hard-core saver mentality ensures that no matter how tough times get, no matter how low-paying their jobs or sporadic their paychecks, most migrants come away from the city with something to show for it.

Yazhen had the means to build a house several years ago, but she wanted to wait until she could afford a really spectacular place without making a dent in her savings. And yet, as she steps into the unfinished courtyard where she's debating whether to install a fish pond or a flower garden, she admits that none of this is really for her to enjoy. She might stay here with her kids for a week or so during Spring Festival each year, but she's not planning to move in anytime soon. Whereas Gan Jia Zhai is a city-village with plentiful financial opportunities, the only work to be done in Yazhen's village is farmwork, and she's not willing to take a big pay cut just to do that again.

As Yazhen and her mother survey a barren concrete space that will eventually become the living room, Yazhen wonders for a moment if she might possibly be able to rent the place rather than just leaving it empty. "Rent this house?" her mother scoffs. "It's not worth one cent. Nobody wants to live out here."

It's a reality Yazhen knew long before construction ever began. Anybody who's from this village already has somewhere to stay and wouldn't pay to live in her house, spacious though it is. And since migration here only goes one way—outward—there's no new influx of people looking for places to live either. The only way for the house to gain value is if the High-Tech Zone eventually expands out to here, turning this village into a city-village in its own right. If and when that happens, Yazhen will add more stories to her house and become like one of those Gan Jia Zhai landlords with nothing to do all day but count rent checks. But until then, she'll have to leave it empty. "Around here, no one lives in any of the nice houses," she explains. "Those people are all out in the city making money. How could someone who's still living in the village afford to build a place like this?"

By afternoon the rain stops, and Yazhen takes a bicycle taxi to visit her older sister in a neighboring village. She finds her sister whisking a broom around as she dances to music playing throughout the house. After talking for a while they climb onto the rooftop to pick persimmons from a nearby tree. They sing and laugh as they work, which makes Yazhen wish she could trade her stale life in the sheet shop for one as upbeat and carefree as her sister seems to have. Who, after all, wouldn't want to stay in the village where the air is fresh and mechanization now makes things easy? "Being a farmer now is very comfortable," Yazhen says. "If I had money, I definitely wouldn't live in Gan Jia Zhai. I'd live here too."

Of course Yazhen does have money—much more than her sister, for sure. But she's not comparing herself to folks who still live in the countryside. If she did that then she'd already be such a success that she wouldn't need to keep plowing ahead. That's especially true in her impoverished village, where money is so tight that local leaders recently had to sell a good portion of communal land just to raise enough to pave the main road. Yazhen bought three plots, and though it was small change to her, it made her one of the biggest and most respected landowners around— which is precisely why they invited her to come back for tonight's planning meeting.

Yazhen leaves her sister to picking persimmons and wanders down to the river where they often played as kids. Now it's dried up a bit and the current seems to have shifted, but otherwise it's much the same as she remembers. She spreads a piece of paper on the hillside and sits on it, careful not to let her black leather pants touch the ground. A woman with her hair tucked under a headscarf washes clothes in the river, while another leads a sheep down the steep embankment toward the water. Yazhen watches them for a while, trying to imagine returning to this type of life again. "The countryside is still pretty pitiful," she finally decides—a nice enough place to live but a major step backward for a person with proven ability like herself.

The last bus back to Xi'an has long since left by the time the meeting finishes, so Yazhen's husband closes the sheet shop and rides his motorcycle out to pick her up. On the way home they stop for dumplings at a roadside diner. When the meal is done they wander over to a makeshift dance hall set up in the parking lot, where a throng of middle-aged couples waltzes beneath flashing colored lights. Yazhen's husband buys two tickets and leads his wife out onto the crowded floor. She moves mechanically through a few songs with him, but her attention is clearly not on dancing: she's too busy calculating how much the clever entrepreneur who opened this place makes each night.

Though Yazhen has run the same shop for so many years, new business plans are always rustling around in her brain. Her own mother opened one of their village's first stores more than twenty years ago and Yazhen grew up helping her out. By age seventeen, she launched her own business, selling kids' shoes and socks on the streets of a nearby town. She would have kept at it, but then she got engaged and felt embarrassed to have her soon-to-be husband's friends and family watch her lug stockings back and forth on her three-wheeled bike every day. Her entrepreneurial spirit lay dormant for several years after that, but when she first saw Gan Jia Zhai she knew she couldn't suppress it any longer. Now she can't imagine doing anything else. "I can do any type of business. I just need to get the goods and find the right location," she says. "But I can't not do business."

The only way Yazhen would stifle her entrepreneurial urges now is if she could somehow go back to school. She never had a chance to study beyond junior high, and her brain is so thirsty that when her kids need help with their homework, sometimes she can't control herself and simply fills in all the answers herself. "Others have the chance to study but don't have the brain for it. I want to study but don't have the chance," she says. "It's a real waste of my brain." The only thing keeping Yazhen from more intellectual pursuits is the belief that her husband is not capable enough to support the family on his own. If he was good at making money, then she'd enroll in a continuing education program, but as it is she brings all the business savvy and he just follows her around—pretending, when the mood strikes, to help her out.

But though his earning capacity falls far short of her standards, she does have to admit that he has a good temper and usually treats her well. "Some people don't have very strong feelings. They can be apart for months and not connect," she says. "But not my husband. If he's away from home for a few days, he can't take it." Even when he leaves Gan Jia Zhai in the morning to putter around their house in the village, he usually calls her by afternoon just to say he misses her. It's an attachment that boggles—and oftentimes frustrates—Yazhen. But while she'd prefer that he had his own busy and lucrative work life, on nights like tonight she is grateful that he's available when she needs him.

Once Yazhen works out the dance-hall financials in her head, she starts shimmying with her full attention. After a few more songs her husband retires to the sidelines, watching as she launches into the cha-cha with a new partner. It's nearly midnight when they finally climb back onto the motorcycle, Yazhen linking her arms around her husband's waist as he revs off toward their abode in the sheet shop.

In the dozen years that Yazhen has spent in Gan Jia Zhai, she's watched it transform from a typical village into a thriving mecca for rural migrants. But now that the High-Tech Zone has fully enveloped it, its end is drawing near. Though it's still not clear when exactly the demolition will begin, people are starting to flee, afraid that all the good spots in other nearby city-villages will be taken if they wait too long. But while the news has others scared about the future, Yazhen sees it as the chance she's been waiting for. "I'm not at all sad about it," she says, as she sits in her shop in early November. "It's perfect because I don't want to do this anymore anyway."

Her plan is to shutter the store once and for all in late January and go back to the countryside to put the finishing touches on her new house. Then she'll enjoy a long vacation before launching into her next endeavor. A few days ago she had no idea what or where that would be, but as she leafed through the newspaper yesterday she noticed several ads looking for people to assemble handicrafts from home. She did a little investigating and realized she had stumbled upon yet another hidden gem of an opportunity. If she sets up a workshop in her new house and pays local farmers to come put the crafts together, it'll be the best of all worlds: the villagers will be thankful to make a little extra money and she'll be content to live in her new house and relax for once while still making a decent profit. Already she's thinking that if it goes well she'll build a separate assembling facility on one of the other lots she owns.

Yazhen's daughter, who is home from school for the weekend, joins her in the front of the shop with a hacky sack in hand. "Let mama try," Yazhen says, shedding her slippers and standing up. As they kick the tiny bag back and forth, Yazhen thinks about her plans to travel and rest and move into her mansion and start her new business in the countryside. "Next year is going to be really great for me," she beams, adding a bit too much oomph and sending the hacky sack sailing out into the street. "Just thinking about it makes me so happy."

Yazhen follows her plan, closing down her shop and moving out of her Gan Jia Zhai cubbyhole about a month before Spring Festival begins. After cleaning and furnishing her new home and celebrating the holiday with her family, she starts looking into the handicraft assembling idea in earnest. Within a few days she realizes the process is too complicated to expect local villagers to do well, and so she decides to scrap the plan altogether.

This conclusion actually leaves her a bit relieved; after spending almost six weeks in the countryside she'd begun to doubt that she really could return to a simpler life after all. She might live like she's destitute back in Gan Jia Zhai, but at least there she can say, do, and wear what she wants. Here in the village it's another story. Over the past few weeks most of the locals gradually stopped associating with her—they weren't comfortable with her fancy clothes and shoes and apparent flaunting of wealth. "I'm the kind of person that loves to pay attention to details," she remarks. "People around here can stand living a dull and boring life, but not me."

With the handicraft idea scuttled, Yazhen shifts her attention to planning her long-cherished vacation. She spends a couple days working out the details, but in the end lounging around doing nothing proves to be too much for her. Bored and restless, she puts her travel plans on hold and heads back to Xi'an to figure out her next big business venture. After three days of scouting potential locations and pumping locals for market insights, Yazhen decides to open a hostel in an emerging city-village near the outskirts of the High-Tech Zone.

She inspects every single home in a three-block area before finding a three-story building perfect for her enterprise. Though the place is already fully occupied by individual renters, Yazhen is not daunted. She offers the landlord substantially more per month than the current tenants pay, and within ten days all seventeen boarders have been kicked out and their keys turned over to Yazhen. From there she and her husband paint and buy TVs, beds, dressers, and blankets for each room. They don't bother replacing the bare cement floors, flimsy doors, and rickety windows, as they have no illusions of attracting an upscale clientele. On April 9, just three weeks after leaving the village with no idea of what she'd do next, Yazhen officially opens her new hostel.

Now, rather than being confined to a small shop, she has the run of the entire place. She's finally even got her own bedroom, though it serves double duty as the hostel's supply closet and the family's kitchen. But despite all the space, for the most part, Yazhen doesn't dare leave the tiny reception room near the entrance for fear of missing a potential customer. This room is just large enough for a single bed, a small desk, and a chair, which means now she's actually more restricted than before. "Originally I wanted to go out this year and travel for a while. Then I got anxious to start making money again, and now I'm locked up inside again," she sighs, as she sits in the reception room pruning a pile of leeks early one mid-May afternoon.

But being cooped up doesn't fundamentally bother her, as long as money keeps rolling in. Since opening the hostel last month, they've averaged about 300 yuan a night, and several times they've completely filled up—not bad for a brand-new business. Yazhen would be ecstatic if it weren't for being so irritated with her do-nothing husband. Back in the sheet shop she didn't mind his laziness so much. There she could close up and go to bed fairly early, and sleep in a bit in the morning. But here she works until at least midnight, and is usually up by 6:00 a.m. Since they don't actually give guests a set of their own room keys, her husband has to stay up until 2:00 a.m., or later, waiting for the last of the guests to straggle back in for the night. But then he doesn't get up until around noon, by which time Yazhen has already checked out most of the customers, cleaned the all rooms, and started lunch. With nothing much left to do, her husband happily eats and spends the rest of the day out roaming.

Though it's not much different than his supposed assistantship at the Gan Jia Zhai sheet shop, Yazhen thought this time would be different. After closing up that store she threatened to stop working altogether if he didn't start pulling his weight, and he spent weeks assuring her that he'd dedicate himself to whatever business she decided to do next. But once they actually opened this place, he fell right back into his old ways. "He talks the good talk, but he doesn't do what he says," Yazhen whines.

She gathers up a couple of bags of vegetables and heads into the bedroom to start cooking a late lunch. Though it's nearly 2:00 p.m., her husband is still lying in bed reading. The sight of him relaxing while she takes care of everything sets her off. "Get up and go mop the second floor," she barks. He shuffles out grudgingly and she pulls out the cutting board, muttering about his intolerable incompetence. She knows he'll probably be back complaining that she's treating him badly, but if she doesn't tell him what to do, he will undoubtedly do nothing. "This guy doesn't know how to use his head. When it gets dark at night, he can't even think to turn on the lights."

When Yazhen emerges with a steaming plate of food, she finds her husband in the reception room scanning the newspaper. "You're still here?" she snaps. He gets up to leave but then lingers in the doorway, finishing his article. While he stands there, a potential customer comes in and asks to see a room. Before he can lead the man upstairs, Yazhen hurries over, snatches the room keys out of his hand, and directs the gentleman to follow her.

While she is eager for her husband to participate in the more menial aspects of running the place, dealing with customers is her domain; he doesn't have enough business sense to properly handle people. A few days ago she was upstairs cleaning when someone started dickering with her husband, wanting a room for 25 yuan rather than the 30 yuan list price. Since the business is still in its infancy, Yazhen almost always agrees to lower the room rate if that's what it takes to make a sale, but her husband wouldn't budge and the customer eventually left. The next afternoon, a guy came in looking for a cheap place to nap for a couple hours, but her husband's inflexibility lost them yet another opportunity. Since then she's forbidden him to interact with customers, afraid that he'll scare more people—and more money—away.

Within minutes Yazhen returns to the reception room with the customer, who says he'll take the room if she gives it to him for 20 yuan. Yazhen negotiates briefly but eventually agrees to his price. Unlike her husband, she knows enough not to turn away cash over a few kuai. She hands the man a thermos of hot water and two paper cups—no tea leaves added for hagglers—and sends him on his way.

As Yazhen turns her attention back to her lunch, her husband stomps in, mop in hand, griping about having to do such grunt work. He doesn't see why they can't hire someone to help out with the cleaning, but Yazhen's not about to throw away good money for something they can easily do themselves. They argue for a while before he retreats to the bedroom, slamming the door behind him. "You let him do a little work and this is the way he gets," Yazhen says, stabbing at a chunk of tofu with her chopsticks. "Sometimes I just want to send him back to the countryside."

By early evening Yazhen's husband is outside, talking with some of his new buddies while Yazhen broods in the reception room, still fuming about his lack of responsibility. After renting another room, she pulls out a little black notebook where she's carefully recorded every transaction since opening the place. As she reviews the day's numbers, she can't help but perk up; usually people just start trickling in about now, but today all but six rooms are already taken. With several more hours of prime customer time still ahead, filling the place tonight is virtually guaranteed. It'll be their third time selling out this week, and if business continues at this pace, she'll easily recoup her 30,000-yuan investment within a year—maybe even make a hefty profit to boot.

After twelve years of slowly and patiently adding to her stockpile, Yazhen has now attained a level of success beyond what most migrants ever hope to achieve—beyond even her own original expectations. But though she has a brand-new home and plenty of money in the bank, it's clear to her that she has farther to go before she can really consider herself successful. Now she wants a car and a house—not the house that's sitting empty back in the village but one that she can live in right here, right now. After all, there's no reason a smart businesswoman like herself should spend her life confined to shabby city-villages when she could be living in proper urban style in the High-Tech Zone just a few blocks down the street.

The way she sees it, the main thing keeping her back now is her husband. In the very beginning, when he quit his job and became her helper at their little shop in Gan Jia Zhai, he heeded her every request. "He was super obedient then," she says. "He couldn't make money and I was making it easily. Think about it. He was obedient to death." Things started to change when the dry cleaner next door closed down. Although Yazhen wasn't planning to open another business, when such a nice space popped up on her doorstep, the entrepreneur in her couldn't pass it by. She launched a clothing shop there and hired two employees—one to cook and do housework and one to help mind the two stores. From then on her husband gradually started relaxing more and working less. "He got spoiled and now he's like this," Yazhen says. "Now he doesn't listen to anything I say."

Opening an additional shop and hiring outside help may have sapped her husband's motivation, but it definitely provided a boost for the couple's finances. They ran the clothing business for seven years, only closing it last September when rumors about Gan Jia Zhai's demise started gaining traction. All those years of pulling in a double income while still living a poorman's lifestyle are what ultimately launched them into a higher echelon of society. If her husband were enterprising enough to start his own business, no doubt they could get even farther this time.

As it is, they technically have enough saved up now to live the city life Yazhen longs for, but then they'd have no safety net. The only way for her to have savings and security and still live the good life is to become a big boss—someone who rakes in enough money not to have to worry about the petty things of life anymore. It's the next logical step on her journey, and she's determined to get there, with or without her husband's help. "I should become a big boss in the future, I definitely should,"

Yazhen says. "I want out of this environment. I want to beautify my life."

She's never told her husband about her goals. He has no idea she's sick of city-village living or that she wants a house beyond the one they only just finished building, and that's the way she intends to keep it. "This is my own private affair," Yazhen says. "He's already satisfied. There's no point in telling him."

By 7:30 p.m. only four vacant rooms remain, and Yazhen is humming with excitement. Now the big question of the night is not whether she can fill the place but, rather, whether she can fill it earlier than she has in the past. When a man who stayed here previously comes in looking for a room, Yazhen jumps up in excitement. "What did you pay before, 30 yuan?" she asks.

"No, you gave it to me for 20 last time," he retorts, retreating a step back toward the door.

"Okay, okay, okay," she concedes, eager to score yet another sale. She motions for him to sit down and then tosses him the receipt book so he can see what a deal he's getting. "Everyone is paying 30 now."

Yazhen collects his money and gets him settled in his room, but he's back a few minutes later to report that his television set doesn't have any reception. "It's not just yours, they're all like this right now," Yazhen explains, turning on the tiny TV at the foot of the reception room bed to show him that every station is static. "There's some problem with the signal." She suggests instead that he take a shower and reminds him where the communal bathroom is located. After he returns to his room, Yazhen flips off the crackling television and jokes: "No TV is good. It saves me some electricity." She laughs for a moment but then grows serious. "Not really. If there's no TV, people won't love staying at my place."

A guest returning from dinner peeks his head in and asks Yazhen to unlock the door to his room. She grabs her key ring and steps into the hallway, where she finds a nervous-looking woman fidgeting in the shadows. Yazhen is annoyed but pretends not to notice; so many guests here are men who bring in women who are obviously not their wives, and while she's happy to take their money, she does feel badly for providing a place for their seedy activities. Though she's never been all that fond of city-village living, ignoring the shadier side of her neighborhood was easier when she was selling sheets. At the hostel, the vagaries of the place are much more up close and personal— which has made her increasingly nostalgic for the simpler China she knew growing up. "Mao was very good. He managed the country very strictly. Everyone was poor and working so hard every day in the collective that there was no time to do bad things," she says. "Now the society's developed, people have money, and there's shady stuff happening everywhere."

Within days of opening the hostel, her husband got his wallet stolen, and last week someone snatched her cell phone out of the reception room. Since then, she's started being much more careful. She still refuses to stash incoming cash in an ugly fanny pack like most bosses do, but now at least she makes a point to regularly hand over money to her husband for safekeeping. Within an hour, another room is taken, and Yazhen heads outside to deposit the funds with her husband. They exchange no words, and after briefly reveling in the novelty of being outdoors, she hurries back inside, leaving him to his loitering. She's itching to take a walk, but there are still two unoccupied rooms left and she's not about to leave them in his hands; she wants to be there to savor the satisfaction of selling out for the night—why waste it on someone who won't get a thrill from it anyway?

The jubilation of renting out the last room comes around 10:30 p.m.—an entire hour earlier than Yazhen's previous record. She waves her arms in the air and taps her feet on the cement floor in the closest thing to a victory dance that the cramped reception room will allow. "Completely finished," she gloats, standing up to stretch. "I'm out of here!"

She changes her shoes and is about to set off on her much-anticipated walk when she remembers that she has yet to add up the day's income in her black accounting notebook. She's in the middle of calculating when her daughter calls. Like Yazhen, she, too, is excited over having just gotten paid. Though only fourteen, the girl dropped out of vocational school in February and now performs in a singing hall where her voice earns 450 yuan a month—150 yuan more than the other kids she works with, Yazhen proudly notes. Whereas other rural migrants stress education as their children's only sure ticket to a better life, Yazhen is not worried about her daughter's lack of scholastic achievement; Yazhen's own successes make her confident that street smarts and a quick wit can take her daughter just as far as higher education would. Besides, as someone who's intent on getting ahead rather than just getting by, Yazhen's own hopes and dreams are pinned largely on herself rather than merely on her kids. Her daughter wants to be a singer, an actress, and a movie star, and those seem like as good of pursuits as any to Yazhen.

Eager to spend a bit of her newly earned money on her parents, Yazhen's daughter asks what she can bring when she comes by for a visit the next day.

"I don't want anything," Yazhen says. "Just that you're doing well."

"No way! You have to want something!" the girl insists.

"Okay, bring me something to eat then," Yazhen says, pleased by her daughter's thoughtfulness. As she hangs up the phone, a smile of satisfaction creeps across her face. Her daughter's future is bright indeed; unlike her father, her brain isn't an empty cup.

When Yazhen finally makes it outside, she strolls to a rice-noodle soup shack at the edge of the city-village. Though only two blocks away, it's the first time she's ventured so far in a long time. She only made the trek tonight because with the hostel already full she has nothing to do for once. "This place has great food," she says, tossing 2 kuai at the clerk. "It's just inconvenient because it's too far from us."

As she sits at a tiny table slurping down the first bite, she watches a donkey cart plod by on the city-village road to her left and a car whiz past in the High-Tech Zone to her right. Over there, to the right, is where she belongs. The three-wheeled bicycles and arguing drunks on her left are all so familiar, as are the brick piles spread everywhere as the village builds up. But the wide sidewalks and the quiet, gated communities of the High-Tech Zone are calling to her, and opening the hostel has only strengthened her desire to get out of the city-village once and for all. "The city-village environment is no good. It's got every kind of person and it's the vilest kind of place," Yazhen sighs. "It's not like being in the city, and it isn't like the countryside either."

When she was a kid, city-villages didn't even exist—people and places were either urban or rural; the distinction was clear and society much more stable. The creation of such an out-of-place kind of place is new—another unforeseen side effect of the country's growing prosperity. Unlike the slums or shantytowns that pop up in other countries, China's city-villages are more of a purgatory—a place where people wait to see what hand fate will deal them. A lot of rural migrants arrive only to go right back from where they came, a select few move on up and out, and still others remain here at the crossroads until they find they don't belong anywhere anymore. After twelve years in the fishbowl, Yazhen may have unwittingly become one of those people.

Yazhen leaves the noodle shack and strolls back toward home. In the distance she can see the sign in front of the hostel and read the two large characters *He Yi*—a name she chose that means "Family Unity." Even when there are no more vacancies, Yazhen always keeps the sign on and the front door open. After all, if other entrepreneurs realize how hot her business is, before long the street will be flooded with copycat hostels. As she approaches the hostel, she sees her husband still sitting there, intently watching a game of pool and totally oblivious of this and the hundred other business concerns that occupy her mind day in and day out. "If he has clothes and food, that's enough for him. But not me. I like to have the kind of life where I'm busy, busy, busy. Develop a profession and do it really well," she says. "I don't mind having the kind of life where we live apart and see each other every few months because we're both out working really hard. For me it's no problem, but he insists on being together—every day together." She rolls her eyes and slowly shakes her head. "Things just aren't going to work this way."

In this regard the changes in China are taking an unexpected toll on her own personal life, just as they are on the society at large, and she can't help but feel nostalgic for the days when their relationship, like the country itself, was far simpler. "When we were young, our thoughts were so pure. When we were first married, our relationship was very good and we worked hard together. We didn't have any money, but still we had nothing but good days," she says, just a hint wistfully. "Now we have money, but he doesn't want to do anything, and we just fight every day."

Although Yazhen told herself she'd go right to sleep after her excursion, when she gets back to the reception room she can't help but take a last quick peek at her black accounting notebook. As she leafs through it, a man wanders in looking for a room for the night. "We're sold out," Yazhen murmurs, without looking up.

"This early and you're already out of rooms?" he asks, clearly surprised.

Yazhen simply nods, but once he's gone she pounds a fist on the desktop. "This is exactly what I was afraid of!" she exclaims. Minutes later she turns away yet another potential customer and can hardly contain her frustration. "This really pisses me off," she hisses. "That's at least 40 kuai that I'll never see." She vows not to take 20 yuan for a room anymore; from now on, it's 30 or nothing. Today she was so eager to sell out that she gave too many rooms away too cheaply and now she's regretting it.

Though annoying, she has to admit that it's better than having too many empty rooms. In fact, if things keep going this well, she's already decided to open another hostel by September. This time she'll find a spot near a university campus, where providing dorm-encumbered students a place for their romantic rendezvous is supposed to be a big business—another venture into the more sordid side of modern life, but one she'll have to live with if she's going to keep moving ahead. She'll have her husband manage that hostel while she stays here at Family Unity. She'll hire both of them a helper and they'll live apart and won't fight and won't even have to see each other that often. Most of all, they'll double their income again and catapult themselves right into the urban lifestyle on which she's set her sights. The key is to make sure her husband stays focused on running a place all alone. "If I'm not there, he'll be forced to do a good job," she says brightly. Then a frown tugs at her lips, betraying her optimism. "Anyway, I'll give him a smaller investment. Just 10,000 yuan. Who cares? However much he can make is what he'll make."

For years, Yazhen has blamed her inability to get out of the city-village on her husband's ineptitude. But the truth is, despite her business smarts, she has never tried to move beyond petty sales. Entrepreneurial genes and an ultra-saver mentality have gotten her this far, but it remains to be seen if they will be enough to propel her to the next level. For all her bravado and seeming confidence, she can't deny feeling trepidation about leaving the city-village. After all, it has been the source of her success for most of her adult life. And as unsettling as it might be, at some level it's still comforting to stay here, where she is the master of her universe. In the city-village she enjoys being a big fish in a little pond, but who knows what will happen if she actually does leap into the vast High-Tech Zone pond down the street?

But these are not issues that Yazhen ever dwells on: she's bought into the progress-at-all-costs mentality wholeheartedly, and for now at least she can't imagine anything more worthwhile than continuing to claw ahead. Even if it shaves another decade off her life or rends another rift in her relationship, these are sacrifices she's more than willing to make in her push toward prosperity; if the last twelve years have proven anything, it's that she can eat bitterness—physically, mentally, and financially—for as long as it takes.

CHAPTER EIGHT

The Big Boss

As Guo Hulin rests in a plush chair at the City Rose Beauty Salon getting his hair groomed, one thing is immediately apparent: the hairdresser put far too much oil on his long locks today. He should know: he spends at least 1,500 kuai here a month, getting his hair washed every few days and even opting for an occasional manicure or facial. Having his tresses smoothed to silky perfection once a week is an essential part of his routine. "This is my personal hobby," he says, chuckling at his own vanity. "It's the only fun I've got in my life."

When the stylist eventually leads him back to the sink to rinse out his hair, Hulin catches a glimpse of himself in the mirror and stops momentarily to flex. The concept of bodybuilding recently arrived in Xi'an, and though he's slight in build and not really a hard-core practitioner, he likes to assess his progress any time the opportunity arises.

His hair proves worse than expected and has to be washed a second and then a third time to make sure it will stay perfectly styled until his next visit. Though he's usually able to laugh off such small mistakes, today he snaps at the hairdresser for her carelessness, which is now costing him valuable time. He's promised his girlfriend, Wang Ni, that he'll cover for her at his convenience store this afternoon, and it's a pledge he's backed out on one too many times already.

Hulin was cool before cool was even a concept in China. Back in the late 1990s he was already sporting shoulder-length, feathered-back hair and wearing sneakers and sweats that put him in stark contrast to the average leather-shoe and dress-shirt clad Chinese man. In the past few years guys have started wearing jeans and T-shirts and some even sport earrings and dyed hair, but Hulin still stands out above the crowd. Nowadays his hair hangs halfway down his back and his wardrobe consists of overseas name-brand athletic gear that has yet to reach the domestic market. He downs imported vitamin supplements by the handful and frequently espouses the benefits of drinking pure whey. He is known to break into song when the mood hits, and his deep, resonant voice only adds to his alluring, rock-star image. Even his Chinese name, Hulin, which literally means "tiger forest," rings of coolness.

He's not the kind of guy you'd expect to be running a small empire in western China's largest High-Tech Zone, and yet, at thirty-two, Hulin is doing exactly that. He's a man who's made it, a man with a big enough bank account to command respect. As of September, he owns six convenience stores, a noodle joint, a fast-food delivery place, and a brand-new 2,500-square-meter fitness center, and he is preparing to launch three neighborhood health clinics in the coming months as well. "These last few years everything's gone very smoothly," he says. "Some people have big dreams, but when they try to make them happen, they run into so many problems. Not me."

As he walks through the front doors of his store in the Maple Leaf Gardens housing complex, Wang Ni and two employees are washing down a dusty load of toys. Though this is his flagship shop, the location that launched his dynasty, it is deceivingly simple: a mere 50 square meters divided into three tiny aisles, with an ice cream freezer serving as the front counter. Since Hulin opened it eight years ago, his product offerings have sky-rocketed from just a few hundred to more than five thousand different types of snacks, beverages, stationery supplies, and novelty items, and sales have shot up to nearly 45,000 yuan a month.

The phone rings and Hulin answers it. A minute later, he hangs up and immediately hollers for one of his employees to take a big bag of sunflower seeds and four little bags of numb-and-spicy chips to a customer in Building 28. One of the girls helping Wang Ni throws the items together and hustles out of the shop.

Soon the Good Bread delivery boy brings in two boxes heaped with an assortment of buns and pastries. "Just two crates today? That's not enough!" Hulin exclaims. "Who said we only wanted two crates?" He scowls, and even from a distance his rising blood pressure is palpable. "Gao Pan!" he barks, calling on one of his longest-standing employees, a twenty-year-old from his home province of Gansu. "Is this enough bread?"

Gao Pan, who's been rearranging laundry detergent at the back of the shop, slides down the aisle and examines the load. "It's enough," the boy reassures him.

"Oh," Hulin mutters, surprised at how out of touch he's become with his shop. When he first opened this place, there was not a single item that came in or out that he didn't personally oversee. Back then, he was just like any other rural migrant, silently and patiently trying to save a bit of money by working here eighteen hours a day and sleeping in a cheap Gan Jia Zhai rental just a few short hours a night. After a few months he brought his sixteen-year-old niece, Taoling, from the village to help out and built her a little bed hidden behind the last rack of merchandise so that she could sleep there expense-free.

The two of them lived like that for two years before Hulin finally broke down and hired another kid from the countryside to assist them. Shortly after that he decided to provide home delivery to people living in the Maple Leaf complex. Considering how hard he and his two employees were already working, the idea seemed a bit crazy. "Everyone said I shouldn't do it," he says. "But to me it was just another kind of good service." The idea turned out to be a hit, and business nearly doubled overnight.

Four years after opening the Maple Leaf store, Hulin started another shop, this one in the Flying Sky housing complex a few miles away. He sent Taoling to run that store while he oversaw the original. From there it was just a matter of time before business exploded in all different directions, and the next thing he knew he'd become a *da laoban,* or "big boss." "But I still need to open more," he says. "If I'm going to do the things I want to do, I need to have a lot of money."

Over the past few years, the staff has ballooned from just Hulin and Taoling to over thirty people for whom Hulin provides room and board. Most of Hulin's employees are like he once was: youth from the countryside with no skills, little education, and no aspirations beyond earning a little bit of cash in the city. That makes Hulin feel personally responsible to help them realize that they can do more than hold down a simple job like this forever. He wants them to believe that they can become big bosses too. After all, if a third-grade dropout with a hot temper, and a secret, sordid past, like his could do it, there's no doubt in his mind that any one of them could do even better.

Recently he's also started hiring local university students from the countryside as part-time weekend help—a novel concept in China, but one he sees as his own special way of enabling them to stay in school and out of poverty once and for all. "Wang Ni always says I have a problem here"—he taps his finger to his head—"but where else are they going to find a job like this? Only from me."

And yet it's not just a sense of responsibility or a desire to be a good role model that keeps Hulin in the game. There's something even deeper behind the near obsession to amass wealth that has seized him as of late—but it's an impulse that, until now, he's kept buried deep inside.

Three weeks ago, without telling Wang Ni or any of his employees, Hulin put several of his stores up for sale. Since then he's been getting a barrage of phone inquiries but still hasn't found the right buyer. When he fields a call from a man who's particularly interested in his location in the Flying Sky housing complex, Hulin tells him as much as he can think of regarding the shop's history, location, and the work involved.

"Do you know how many buildings are in that complex?" the man asks.

"Of course I know," Hulin laughs. "How could I open a store there if I didn't even know such a simple thing as that?"

"What's the busiest time of year?"

"Spring Festival," Hulin says, a bit put off by the man's obvious lack of experience. After a few more similarly silly questions, Hulin interrupts. "Look, if you do this for a while, you'll know. But what you really have to realize is that kids buy their milk there in the morning on the way to school. You've got to get up really early and that's the most tiring part. So if you're going to get into this type of business, you've got to think about how long you're willing to work in a day."

"Can I come by and take a look?"

"Yeah, but you can't interrupt my business. And you can't tell my workers I'm trying to sell it. They've been with me a long time and I haven't told them yet."

When the man finally asks him why he's selling the place, Hulin takes a deep breath. This is the point in the conversation where he's never quite sure how to answer. Sometimes he tells callers that he needs to devote more time to his new fitness center, and other times he opts for the "I'm about to open three health clinics" excuse. But what he doesn't tell them is that, despite all his outward success, he has recently started running into problems of the less tangible kind. Having already blown past all the traditional barriers in a migrant's path and launched himself into the upper echelon of society, he's now started turning his attention to concerns beyond his own; he's encouraging shoppers to use baskets rather than plastic bags, helping employees recognize their own potential, and launching neighborhood health clinics to give back to the communities responsible for his success. But none of this has proven enough to quell his longing for meaning, and so, unbeknownst to anyone else, Hulin has now set his sights on opening and running an orphanage.

The way he figures it, he'll need to sell at least three of his current businesses to raise the necessary start-up capital, and

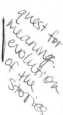
quest for meaning. evolution of the story.

then it'll take steady income from at least three more enterprises to keep it up and running. He's promised himself that he'll do it before he's thirty-five, which leaves just three more years to accomplish his goal. It's the *xinli hua*, or "heart talk," that he doesn't share with anyone. "If you tell other people, they'll think you're talking nonsense, think you're crazy," he says. "They'll say, 'Doing business is exactly for the purpose of making money. Why do you have to think so much beyond that?'"

In a country where vehicle ownership in large metropolitan areas is a mere 12 percent, Hulin now has three vehicles. There's a car for his fitness center, a minivan to deliver fast food, and, most recently, a new Buick for his personal use. But on this bright, October morning Hulin decides to forgo his ride and walk eight blocks to the High-Tech Zone hospital, where a close friend is scheduled to have minor kidney surgery.

When he gets to the kidney ward, Hulin finds his friend lying in bed. The man's wife is perched beside him, gently stroking his head. These are Hulin's nearest and dearest friends, people he met during the lowest point in his life back when he'd just arrived in Xi'an without a penny in his pocket and worked as a measly dishwasher. They ran a nearby convenience store and, despite his lowly status, didn't hesitate to befriend him. Spending time with them proved a great boost to his spirits and a much-needed respite from the tedium of his menial life. To Hulin they are more than just good friends—they are his *ge* and *saozi*, his big brother and sister-in-law.

"Where's Wang Ni?" big brother asks, as Hulin settles in a chair at the foot of the bed. Like a good Chinese older sibling, *ge* almost always starts with this question, though he well knows that Hulin and Wang Ni almost never go out at the same time;

one of them is always on duty at the Maple Leaf store, and these days it's usually Wang Ni.

"Why don't you two hurry up and get married already?" big brother cajoles from beneath his comforter. "You've already been together something like six years now, right? And still you're not married. Is that terrible or what?"

Sister-in-law nods in agreement. "Hurry up a little!" she throws in for emphasis.

In fact, Hulin and Wang Ni are supposed to marry next month—at least that's what he proposed a few weeks ago when things were going smoothly. But now he's wavering again. She was just a student and he a fledgling shop owner when they met, and though he feels indebted to her for all her help over the years and grateful that she loved him first as a poor man, he's not sure they have the requisite understanding for a good marriage. Thankfully no one else knows about their wedding plans, so he still has a chance to fix things without losing too much face or having to call the relationship off altogether.

Big brother's surgery gets pushed back a few hours, so Hulin and sister-in-law head down to the cafeteria for an early lunch. Sister-in-law is in good spirits today considering that her husband is about to go under the knife. Somehow, she explains, today feels strangely like a vacation day. She and big brother run a true mom-and-pop place, with both of them usually working in their little convenience shop all day, every day. They have no employees, and so on a day like today they have no choice but to close their doors.

For years now, Hulin has been urging them to break out of their small-time mind-set and move into the big leagues. He wants them to follow his lead and hire some help and start expanding, but until now they've resisted, scolding him instead for focusing too much on work. While he prides himself on never once having closed his shop in all these years, they pride themselves on being sane enough to take a rest every once in a while. "A lot of people sacrifice a lot, and they do it all for money," sister-in-law explains as she stirs her bowl of porridge, obviously but indirectly referring to Hulin. "But time is going by, and people are getting older. Before they ever get to the point of having time to live their life, they're too old to enjoy it."

It is true that the stress of constant wheeling and dealing is taking its toll on Hulin and making it harder for him to enjoy life. First he was incapacitated by lower back pain, then a barrage of stomach problems that turned into ulcers, and finally a tumor that landed him in the hospital twice—once in March for ten days and then again in May for eight days. Now he's supposed to stay away from salty, spicy, sour, and fried foods, wheat products, and meat, eliminating virtually everything he likes to eat.

But even through all that, he never closed a single one of his shops for a single hour. "When he was in the hospital, as soon as Wang Ni would come visit, he'd tell her to hurry back and make money," sister-in-law says, shaking her head in disapproval. "Everything with him is about the money."

There's still an hour or so before big brother's surgery begins, and the conversation in the hospital room turns to some of the failed business exploits of their mutual friends. A few minutes later, big brother lists off some of their wealthier acquaintances and asks rhetorically of each, "Is he a great man?" No, the three of them agree, none of these men are great.

Then big brother names a rich friend who recently made a substantial donation to build a school in a poor village. "Now *he* is a great man," he declares.

[handwritten margin note: make $ but no time to enjoy it. constantly stressed about making more $.]

"Yeah, but where did his first round of money come from?" Hulin asks, implying something shady in the man's past. But big brother discounts that almost immediately; getting start-up money by not-quite-legal means is so common as to be a nonissue in his mind.

Hulin thinks about all the hoops he had to jump through to get the needed approval for his fitness center—nothing illegal, exactly, but enough servile back-scratching to leave him with a permanently sour taste in his mouth. No doubt he'll have to jump through similar hoops in order to get his health clinics properly licensed. "Being rich isn't at all a happy thing," he murmurs.

"That's right," big brother agrees, then pauses and flashes Hulin a sly grin. "So who's to say you wouldn't have been better off with just the one store and not ten?"

Hulin squeals in frustration while big brother and sister-in-law laugh. He hates not being able to set the record straight, hates not being able to tell them that, despite what it may look like, for him this isn't just about money—at least not anymore. Sure, it seems like he's greedily opening business after business after business until he and Wang Ni and Taoling are exhausted to death, but unlike so many Chinese clamoring after wealth these days, at least he's doing it with a higher goal in mind.

If Hulin were going to tell anyone about his plans for the orphanage, it would be big brother and sister-in-law. But for as close as they are, and as much as they heckle him for focusing too much on money, even they wouldn't understand the promptings of his heart. His expensive clothes and spa treatments might earn him an eye roll now and then, but they are implicitly condoned and even respected as the entitlements of a big boss.

Spending time and money opening orphanages is another matter altogether.

Besides, in China, orphanages are usually state-run and seen as the responsibility of the government or large charitable organizations, not individuals like Hulin. In fact, giving to charity at all is something of a new concept in a country that was consumed with poverty just a few decades ago. And though rich people like their friend, who throw money at some school project and then never bother with it again, are widely respected, for Hulin part of the appeal of an orphanage is that he will be directly involved in it; having so many lives depend on him just might bring the fulfillment he's been looking for.

No doubt others will want to donate money once they see what he's doing, but he can't count on it at this point. He can only count on himself, and that means dedicating himself to his work and keeping all his intentions quiet for fear that others— even those as close as big brother and sister-in-law—will try to derail his plans. "By the time I let them know what I'm doing, the kids will already be in the orphanage."

Big brother's surgery is quick and seamless and he's back in his room dozing when sister-in-law suddenly remembers that today is Thursday—the day money must be deposited into the alcohol and cigarette wholesaler's bank account to ensure Monday delivery. Hulin needs to make a payment for his stores, too, and so he leaves the hospital with sister-in-law's bank card in hand, assuring her that he'll take care of it.

He takes a taxi to the front of the High-Tech Zone district where he has a few errands to run and then walks along the main road toward the bank. For him, traveling through this area is like wandering through a minefield of former and future business opportunities—locations that he's either bought or sold, or those that are in negotiations, are scattered everywhere. As he walks, he keeps a close eye on traffic, looking for beautiful cars and good license numbers. The license plate he currently uses has three 7's in a row, which makes it quite auspicious. He paid over 10,000 yuan to acquire it and now another big boss wants to buy it off him for much more than that. But though Hulin owns two other lucky numbers, neither is quite as good as this one, and he has no intention of selling.

Collecting propitious license plates is a growing business among big bosses—another way for those with money to keep themselves entertained. In the three decades since the country's economic reforms began, rural and urban Chinese alike have set their sights on material progress with single-minded devotion, driven by the belief that material prosperity is an essential foundation for just about everything else. After all, Chinese from all walks of life frequently explain, people must first *chibao*, or "fill their stomachs," before they can consider extraneous things like helping others. Though the vast majority of China's citizens have long since transcended the hand-to-mouth stage, the saying—as well as the associated focus on one's own financial well-being—is still pervasive.

But while countless millions of Chinese remain too preoccupied to look beyond the demands of each day, people like Hulin finally have the luxury to ponder the question being whispered across the nation: Now what? What do you do when you've eaten bitterness so long and so hard only to accomplish all that you set out to do and more? While buying cars and lucky license numbers are nice distractions, they are clearly not permanent fixes. These days, growing contingents of Chinese are embarking on the search for meaning—embracing religion, resurrecting traditional philosophies, and espousing social activism. In the midst of the country's climb toward superpower status, even the central government has officially shifted its attention away from mere economic growth toward the broader goal of building a balanced and harmonious society. But as someone struggling to achieve that equilibrium in his own life, Hulin knows just how difficult—and lonely—an aim that can be.

As Hulin nears the bank, he points to a new luxury high-rise where he was planning to buy a flat before deciding it was too expensive. "People say I should buy an apartment, but I don't need an apartment," he says. "You buy it and it just sits there. Why should I spend 430,000 yuan for that?"

Hulin may be a big boss now, but despite his pricey pastimes he still maintains a frugal migrant mind-set in many ways. Sure, now he's upgraded from a single room in Gan Jia Zhai to a three-bedroom rental in the Maple Leaf Gardens, but he shares the place with so many employees and such a clutter of cast-off supplies from his numerous business ventures that it's impossible to use the place for anything other than sleeping. And though he has nearly 1.5 million yuan sitting in the bank, on top of the 2 million yuan he just sank into his fitness center, he still returns to the Maple Leaf shop nearly every night to close it down a couple hours after midnight.

Like so many small-time Chinese businessmen, Hulin started out by surrounding himself exclusively with trusted family members, and he still tries his best to keep it that way; Wang Ni, Taoling, and a couple other relatives are each stationed at one of Hulin's businesses every day from morning until evening. Though he could easily hire a few managers to keep an eye on things and ease all their burdens, that would be a real waste of money to him. Besides, in his mind, outsiders can never be totally trusted when it comes to financial matters—though now with so many different businesses he sometimes has no other choice.

By the time Hulin deposits the cigarette money and heads over to the Maple Leaf store, it's nearly 5:00 p.m.—the slow time, right before people start coming home from work. He finds cases of ramen noodles strewn outside the shop and scolds Wang Ni as soon as he walks in. "What's that about?" he asks. "It looks terrible!" But Wang Ni simply ignores him and continues watching TV from her post behind the counter. "You're a real farmer," he mutters, tossing out one of China's newest jibes for someone who's uncultured.

Hulin calls for Gao Pan to come take care of the mess, but a quick scan of the shop reveals that all the employees are out right now. "Errrrr!" he squeals, face flushing with anger as he hurries outside. He starts moving the boxes himself, stacking them neatly against the front of the shop. He's calmed down and almost finished when an old woman walking by stops and watches him for a moment.

"Hello, auntie," Hulin calls to her.

"I haven't seen you here for a long time," she says.

"I'm always here."

She looks at him again, boxes in hand, and finally says, "Well at least I haven't seen you *working* much in a long time."

It's true, Hulin doesn't work like he used to. He doesn't normally stock shelves or make deliveries or clean up like he did in the early days. He has plenty of employees for all that. Now it's more a matter of controlled roaming among all his different enterprises while still looking for new opportunities and trying to unload some of the old. Since he can no longer maintain as tight a rein on his holdings, he's installed computerized accounting and tracking systems to prevent employee theft. He also insists on being around when big shipments come in at each shop, just to give the impression that he still knows what's going in and out of his stores.

Tonight it's time to stock up at Flying Sky, so Hulin has a quick dinner and then drives over. He's laughing as he fiddles with the car radio on his way there, but by the time he walks through the shop doors, he's assumed his stern, big-boss style. He points to a pile of empty boxes by the doorway. "What's all this?" he growls.

None of his three employees respond. Instead, they all keep their eyes fixed straight ahead, faces emotionless, as if totally absorbed in the task of making way for the week's new goods. Hulin lets out a long sigh and joins them in stacking and stocking. Though, on the one hand, he wants to encourage his workers to attain bigger and better heights, on the other hand it seems that there's always something to be mad about when dealing with them. Before long they settle into a familiar rhythm: every time Hulin enters the store with a load of merchandise he spews out a new complaint and the workers do their best to ignore him—or at least his attitude—until he calms down.

Hulin is stacking mahjong sets along the back wall when a small boy, about seven years old, comes into the store. He pokes Hulin in the ribs and asks if he has any notebooks. Hulin leads him down an aisle and points to two long shelves full of them. "Here they are," he says, smiling widely for the first time since

Guo Hulin talks with a child in his village.

arriving at Flying Sky. "Take a look for yourself and see what kind you want."

Hulin has always had an affinity for kids. He's been donating books and supplies to a nearby orphanage for several years now and feels compelled to open his own not just because it's a good thing to do or because it will give him a sense of purpose but because he feels especially close to such kids. "I've got a mama and a baba, but from the time I was little, it was just like I was an orphan," he explains.

Though he's the youngest of five children, his mother actually had several more kids who died because of the harsh conditions at the time. His father also passed away unexpectedly in his fifties, when Hulin was just eight years old. He wasn't yet old enough to understand the full impact that it had on the family but the effect on his own life was clear. "From that time on, I was basically on my own," he says.

With his mother and older siblings too busy trying to keep everyone fed to bother with the needs of a young boy, at age ten Hulin did the Western equivalent of running away—though in his mind he was simply moving on. He didn't leave a note, didn't tell anyone what he was doing or why, because, as he saw it, there was nobody who could understand his heart. He made his way to the nearest big city and snuck on a train heading to Xinjiang, China's most remote, northwestern province. "It didn't matter to me then if I lived or died," he recalls. "Life was just about eating and passing the time away. If I died, then I wouldn't have to worry about those things anymore."

When he reached his destination several days later, he slept along the roadside until he was taken in by a shepherding family who provided him room and board in exchange for labor. Though they never treated him like just another worker, they never treated him like a real part of their family either. After a couple of years he wandered off again, looking for something else to do and hoping, somehow, to find someone who could truly love and understand him.

It's a quest that, until today, has proved elusive. But when Hulin opens his orphanage, he's sure that he will finally find what he's been looking for all these years. "Those kids will love me," he says. "They'll definitely love me very much."

By the time Hulin parted ways with the shepherds, he was nearly fourteen and quickly turned his attention to having fun. He would hitch his way to somewhere new, make a little bit of money, and play until he was bored and broke. Soon enough, he'd move on to the next place and do it all over again. After several years of drifting, he discovered a passion for vehicles and started trucking produce across the country with a friend. When the novelty of that eventually wore off, he decided the time had come to take making money a little more seriously. "I realized that that was the only way to have a good life," he says. "Otherwise people see you as pitiful. Everyone else has a profession, but you can just scrape together enough to keep your belly full."

And so he saved up some money, returned home to Gansu province, and opened a little convenience store in Tianshui, the city near his home village. He was only nineteen but by then he felt ancient, having been on his own already for nearly a decade. Business was surprisingly good, and soon he opened a second shop. Not long after, he expanded them both. The next thing he knew he was on his way to becoming rich.

It was quite an unexpected turn of events for a third-grade dropout runaway wild child, and soon his remarkable success was the talk of the town. He was still quite rough-and-tumble, with late-night drinking and fighting and carousing more a way of life than an aberration, but he seemed settled nonetheless and destined to have a prosperous life close to home.

In early 1998 two friends approached him with plans to open a gold mine. It was a hot business opportunity in the area at the time, and Hulin knew quite a few people who had made millions that way. "It was like gambling," he says. "If you lose, you lose everything, but if you win, suddenly you have everything."

He decided to take his chances. Without doing any research or even giving it much of a second thought, he promptly sold both his stores and took out a loan in order to bring his total investment to 1.8 million yuan. His two partners put in similar amounts.

But luck was not on their side. That year the government created new policies to more closely monitor the area's rapid development, and as part of that crackdown they decided there would be no more private mines. After Hulin and friends had bought all the necessary equipment, set up the entire operation, and were just about to start mining, they were officially given three days to get their supplies and people out.

One of Hulin's partners had borrowed nearly all of his investment money and was so distraught over this turn of events that he promptly jumped off a cliff and killed himself. Shocked and grieving, Hulin informed his bank that he had no way to pay back his loan. Within a matter of days he surrendered both his house and his car. "Helpless," he says, squealing with irritation at the mere thought of those times. "At that time I was totally helpless."

Hulin couldn't even think of staying there, nor could he possibly stand to go back to his village. The failure was simply too great; he'd lost everything, including his newly won identity as a success. Rather than ask anyone for help, he threw two changes of clothes in a bag, gathered together enough money to buy a train ticket to Xi'an, and slipped away once again. "That's just my character," he says. "I can't depend on other people. I know that everything here"—he points to his head and arms and legs—"is working, so why shouldn't I be able to survive on my own?"

Hulin is just finishing up at the Flying Sky store when big brother calls to say that he has trouble sleeping in strange places and doesn't want to stay at the hospital overnight. Sister-in-law has already gone back to open the shop for the evening, so he needs Hulin to come pick him up. Though Hulin usually takes over for Wang Ni around this time, she'll just have to wait; big brother and sister-in-law are two people that he never refuses. Not only are they the first real friends he made in Xi'an when he arrived desperate and depressed after the failed mining fiasco, but they are also the reason he's not still working in some restaurant, up to his eyeballs in dish soap.

They'd already been fast friends for nearly two years when big brother and sister-in-law stumbled upon the chance to open a shop in the Maple Leaf Gardens. Though it was one of the High-Tech Zone's nicest housing complexes at the time, they decided to give the opportunity to Hulin rather than take it for themselves. They put up 10,000 yuan to purchase the initial batch of merchandise, and he pitched in as much as he could toward the first month's rent and utilities. Though he'd already proven his business acumen once before, at that time he was in no state of mind to track down a new venture on his own; it was big brother and sister-in-law who enabled him to become a full-blown shopkeeper once again. "If we hadn't seized that chance, I'd probably still be just a worker today," he says.

By the time Hulin gets to the hospital it's after 8:30 p.m. and quiet pervades the kidney ward. He tells the doctor on duty that big brother wants to leave for the night and come back in the morning for his checkup, but the doctor doesn't agree. He may seem fine now, the doctor says, but tonight he needs to stay put—just in case.

"What should we do?" big brother asks when Hulin relays the doctor's orders to him.

"Sneak out," Hulin shrugs. "The night doctor's got to play it safe and say you should stay."

Big brother ponders for a moment and then agrees. "All right, let's go then." He asks his fellow roommates to cover for him if anyone comes in to check on him during the night, then cracks the door open, peers down the hallway, and nonchalantly strolls out as if he were merely getting some exercise. A minute later,

Hulin leaves the room and heads for the exit, whistling as he goes.

It's almost a repeat performance the next morning, as the pair take turns casually sneaking back into the hospital room. Then Hulin goes to the nurse's station to find out when big brother will be discharged.

"Did he stay here last night?" the nurse questions suspiciously.

"He stayed," affirms Hulin.

"I tried three times to find him this morning."

"I don't know, maybe he went out for a walk or something."

She comes back into the room with Hulin and hooks big brother up to an IV, one of the many medications he'll need to take before he can be released. Sister-in-law is running the shop today, so Hulin will have to take big brother home again when the time comes. In the end, the kidney operation didn't even close their store down for a full day, but Hulin is still not satisfied. They helped launch his career in Xi'an, and now he wants to jump-start theirs—and that means getting them to take their business a bit more seriously. "They haven't really put in the effort. They'll open for a few days, and then close up and go out for a while," Hulin says, though big brother and sister-in-law estimate that they work at least 340 days a year. "It makes a big difference. I haven't closed for a single day in six years. Not one day."

When Hulin first struck it rich in Tianshui in his early twenties it was by dumb, blind luck. He lacked diligence, discipline, business smarts, and strategy, and even when the money started rolling in, he was still just a hot-tempered kid who suddenly had the means to play and fight to his heart's content. "At that time I didn't have any set ideas; I just wanted to make money to have fun," he explains.

This time around, he is much more serious about his professional undertakings. He quit smoking and drinking as soon as he opened the Maple Leaf store and started focusing all his attention on moving forward. But even so, he can't explain why he was able to leapfrog his way to wealth twice when so many other equally hardworking migrants remain forever stuck in their daily struggles. It's true that he's outgoing, confident, and flashy in ways most other rural people are not, and that helps him rack up the personal relationships essential to doing business in China. It's also true that he's not afraid to bend the rules when needed—incentivizing inspectors, underestimating his income, and overinflating his accomplishments as the situation demands. But when he looks at himself, he still sees rough edges everywhere and feels as bewildered by his victories as others do by their failures. The best he can do is chalk it up to fate—and his audacity to keep going despite the hard knocks life has dealt him. "This kind of courage is essentially all that I've got," he explains.

By noon, big brother still has several more IVs to finish, so Hulin leaves him at the hospital and drives across the city to meet up with two truck drivers he knew back in Tianshui. They drove to Xi'an yesterday to drop off a shipment of furniture, and they'll be leaving tonight to transport another load back home. Hulin picks them up at the wholesale furniture market and then heads downtown to a fancy hotel, where a guard directs him to park up on the sidewalk.

After they're seated, the two drivers ogle the opulent, crowded dining room, while Hulin scans the menu. He tries to flag down several servers but, to his dismay, they keep hustling past him without notice. "The management here is terrible, a real mess,"

Hulin complains to his guests, who don't have enough experience in such places to have any expectations.

A waitress eventually arrives and Hulin orders a beer for each of his visitors. They urge him to have one, too, but he insists that he no longer drinks. Only red wine, he tells them, and then only a certain kind that the doctor says is good for his stomach. He scans the drink menu to see if they have it, and his friends' eyes bulge as they realize that a single bottle costs more than their weekly salary. They look at each other quizzically; though Hulin had money before, this time he's clearly moved into a new socioeconomic class, and they're no longer sure what to make of him.

Hulin doesn't consult with them when it's time to order but just starts firing off a list of dishes, including chicken, pork paws, and meatballs. When the food arrives, they urge him to dig in, but he says he doesn't eat meat anymore either. He's ordered a bowl of spinach noodles and shredded potatoes for himself. They keep trying to press choice pieces of meat on him, but when he starts detailing his recent surgeries they raise their eyebrows at each other and leave him to his potatoes. An awkward silence settles over the table, and the two truck drivers focus on their food with exaggerated attention, clearly glad for the diversion. As the meal draws to a close, Hulin takes the check—there's no doubt that, as the only *da laoban* at the table, it's his treat.

When they finally pile back into the Buick, the guard is no longer standing there, and Hulin ends up going the wrong way down the sidewalk. Soon he finds himself at the corner with no outlet. Rather than back up, he simply accelerates over the curb and onto one of the busiest streets in the city. As they pull up to the furniture market, Hulin tells the two drivers that they should stay with him the next time they come to Xi'an. They look at each other and nod noncommittally, then hurry out of the car with a sigh of relief. Hulin pulls onto the main road again and lets out a deep sigh of his own. "For me, every day is like this," he says. "I never get to rest."

When big brother finally gets discharged from the hospital late that afternoon, Hulin drops him home and then proceeds directly to the City Rose salon. He asks for a shampoo and the stylist has just started lathering his hair when he gets a phone call. At first she continues on while he talks but then stops as his conversation gets heated. Eventually he hangs up, crosses his arms, and lets out his trademark squeal of frustration. He sighs deeply, and the stylist starts massaging his head again.

Hulin may already be a much-envied big boss, but he has no desire to become an even bigger one. It's not just that it's stressful and taxing on the body; the worst part is growing out of touch with people, like the two truck drivers he used to be able to call friends. "All I am now is a money-making machine," he laments.

Last year, during Spring Festival, Hulin was standing among a group of spectators watching a fireworks display near an alcove of ritzy single-unit estates. Everyone was laughing and enjoying themselves when Hulin noticed the owner of *Ai Jia*, a wildly successful chain of superstores in this province, peek his head out of one of the villas. A few minutes later the man stepped outside, bodyguards in tow, but it wasn't long before he hurried back into his house to watch from inside. "These big bosses are so pitiful," Hulin says. "They're not like everyone else, the ordinary people on the street, who can just enjoy themselves."

Though Hulin is nowhere near that rich or that isolated, there's already so much he can't share with others and so much they can't understand about him. He was a complex character with a complicated past to begin with, but being a big boss has now made him inscrutable to those around him. The problem is especially acute in his relationship with Wang Ni, who resents that he spends so much time shuttling people around and taking them out for fancy meals while she's stranded in the Maple Leaf shop day after day. And though she can see he's also tired, most of the time she can't fathom why; from her perspective, he's out playing while she's busy working away. Hulin can't seem to explain why such activities have become tasks he must complete rather than forms of enjoyment, nor can he impress upon her how exhausting the nonphysical demands on a big boss can be. And if the daily struggles of his life are beyond her understanding, how can he ever hope to share his more abstract feelings, like his need to find meaning or determination to open an orphanage?

No, Hulin asserts, he has no desire to become much bigger of a boss than he already is. As it is now, he can barely stand his life, and he's itching to take off, leave everyone and everything behind, and start over from rock bottom once again.

Even now, after redeeming himself for a second time, Hulin still doesn't like to go back to his native village; there are simply too many bad memories there and too much lost face. He makes the six-hour trek only once or twice a year. In mid-October, after much nudging from his oldest brother, he agrees it's time for a brief visit.

He takes the train and gets into Tianshui a little before midnight. One of his brothers and three of his friends meet him at the station, and they all walk to a neighborhood restaurant for a late-night dinner, compliments of *da laoban* Hulin, of course. The next morning he pays a taxi driver friend to take him around for the day. Within an hour they're at the city's outdoor produce market and Hulin buys groceries like he owns a restaurant. He takes 5 kilos each of tomatoes, eggplant, baby bok choy, bean sprouts, and garlic tops and smaller quantities of many other vegetables. Then he goes to a nearby department store for bulk candy, crackers, cakes, and tea. In all, it takes nearly two hours and more than 500 yuan to prepare for the short journey home.

Once he finishes shopping, the taxi speeds beyond the city limits, where the road narrows, and begins a steep climb up a terraced mountainside. This is plateau country, and the yellow soil spills down in steep banks, blending in with the hand-packed dirt walls that mark off each home's courtyard. After a long while the driver turns onto a footpath that seems impossible to traverse by vehicle, but he plunges forward undaunted, having successfully made it on previous visits. They pass by orchards and fields until they eventually enter Hulin's village and stop in front of a compound similar to all the others—an earthen wall with a set of ancient double doors framed with recently harvested corn on each side. Hulin enters the courtyard and walks past row upon row of drying corn and pepper strings, while a group of chickens scatters as he passes by.

Suddenly there appears his mother, older and frailer than he remembers, clad in the same tattered-blue Mao suit she's worn for decades. Her disheveled white hair is pulled into a tiny bun at the nape of her neck, which she pats down as she eyes him. At first she's confused, not sure he is who she thinks he is, but once he puts his arms on her shoulders and says, "Mama, it's me," her tears start streaming.

"You forgot me," she says over and over. "You forgot your mother."

Hulin tries to explain that he didn't forget her, tries to explain how busy work has been, and tries to hint that maybe she's forgotten the last time he visited, but she's hearing none of it. "How could you forget me?" she cries even louder. He holds up the bags of freshly purchased goodies and shows them to her. "Look, see, I didn't forget you," he says. "I brought all this for you."

He guides her past the tiny earthen structure where he and his siblings grew up, and where his mother still prefers to sleep at night, and into the adjacent three-room tiled house that his oldest brother built three years ago with Hulin's money. He sits on the edge of a bed, takes a small cake from his stash, and starts feeding it to his one-toothed mama, bite by bite. Between mouthfuls, she continues scolding him, and he, like his own employees do so often, sits with his head down, staring at the floor and taking it all in without reply. His oldest brother, who lives here with his wife and two kids, sits on a nearby chair watching TV; he smiles at the scene that is reminiscent of their childhood.

After his mother has cleared her heart, they talk for a bit about his life, and then Hulin stands up, stretches, and says it's time for him to go. He's been here for little more than a half hour, but that seems to be all he can take. His mother looks as if she's about to cry again, but he consoles her before a tear can drop, assuring her that he will be back for another visit soon.

Before he can go, there's one more stop to make, and he and his brother navigate the dirt path that winds through the village, while the taxi follows behind them. As they walk, Hulin notices how empty the place is now—no longer bursting with life as it

Guo Hulin and his mother.

did when he was a kid. He also notes how many new tile and brick houses there are, thanks in large part to the money flowing in from people like him who've moved to the city. A few minutes later they reach their destination: the small red-brick village temple perched up on a plateau about 4.5 meters above the trail. Hulin burns a few sticks of incense, kowtows several times, and raises his hands toward the heavens. Then he zips up his red-and-black Wilson warm-up jacket and hurries down the steps, where his brother and the taxi driver are waiting.

Along with his newfound interest in philanthropy and an emerging thirst for spirituality, Hulin has been looking for ways to improve himself—particularly his temper. It's no secret to those around him that he can be a bit hotheaded, and when something sets him off, he usually acts immediately and without seeming restraint. Just last week he got upset at a handful of his workers and gave them until sunset to get their things together and move out of the dorm. Several of the youth he fired were Wang Ni's relatives, but he never gave a thought to ruining his relationship with her family—typically a major consideration in China. "They know they've done a bad job," Hulin says simply. "I just don't understand how they can treat me so badly after all I've done for them."

But even if he still gets angry and impulsive when things don't go according to his expectations, to him those are just minor things that he wishes other people could overlook. "If they saw where I came from, they'd realize I'm doing pretty well."

"I've done a lot of bad things in my life," he explains, pushing up his sweatshirt sleeves and revealing forearms filled with scars. "My whole body's full of them." He's been in so many fights—fistfights, knife fights, broken beer-bottle fights—that he can't even begin to count them all. "Others would be embarrassed to talk about such things, but I feel happy to say it because I've improved so much."

When he talks about his life before becoming a High-Tech Zone big boss, he typically uses the pronoun *he* rather than *I*. "That person is already finished. I'm a different person now. I can love other people. I can accomplish things. I've grown up," he says. "Now if an employee makes me mad, I don't even yell—and I can yell really loudly. Instead I just stamp my foot and bottle up. Really, I've improved so much."

It might be an effective way to control his temper, but all that bottling up is apparently not so good for Hulin's health. By the end of October he finds himself back in the doctor's office again, this time for a cold that won't go away. His head is stuffy, he's always tired, and he's been having a hard time with his stomach for several weeks now. They start him on a regimen of intravenous fluids and antibiotics for at least the next three days. Perturbed, he forces himself into one of the clinic's beds and flips through the TV channels. "It's not fair," Hulin complains. "Getting sick is for people who have nothing to do. They have time to be sick. It's not supposed to happen to people like me."

He knows, of course, that most of his health problems are stress-related, what with his new fitness club off to a somewhat sluggish start and permissions to open the medical clinics proving stickier and more back-scratching-intensive than he'd imagined. To top it all off, Wang Ni isn't talking to him again. He's not sure what the problem is this time, but he suspects that it's the same thing she's been grumbling about for months; she thinks he spends too much of his time taking care of other people's affairs and not his own—and certainly not her own.

Hulin can't deny that a good amount of his time is occupied by things not directly related to his businesses, but he sees it as more of a responsibility than a choice. After all, he has proven his abilities more than once, and somehow people naturally seem to turn to him for help—be it professional, financial, or personal. Last night, for example, the friend with whom he opened the fitness center called and said his grandma had hurt her back, so Hulin spent this morning taking her to several hospitals in search of one that could perform the surgery she needs. Then today at lunch he helped another friend negotiate a deal on a shop she wants to buy, and tomorrow he'll accompany her to sign that contract. No doubt Wang Ni will be unhappy about that, if not a little jealous, too, but what can he do? He just hopes that one day she'll understand him and see that he's a good person at heart. "If someone asks me for help, I can't say no. I might come back and say I couldn't do it, but I'll never say no to trying."

Even when people don't ask for his help, Hulin can't seem to resist giving it. A few days ago he sold the Flying Sky store to three young university graduates who work together at China Mobile. It's their first time opening a business and Hulin is worried about them—not just because they could barely scrape together the 150,000 yuan needed to purchase the shop, but because, as Hulin sees it, they don't have any experience in the outside world. They've been cloistered in schools and offices their whole lives and have no idea how to really get by. "I'm afraid they're not familiar enough and will do badly. I'm afraid they'll fail," he says. And so he's decided to spend some time training them—accompanying them to order stock, handle larger deliveries, open in the morning, and close up at night. "No one else would do that, but it's just the way my heart is."

The three young men are so thankful that they're already calling him *ge*, or "older brother," in much the same way Hulin feels indebted to the honorary big brother and sister-in-law who helped him start his first shop in Xi'an. But what he really gets a kick out of is that he, a grade-school dropout, is able to help these college boys survive. "They're not the same type of person as I am. They wore leather dress shoes when they were out with me," he says with a laugh, looking down at his own sturdy Nikes. "After two days, their soles were all worn out."

By March, Hulin's health is much improved. He hasn't caught a cold in months and his stomach has calmed down considerably. That doesn't mean he's been taking it easy though; if anything, he's busier now than ever. He recently launched another noodle joint as well as a breakfast nook that is just four doors down from his Maple Leaf store. Though that place has been open for only three days, so far they've sold out of soy milk, soy pudding, stuffed buns, and rice porridge every morning, and Hulin is already looking to expand into lunch and dinner too. "I'm still just a money-making machine," he complains.

The breakfast nook is a bit too stuffy for Hulin's liking, so today he hovers outside, overseeing the installation of a new air conditioner. One of his employees brings him a bowl of noodles. As he stands there eating, Wang Ni emerges from the Maple Leaf shop with their new puppy, Little Bear. The dog clamps on to her pant leg and she pulls it along behind her, teasing and laughing as she goes. Over the past few months Hulin successfully postponed their wedding again—twice. Now the plan is to wait until after his health clinics are up and running which, given the current stalled negotiations, might be quite some time, he notes with just a trace of a smile.

Wang Ni hurries him back into the shop, where a potential part-time employee is waiting for him. The boy, a nineteen-year-old college student from the countryside, has already interviewed with Wang Ni and now just needs Hulin's final approval. Hulin tosses out a few questions and then hires him, telling him to come each Saturday from noon until 10:00 p.m. The boy timidly explains that the last bus back to his university leaves this area at 8:30 p.m., so staying so late would be impossible.

"Why would you take the bus? You'd just waste the money you'd make," Hulin scolds. "Don't worry about it. I'll buy you a bike."

Hulin's desire to help countryside kids escape poverty is stronger than ever, but his plans to open an orphanage are now on hold. In January, his mother passed away, before he had a chance to make good on his promise to visit again. While he was home for the funeral he talked to some local officials who offered to give him a parcel of land on which to build an old folks' home. The details are still fuzzy, but it looks like he'll get the green light to proceed within the next couple months. It's exciting for Hulin—his first chance to do something really worthwhile. Though it means taking his focus off the orphanage for the time being, he's okay with that. After all, he explains, old people whose families don't look after them are nearly as needy as young kids who are parentless.

In the end, Hulin never did tell Wang Ni or anyone else about his ideas for the orphanage, and he's not about to share this new plan either; he'll just lock it up in his heart with all his other good intentions. No matter what anyone else may say or think, he's determined to blaze a new life path for himself, and that means turning his sights outward, toward helping the society at large, and inward, toward taming his temper and improving his character. But though he always knew that stepping off the beaten path was going to be lonely, he never imagined it would be even more challenging than building a business empire. In fact, the more he struggles to revamp the focus of his life, the more he understands why so many of his countrymen simply concentrate on filling their stomachs—even when they are too well-fed already.

In this regard Hulin may not be a typical Chinese, but he is typical of the direction in which China is headed. If the economy continues to rocket ahead at its current pace, the nation's GDP will double every seven years. Even if most rural migrants never attain the wealth that Hulin has, their incomes will rise, their lifestyles will improve, and at some point blindly eating bitterness will cease to make sense anymore. When these folks finally do stop to reevaluate the journey on which they've embarked, they just might find a similar restlessness burning in their hearts. Hulin is simply leading the way.

EPILOGUE

I finished the interviews for *Eating Bitterness* in the summer of 2007. Soon thereafter the western side of Gan Jia Zhai fell victim to urbanization. Men with sledgehammers simply appeared one day and, without fanfare, began whacking. Within a matter of weeks, all that remained was rubble; before long, a six-lane street was laid in its stead.

By that time, I had moved to Beijing, where I once again gravitated toward the city's High-Tech Zone. I now live in Zhongguancun, the Silicon Valley of China, in an apartment just minutes away from Google and Microsoft. Getting to their buildings, however, requires walking through a ramshackle old city-village that's strikingly similar to Gan Jia Zhai: packed with rinky-dink diners, produce stands, and gaming halls, teeming with an eclectic mix of hardworking rural migrants, and swirling with rumors of its imminent demise.

From this standpoint, *Eating Bitterness* provides more than a mere snapshot of a moment in time and place; rather, it chronicles a decades-long process unfolding across the country. The rest of

A Gan Jia Zhai recycling center with the High-Tech Zone in the background.

Gan Jia Zhai may soon be demolished and the people who live there scattered in all directions, but for every place pushing migrants to the periphery to make way for more highly skilled workers, there are dozens of up-and-coming new urban areas eager to accommodate them. As China's urbanization swings into ever-higher gear, today's tiny townships will turn into cities, and cities will grow into metropolises. City-villages will rise, mature, and then finally fall. These places will need a hefty input of rural labor to help build infrastructure, contribute to industry, and provide basic services; in some rapidly expanding cities, migrants are projected to comprise upward of 40 percent of the local population.

As a testament to the valuable role migrants play, migrants' salaries have risen rapidly in recent years and are now just 300 yuan lower, on average, than a college graduate's starting salary. But such figures are deceiving. College graduates have significantly higher social status and typically witness a significant climb in income within a few years. Migrants, on the other hand, tend to work much longer hours and face a range of obstacles that includes lack of access to affordable housing, education, health care and insurance, minimal labor law protections, and an outmoded housing registration system that distances them from their urban counterparts.

The government is not indifferent to these issues, but the enormity and complexity of the task at hand are staggering. Even if policy makers can accommodate the movement of 300 million people to urban areas in just two decades, accomplishing it in an even semi-orderly, efficient, and fair manner is an undertaking of monumental proportions. Repeal of the *hukou*, or household registration system, is often hailed as the key to leveling the playing field between rural migrants and their urban brethren, but that is not as easy as it might seem. Some city governments have dabbled with *hukou* reform by offering temporary urban residency to migrants, only to discontinue their programs after funding social benefits for these new citizens proved prohibitively expensive. Indeed, extending public services to migrants across China would take an estimated 1.5 trillion yuan, or almost 2.5 percent of the urban GDP.

More importantly, changes to the *hukou* system may not necessarily be welcome by the very people they are meant to serve. Several pilot programs allowing migrants to trade in their rural *hukou* for permanent urban residency status have been met with lukewarm reception. In 2009, for example, more than thirty thousand migrants qualified for one such program in southern China, but less than two hundred actually took advantage of it.

And in Sichuan province, a 2010 policy designed to grant 10 million farmers urban residency status had less than 45,000 takers in the opening months of the program.

It may well be that government efforts to improve the rural quality of life are taking effect: in recent years the country has eliminated its burdensome 2,600-year-old agricultural tax, dramatically extended the reach of a subsidized health care program for rural *hukou* holders, and provided subsidies for the purchase of items such as appliances and farm vehicles. And then there is the land. During my interviews for *Eating Bitterness,* migrants told me time and again that they may not have much, but at the very least the parcel of farmland granted by their rural residency status ensures that they will always be able to feed themselves. In a country beset by starvation a few short decades ago, that is not a benefit taken lightly. Nor, it seems, is it one that many migrants are willing to exchange for urban-style benefits just yet—even if they have no intention of returning to the countryside in the foreseeable future.

Such an attitude underscores the great irony underlying China's urban migration. Those who undertake this journey are neither able to completely abandon their rural lifestyles nor are they able to fully join the urban ranks; they belong neither to the nation's traditional past nor to its modernized future. ~floaters~ Though they navigate between these dramatically different worlds with varying degrees of success, as a people in transition in a nation in transition, they remain largely in limbo, stuck somewhere between their point of origin and their intended destination. And though much of urban China's progress depends upon their efforts, as does that of the rural communities they've left behind, they themselves are often the most browbeaten of all.

It could be a recipe for disaster in a place with a strong sense of personal entitlement, but not in China. At least not yet. Never mind their cheap and plentiful labor—migrants' willingness to patiently plod ahead while this great social experiment unfolds around them has in itself proven to be an invaluable asset to the country. But while eating bitterness in all its varied forms has helped carry China forward, the nation can't rely on it indefinitely. China is not just experiencing the greatest migration and the biggest economic comeback in history but also the fastest. Centuries-old, if not millennia-old, values long considered the crowning achievement of Chinese civilization are being pushed to the wayside. Attitudes toward family life, status, beauty, money, individuality, and ethics are in flux, and views regarding *chiku* are no different. Already, younger generations, those like M. Perfumine's teenage beauty therapists, are unwilling to eat bitterness without clear expectations of it being a temporary means to a more comfortable end, and members of the older generations are gradually following suit.

Perhaps that is as it should be. Eating bitterness is undoubtedly a virtue worth preserving, but, like everything else, it is best tempered with moderation. So many migrants sacrifice so much—parting ways with their families, living in overly cramped accommodations, subsisting on substandard food, and working interminable hours—long after they've secured the means to live otherwise. Over the last few decades, China has employed a sort of brute-force, economic-growth-at-all-costs model of development. That type of *chiku* mentality made sense up to a point, but now that the economy has clearly been kick-started, the government is steering the country toward a saner, more sustainable model that values harmony as well as material gains.

If migrants undertook a similar reassessment of personal strategy, they could greatly enhance the quality of their lives, without necessarily impacting their prosperity.

It's clear from the trials of people like Guo Hulin, however, that rethinking oneself is not without its own hardships. China's whiplash-fast development has left citizens from all walks of life disoriented, not quite sure where they are going or who they will be when they get there. For many migrants, who've spent years reining in their desires, moving beyond brute-force *chiku* means wrestling with a whole new set of possibilities and ultimately struggling to find a self-identity beyond simply their ability to endure.

In late 2010 I returned to Xi'an to take a look at the old neighborhood. Though I'd lived there for years, I immediately got lost. The Gan Jia Zhai corner once prone to late-night fights had become an intersection, the row of mahjong parlors had been replaced by upscale cafes and restaurants, and the spot where I had watched one of the city-village's only remaining trees fall had transformed into a boulevard lined with flowering shrubs. What remained of Gan Jia Zhai was now tucked behind a new series of billboards, bigger and bolder than before, each one proclaiming the virtues of the luxurious housing developments yet to come. There was a sign for the Honorable Mansion Kingdom Palace, the VIP Crystal City Plaza, and, largest of all, the Substantial Residential Complex, with over a million square meters of floor space for upper-class comfort.

The transformation of the place was so quick, and so dramatic, that initially I didn't even realize I was less than a block away from the apartment complex where I'd lived for years. It took quite some time for me to process all the changes that had taken place and to finally find my bearings. As China continues hurtling ahead at an unprecedented pace, I can only hope it will be so easy for folks like those featured in *Eating Bitterness* to find theirs.

RESEARCH NOTES

Back in 1997 I was running a small technical writing company in California when I received an unexpected invitation to work in China. I was given two days to make a decision and two weeks to make the cross-Pacific move. Assuming that it would be an intriguing but brief dalliance, I put my business on hold and headed for the southern seaport of Zhuhai.

My time in China has proven longer—and infinitely more intriguing—than expected. Over the past thirteen years I've served on the board of directors of an educational research organization, written a language-learning textbook for kids, cohosted a call-in radio program, headed a software company's educational products division, and launched a business consulting company. I've witnessed the impact of Macau's return to China, China's entry into the World Trade Organization, SARS (severe acute respiratory syndrome), the Sichuan earthquake, and the 2008 Summer Olympics. Along the way I've befriended people from every level of society and learned much about the realities of life in the world's most populous nation.

From among my varied experiences, it was a six-month sojourn in a remote banana-farming village that inclined me toward the issues presented in this book. My stay there acquainted me with the nuances of modern-day China from the peasant point of view in a way that nothing else could. When I subsequently moved to Xi'an, the contrast between life in the village and that in the booming new High-Tech Zone was so great that I felt dazed; I could only wonder how newly arrived rural migrants dealt with such a dramatic shift.

As the development of western China continued to gather momentum over the next few years, the desire to chronicle this unfolding transformation ultimately led me back to the United States to pursue a master's degree at the Missouri School of Journalism. Upon graduation, in 2006, I was awarded the school's top accolade, the McIntyre Fellowship, which provided funding to undertake the research for *Eating Bitterness*.

When I returned to Xi'an, my initial challenge was to track down a mix of stories that together captured the breadth of the migrant experience. Above and beyond more obvious factors like occupation, age, gender, and family circumstances, I wanted to illustrate the diversity that exists in terms of the obstacles migrants face, the sacrifices they make, and the risks they are willing to take. Additionally, I looked for variation in how successfully individuals integrated into city life and how closely they maintained ties with the rural communities they'd left behind.

How I ultimately settled on the eight stories featured in *Eating Bitterness* was a combination of planning, luck, and *yuanfen*, or fate. I'd bought produce from the veggie vendors for years and had lived in the Maple Leaf Gardens during Guo Hulin's metamorphosis from fledgling shop owner to increasingly dissatisfied big boss. I'd stumbled across Er Huan in the recycling center as I strolled through Gan Jia Zhai looking for ideas and had befriended Yazhen after buying sheets from her that very same day—though I didn't seriously consider including her in the book until she invited me to her new home in the village and I realized the sort of double life she lived. I'd been looking for a woman who'd left her family behind to head city-ward when a friend introduced me to Cui, who suggested I talk to her nanny, Xiao Shi. I'd met with numerous youth who'd migrated to Xi'an fresh out of junior high, but when I happened upon a couple of M. Perfumine beauties distributing free facial certificates in the street one day, the choice became clear. A few weeks later I was interviewing Jia Huan at the salon when Wang Jing and her mother Liping came in for a beauty treatment. I hadn't planned on using a peasant-turned-landlord story, but when, unasked, they started describing the incredible highs and lows brought on by Gan Jia Zhai's changing fortunes, I knew it belonged in the book.

I found the Knife Sharpener last, and this proved to be the most difficult task of all. I wanted to include the story of an older man who did some sort of petty sales from the back of a bicycle, but while finding such men was easy, getting them to stick around long enough to record their full stories was not. By then I was seven months' pregnant and all of the older migrants I approached seemed leery to have me around. To make matters worse, none of them had a phone, or even a consistent work time and place, which made it almost impossible to find them again if they didn't show up for an appointment. I was standing on the street corner early one morning waiting for yet another no-show when the Knife Sharpener trudged past. I tagged along with him all morning and when he predictably failed to meet me at the agreed-upon time the next day, I roamed the High-Tech Zone until I eventually heard his bullhorn blaring.

I knew early on that I wanted to keep myself out of the book and write in the third person rather than the first, as I wanted the focus to remain on the migrants' stories and not my own. But in Xi'an, where foreigners (and especially foreigners able to speak Chinese) were still something of a novelty, that proved challenging. Most of the people in *Eating Bitterness* had never talked to someone of non-Chinese origin before and were more interested in knowing about me and my life experiences than in talking about theirs. In the end, time proved to be the best means for taking myself out of the spotlight. I simply spent enough time with each person—answering questions, asking questions, and just sitting on the sidelines observing—that they eventually felt comfortable carrying on as usual. Sometimes I visited people in couple-hour spurts, other times entire days. On average, I spent about three weeks with each individual, though that was often spread out over several months. The most difficult, again, was the Knife Sharpener, who was too busy hunting down knives to stop and talk to me and who, to his credit, refused to let a pregnant lady traipse across the city with him in the blistering heat for days on end. Even when I offered to reimburse his lost wages if he'd just sit in the park and tell me his story, he hesitated, not at all eager to take an afternoon off like I'd expected.

Long before I started writing *Eating Bitterness* I had come to admire the Chinese ability to weather the multitudinous tests and trials of life with grace, courage, and persistence. It is impossible to capture this spirit, or the historical, cultural, and economic forces that necessitate it, in a single volume. Fortunately, a body of skillfully crafted China-related literary nonfiction has developed over the past decade, and it is my hope that *Eating Bitterness* adds yet another dimension to the multi-faceted picture that is now emerging. Works that explore the impact of China's recent transformation on the lives of ordinary citizens include: Peter Hessler's *River Town* (HarperCollins, 2001), *Oracle Bones* (Harper-Collins, 2006), and *Country Driving* (Harper, 2009); Ian Johnson's *Wild Grass* (Pantheon, 2004); John Pomfret's *Five Lessons* (Henry Holt and Co., 2006); Rob Gifford's *China Road* (Random House, 2007); and Michael Meyer's *The Last Days of Old Beijing* (Walker, 2008). Oral histories include Sang Ye's *China Candid* (University of California Press, 2006) and Liao Yiwu's *Corpse Walker* (Anchor, 2009), as well as memoirs such as Lijia Zhang's *Socialism Is Great!* (Atlas, 2008) and Kang Zheng-guo's *Confessions: An Innocent Life in Communist China* (Norton, 2007), which is set in and around Xi'an following the Communist revolution.

Leslie T. Chang's *Factory Girls* (Spiegel & Grau, 2008) is essential reading for anyone interested in learning more about China's rural migrants. As the title suggests, it takes as its focus young women tucked away in factories and largely isolated from the broader society. Though their experiences are distinctly different than those of the people in *Eating Bitterness,* similar struggles for meaning and progress pervade. In recent years, feature films like *The World* and documentaries like *Up the Yangtze* and *Last Train Home* have also brought to light both the diversity and uniformity of the migrant experience.

On the academic front, Dorothy Solinger's *Contesting Citizenship in Urban China* (University of California Press, 1999) provided one of the earliest detailed explorations of migration in China. Since then, an expanding repository of scholarly literature has developed, including, but by no means limited to, the works that follow.

Fan, C. Cindy. "China on the Move: Migration, the State and the Household." New York: Routledge, 2008.

Gaetano, Arianne M., and Tamara Jacka. *On the Move: Women and Rural-to-Urban Migration in Contemporary China.* New York: Columbia University Press, 2004.

Merkel-Hess, Kate, and Jeffrey N. Wasserstrom. "A Country on the Move: China Urbanizes." *Current History* (April 2009): 167–72.

Murphy, Rachel. *How Migrant Labor Is Changing Modern China.* Cambridge: Cambridge University Press, 2002.

Ping, Huang, and Frank N. Pieke. "China Migration Country Study." Presented at the Regional Conference on Migration, Development and Pro-Poor Policy Choices in Asia. Dhaka, Bangladesh. June 2003.

Zhang, Li. *Strangers in the City.* Stanford: Stanford University Press, 2001.

Throughout *Eating Bitterness* I've tried to present an overview of the major themes relevant to rural migration, but a more detailed exposition is beyond the scope of this work. For those interested in gaining a deeper understanding, a list of sources that proved useful in clarifying and completing the picture I gathered in the field follows.

URBANIZATION

Friedman, John. *China's Urban Transition.* Minneapolis: University of Minnesota Press, 2005.

Preparing for China's Urban Billion. Research report by McKinsey Global Institute, 2008.

Yusuf, Shahid, and Tony Saich. *China Urbanizes: Consequences, Strategies and Policies.* Washington, D.C.: The World Bank, 2008.

CITY-VILLAGES

Liu, Yuting, and Fulong Wu. "Urban Poverty Neighbourhoods: Typology and Spatial Concentration Under China's Market Transition, A Case Study of Nanjing." *Geoforum* 37, no. 4 (2006): 610–26.

Pu, Hao, Richard Sliuzas, and Stan Geertman. "Open Villages within the Exclusive City: An Empirical Study on Urban Villages in Shenzhen, China." Proceeding of the 10th N-AERUS Conference: Challenges to Open Cities in Africa, Asia, Latin America and the Middle East: Shared Spaces Within and Beyond. October 2009, Rotterdam.

Song, Yan, Yves Zenou, and Chengri Ding. "Let's Not Throw the Baby Out with the Bath Water: The Role of Urban Villages in Housing Rural Migrants in China." *Urban Studies* 45 (2008): 313–29.

Zheng, Siqi, Fenjie Long, Cindy C. Fan, and Yizhen Gu. "Urban Villages in China: A 2008 Survey of Migrant Settlements in Beijing." *Eurasian Geography and Economics* 50, no. 4 (2009): 425–46.

HUKOU, OR HOUSEHOLD RESPONSIBILITY SYSTEM

An, Baijie. "Farmers in Chongqing Say 'No Thanks' to Hukou." *Global Times,* September 29, 2010. http://china.globaltimes.cn/society/2010-09/578274 .html.

Chan, Kam Wing, and Will Buckingham. "Is China Abolishing the Hukou System?" *The China Quarterly* 195 (2008): 582–60.

Garst, Daniel. "Rural Economies May Break Invisible Shackles of Hukou." *China Daily,* June 7, 2010. http://www.chinadaily.com.cn/metro/2010-06 /07/content_9942264.htm.

"Invisible and Heavy Shackles." *The Economist,* May 6, 2010. http://www .economist.com/node/16058750?story_id=16058750.

Kong, Sherry Tao. "China's Migrant Problem: The Need for Hukou Reform." January 29, 2010. East Asia Forum. http://www.eastasiaforum .org/2010/01/29/chinas-migrant-problem-the-need-for-hukou-reform/.

"Urban Hukou or Rural Land? Migrant Workers Face Dilemma." *China Daily*, March 10, 2010. http://www.chinadaily.com.cn/china/2010npc/2010 -03/10/content_9568726.htm#.

Yusuf, Shahid, and Kaoru Nabeshima. *China's Development Priorities.* Washington, D.C.: The World Bank, 2006.

RURAL LAND RIGHTS

Brandt, Loren, Jikun Huang, Guo Li, and Scott Rozelle. "Land Rights in Rural China: Facts, Fictions and Issues." *The China Journal* 47 (2002): 67–97.

LAO XIANG, OR NATIVE PLACE, NETWORKS

Ma, Laurence J. C., and Biao Xiang. "Native Place, Migration and the Emergence of Peasant Enclaves in Beijing." *The China Quarterly* 155 (1998): 546–81.

Mobrand, Erik. "Politics of Cityward Migration: An Overview of China in Comparative Perspective." *Habitat International* 30 (2006): 261–74.

SCHOOLS AND EDUCATIONAL OPPORTUNITIES

Goodburn, Charlotte. "Learning from Migrant Education: A Case Study of the Schooling of Rural Migrant Children in Beijing." *International Journal of Educational Development* 29 (2009): 495–504.

Liang, Z., and Chen, Y. P. "The Educational Consequences of Migration for Children in China." *Social Science Research* 36, no. 1 (2007): 28–47.

Woronov, T. E. "In the Eye of the Chicken: Hierarchy and Marginality Among Beijing's Migrant Schoolchildren." *Ethnography* 5 (2004): 289–312.

Wu, Xiaogang, and Zhuoni Zhang. "Changes in Educational Inequality in China, 1990–2005: Evidence from the Population Census Data." In *Globalization, Changing Demographics, and Educational Challenges in East Asia (Research in Sociology of Education, Volume 17),* edited by Emily C. Hannum, Hyunjoon Park, and Yuko Goto Butler, 123–52. Bingley, UK: Emerald Group Publishing, 2010.

RECENT CHINESE HISTORY

Fairbank, John King, and Merle Goldman. *China: A New History*. Second enlarged edition. Cambridge, Mass.: Belknap Press of Harvard University Press, 2006.

Wasserstrom, Jeffrey N. *China in the 21ˢᵗ Century: What Everyone Needs to Know*. New York: Oxford University Press, 2010.

CHINA'S REFORM POLICIES AND THEIR IMPACT ON MIGRATION

Fleisher, Belton M., and Dennis Tao Yang. "Problems of China's Rural Labor Markets and Rural-Urban Migration." *Chinese Economy* 39, no. 3 (2006): 6–25.

Li, Bingqin, and David Piachaud. "Poverty and Inequality and Social Policy in China." Center for Analysis of Social Exclusion, London School of Economics. CASE Paper 87, November 2004.

Lindbeck, Assar. "An Essay on Economic Reforms and Social Change in China." World Bank Policy Research Paper No. WPS 4057, November 2006.

DEVELOPMENT OF WESTERN CHINA

Bao, Shuming, Anqing Shi, and Jack W. Hou. "Migration and Regional Development in China." In *The Chinese Economy after WTO Accession*, edited by Shuming Bao, Shuanglin Lin, and Changwen Zhao, 307–34. Burlington, VT: Ashgate Publishing, 2006.

Goodman, David S. G. "The Campaign to 'Open up the West': National, Provincial-Level and Local Perspectives." *The China Quarterly* 178 (2004): 317–34.

Zhao, Rong, and Guo Zheng. "Shaanxi." In *Developing China's West: A Critical Path to Balanced National Development*, edited by Y. M. Yeung and Jianfa Shen, 351–72. Hong Kong: Chinese University Press, 2004.

ONE CHILD POLICY

Gu, Baochang, Feng Wang, Zhigang Guo, and Erli Zhang. "China's Local and National Fertility Policies at the End of the Twentieth Century." *Population and Development Review* 33, no. 1 (2007): 129–47.

SOCIAL SECURITY BENEFITS

Zhu, Yukun. "A Case Study on Social Security Coverage Extension in China." Working Paper No. 7. International Social Security Association, Geneva, 2009.

LITERACY

"Illiteracy Rate among Adult People in China Slashed." *People's Daily*, November 18, 2002. http://english.peopledaily.com.cn/200211/18/eng20021118_106987.shtml

Plafker, Ted. "China's Long—but Uneven—March to Literacy." *New York Times*, February 12, 2001. http://www.nytimes.com/2001/02/12/news/12iht-rchina.t.html?pagewanted=1..

BEAUTY INDUSTRY

"Chinese Women Go Crazy for Cosmetics." *China Daily*, June 7, 2005. http://www.chinadaily.com.cn/english/doc/2005-06/07/content_449333.htm.

ACKNOWLEDGMENTS

There is no way I would have had the courage to drop every-thing and head off to China on such short notice all those years ago if it hadn't been for the enthusiastic support of my parents, Randy and Cheryl Dammon. I can't imagine where I would be today (though almost certainly not in China) if they hadn't kin-dled in me the desire to explore and give back to the world. For that—and everything else—I am forever grateful.

Getting to China was merely the first step on the winding path that led to this book; returning to the United States for grad school in 2004 was an equally crucial step in the process. I learned much at the Missouri School of Journalism and would especially like to thank Mary Kay Blakely, Katherine Reed, Marty Steffens, Michael Grinfeld, and Byron Scott for their guidance and encour-agement. In 2006 I was awarded an Overseas Press Club (OPC) Foundation scholarship for an essay that ultimately grew into this book. I would like to thank Jane Reilly, Bill Holstein, and all the other folks at the OPC for their continued support of journalists with an international focus. I am also extremely grateful to have been named the 2006 recipient of the J-School's O. O. McIntyre Postgraduate Writing Fellowship, without which this book most assuredly would have gone unwritten.

Many thanks to my agent, Diana Finch, for taking on this project, and to my editor at UC Press, Niels Hooper, as well as UC-Irvine professor Jeffrey Wasserstrom, whose thorough review of the manuscript proved extremely helpful.

Heartfelt gratitude goes out to my other set of parents, Sudarshan and Nirja Loyalka, who have taken me into their family with such unfailing love, generosity, and good humor as to open up a whole new arena of life possibilities. My two children have, quite literally, accompanied me through every stage of this book. I was pregnant with my daughter, Zayha, during the interview process, and then with my son, Breakwell, during the writing phase. It's impossible to imagine two more delightful, or patient, companions. My husband, Prashant, has labored through every page of *Eating Bitterness* with me. He acted in turns as researcher, editor, critic, and manager, but above all he remained, always, a true best friend. For the opportunity to be navigating the road of life with him, I am eternally grateful.

There are many others to thank, but a few stand out as having been truly indispensible to the completion of this project: Nikhil Ravi, a meticulous editor, the most giving of friends, and a true and exemplary *didi* in all respects; Christi Lawson, for being a real member of our family team when we needed it most; Xiao Li, without whose supreme competence things would surely have fallen apart along the way; and Dictionary.com, for making it infinitely easier to find the right word every time.

I am so thankful to have come across the writings of 'Abdu'l-Bahá shortly after moving to China. His insights into the qualities of the Chinese people and the country's importance in world affairs were truly visionary. I'd also like to express my heartfelt love and appreciation to the numerous Chinese friends—Lu Ping, Lian Jianhua, Spring Liu, Xu Rui, Zhao Yan, Wang Xin, Ye Fei, and Yan Zhiming, to name a few—who have made this vast country feel like the coziest of homes. Finally, my deepest thanks go to those who so generously shared the trials and triumphs of their lives with me so that I in turn could share them with the readers of *Eating Bitterness*. I have learned much about humility, optimism, and perseverance from them, and for their strength of character, I admire them tremendously.

INDEX

Note: Page numbers in *italics* indicate photographs.

Ai Jia (Love Home superstore),
30–31, 229

beauty and cosmetics industry.
See teenage beauty queens
big boss: beauty queens and, 76;
Hu Yazhen and, 197–98, 199;
Zhang Erhua on, 107. *See also*
Guo Hulin
Big Rice Pot (*Da Guo Fan*), 45, 62,
109. *See also* collective farming

Ceri Silk, 87–88, 93–95
chiku (eating bitterness), 8, 16–17,
185–86, 244–45; Wang Quanxi
and, 40; Wang Tao and, 149;
Xiao Shi and, 171, 180–81
China: city villages and, 128–29;
literacy and 41; modernization,
economic growth, and urbanization of, 1–4; one-child policy
of, 160, 170; savings rate in, 185.

See also collective farming;
education
Chuan Shuanghai. *See* Li Donghua
and Chuan Shuanghai
city-villages, 128–29, 201–2, 241.
See also Gan Jia Zhai
collective farming: floaters and,
109; Wang Quanxi and, 45–46,
48; Wang Tao and, 122–24, 143,
147–49
Communist Party/communism, 1,
4–5, 41, 123. *See also* collective
farming
Cui Yanwen, 153–58, 166–69, 171–78

Da Guo Fan (Big Rice Pot), 45, 62,
109. *See also* collective farming
da laoban. *See* big boss

eating bitterness. *See chiku*
education, 3, 11, 26, 41, 79, 200;
hukou system and, 102, 136, 176–77

floaters, at recycling center, 97–118; *hukou* system and, 101–2, 109–10; *laoxiang* network and, 110–11, 114–15. *See also* Wei Laifu; Zhang Erhua

Gan Jia Zhai, 5–6, *6*, 7, 21, 126–27, *241*; map of, ii; transformation of, 240–41, 245–46
Gao Pan, 208, 219
Guo Hulin (big boss), 206–39, *221*, *233*; business success of, 207–11, 226–27; childhood and youth, 221–23; as employer, 218–21; first businesses of, 223–24; health of, 214, 228, 234–36; helping of friends, 212–14, 224–29, 235–36; lifestyle of, 206–7, 216–17, 229–30; restlessness and plan for orphanage and charity work, 211–12, 214–15, 217–18, 230, 237–38; returns to home village, 230–33, 238

High-Tech Zone, ii, *5*, *6*, 20–21, *241*
Hong Li, 64–65, 67, 70–74, 77, 81, 86–88, 91–92
hukou system: changes in and loss of security, 242–43; education of children and, 102, 136, 176–77; floaters and, 101–2, 109–10; urban job-hunting and, 135–36
Hu Yazhen (opportunity spotter), 182–205, *186*; admiration for Mao, 199; education and, 189–90, 200; entrepreneurial spirit and business ventures of, 182–83, 189–201, 203–4; home life, 183–85; reluctance to leave city-village, 187–88, 202–5; savings of, 185–87

Jia Huan (beauty worker), 72, *83*; educational opportunities missed, 78–79; goals and expectations of, 77–78, 83, 85–86, 92–93; move to city and visits home, 79–85; outward transformation of, 80–81; training of, 64–68, 74–76, 86; work life of, 68–74, 86–96

knife sharpener. *See* Wang Quanxi

landless landlords. *See* Wang Tao; Zhang Liping
land policies. *See hukou* system
laoxiang network, floaters and, 110–11, 114–15
Liang Hongxia, 97–101, 105, 108, 110–13, 115–16
license plate collecting, 217
Li Donghua and Chuan Shuanghai (veggie vendors), 9–35, *19*; decision to leave rural life, 15–16, 28–29; home life of, 21–26; hopes for daughter, 18, 21–26, 29, 35; precariousness of marketplace, 20–21, 33–35; work life of, 9–15, 18–20, 26–33
literacy, 41. *See also* education
liudong renkou (floating population), 3. *See also* floaters, at recycling center

Ma Haiying (beauty worker), 68–70, 73, 81, *83*, 87, 92, *93*, 95–96
Meng Wei (beauty worker), 81, *83*, 84
migrant workers: importance to China's economic growth, 3–7, 30; lack of legal protections for, 58; rising salaries of, 241–42. *See also specific individuals and occupations*

M. Perfumine. *See* teenage beauty queens

nowhere nanny. *See* Xiao Shi

one-child policy, of China, 160, 170
opportunity spotter. *See* Hu Yazhen

savings rate, in China, 185
Songling (beauty worker), 91, 93

Taoling, 209, 215, 218
teenage beauty queens, 64–96; beauty work as best available employment alternative, 96; goals and expectations of, 85–86; marriage option and, 86, 91–93; training of, 64–68, 74–76, 86; urban reliance on rural labor, 76–77; work life of, 68–74, 86–96

veggie vendors. *See* Li Donghua and Chuan Shuanghai

Wang Jing: father's addiction to mahjong and, 119–22, 145; job-hunting and, 125–26, 135–36; need to relocate for High-Tech Zone expansion, 129–30, 132–34
Wang Kai, 124, 125, 151
Wang Mei, 124, 125, 141, 149–50, 151
Wang Ni, 207, 208, 210, 212–15, 218–19, 224, 230, 234, 235–36, 237–38
Wang Quanxi (knife sharpener), 36–63, *40, 52*; brick-factory work, 46, 48–49; collective farming's effect on, 45–46, 48; home life of, 48, 60; missed opportunities of, 41–42, 55–56; petty entrepreneurs and outdated skills in high-tech area, 50–52, 62–63; support of rural-dwelling family, 53–55, 60–62; work life of, 36–40, 42–44, 46–50, 56–58
Wang Tao (landless landlord), *148*; addiction to mahjong, 119–22, 125, 138–39, 143–47, 148–50; rental properties and need to relocate for High-Tech Zone expansion, 125–37, 140–43, 145, 150–52; work during collective farming, 122–24, 143, 147–49
Wei Laifu (recycling center worker), 97–100, 102, 105, 108, 113, *114*, 115

Xi'an, 5, 20–21
Xiao Shi (nanny), 153–81, *164*; decision to leave rural life and daughters, 163–69, 173–76; dreams of house and education for daughters, 161, 179–81; parental manifestations of love, 180–81; support of extended family, 159–60, 168–69; work life of, 153–59, 161–74
Xibu Da Kaifa (Great Opening of the West), 5, 20

Zhang Ai, 141–42
Zhang Erhua (recycling center worker), *104*; enterprises of, 105–8, 113–15; *laoxiang* network and, 110–11, 114–15; rejection of money-at-all-costs mentality, 104–5, 116–18; on shift in culture, 116–17; work life at recycling center, 97–105, 108, 110, 112–13, 115

Zhang Jing (beauty worker), 64, 66, 68–70, 88–91, 95–96

Zhang Liping (landless landlord), *133*; collective farming and, 123–24; husband's addiction to mahjong and, 119–22, 125, 128, 143–47; rental properties and need to relocate for High-Tech Zone expansion, 125–37, 141–44, 151–52

Zhang Rui, 156, 159, 166, 167–70, 172–73, 174–76, 179

Zhang Yuan, 161–62, 163, 164–66, 169–76

Text:	10.75/15 Janson
Display:	Janson MT Pro
Compositor:	Westchester Book Group
Printer and binder:	Maple-Vail Book Manufacturing Group